This copy of The book is for
O/C, friend and fellow
journalist. The full story
of his achievements would
require many volumes!

Anthony Burgess.
Feb. 1984

FROM THE ARCHIVE OF

JON & NANCY WILKMAN

THE LIFE AND *TIMES* OF LOS ANGELES:

A Newspaper, A Family and A City

THE LIFE AND *TIMES* OF LOS ANGELES:

A Newspaper, A Family and A City

MARSHALL BERGES

ATHENEUM

New York 1984

Excerpt from *Vision or Villainy: Origins of the Owens Valley–Los Angeles Water Controversy* by Abraham Hoffman used by permission of the author and Texas A & M University Press.

Library of Congress Cataloging in Publication Data

Berges, Marshall.
The life and Times of Los Angeles.

Bibliography: p.
Includes index.
1. Los Angeles Times. I. Title.
PN4899.L64L662   1983   071'.9494   83-9243
ISBN 0-689-11427-3

Published simultaneously in Canada by McClelland and Stewart Ltd.
Composed by Maryland Linotype Composition Company, Baltimore, Maryland
Manufactured by Fairfield Graphics, Fairfield, Pennsylvania
Designed by Mary Cregan
First Edition

TO MILDRED

enchanting companion on my journeys

Contents

List of Illustrations

Author's Note

A newspaper's pages deal with adventure, some of it so exciting and colorful that it borders on theater. Behind the scenes
there is another kind of adventure, a round-the-clock effort
to fulfill a wide-ranging set of responsibilities: to be accurate
always, even though accuracy is often elusive and sometimes
arguable; to be fair and balanced, even though the news does
not break in a fair and balanced way; to give readers the best
account of public affairs that the newspaper is capable of delivering; to strive always for a recognizable and sensitive picture of the immediate environment and of the world at large,
telling how people work, play, live, govern, seek self-improve-
ment, achieve and otherwise engage in the full spectrum of
human activity.

This is the fascinating story of one newspaper—of its people and of its extraordinary metamorphosis. Just a century
ago it was an owner-directed paper, the singular (and often
shrilly partisan) voice of its tempestuous proprietor. But today
the old-fashioned press boss is, by and large, as extinct as hand-
set type. Gone are William Randolph Hearst, Adolph Ochs,
Robert R. McCormick, Roy Howard, Joseph Medill Patterson
and others who—admired by some, despised by others—practiced an intensely personal journalism, a tyranny from the top.

Perhaps nowhere is the change more evident than in the

Los Angeles Times. Once the private preserve of Harrison Gray Otis, the *Times* of the late twentieth century is a newspaper where the only dominant voice is quality. In an ironic thrust across the years of dynasty, the extraordinary emphasis on quality has come from Otis Chandler, great-grandson of the man who practiced tyranny from the top.

Quality is evident throughout the paper in the work of a remarkably talented staff. Among them are some of the most fluent, wise and witty characters I have ever known. Beyond their professional lives they have developed a vast range of interests and activities: scratch a newspaper person and you may find variously a poet or an aviator, an athlete or a musician, a zealot, a patriot, a social and political and economic philosopher.

In these pages you will meet behind the scenes Jack Smith, who day after day enables us to look whimsically at each other; Jim Murray, a master of hyperbole who pretends to be a sports columnist but who really writes about people; book review editor Art Seidenbaum, who strives valiantly to make worthy choices for review among some 42,000 books published each year; David Shaw, whose incisive critiques of the media (including the *Los Angeles Times*) make him the lively equivalent of a one-man school of journalism; William Thomas, the top-ranking editor of the huge enterprise (an editorial staff of more than 850). You will hear their voices as they talk about their work.

You will meet them and others—writers and editors and foreign correspondents. I interviewed scores of them, not only in the *Times* but in the parent company, Times Mirror, which during the past century has grown from a tiny printing shop to become a $3 billion communications empire, owner of such metropolitan newspapers as *Newsday,* the *Dallas Times Herald,* the *Denver Post,* the *Hartford Courant*; groups of book publishing companies including New American Library and

Harry Abrams; seven television stations plus cable television companies; a cluster of magazines including *Popular Science, Outdoor Life, Golf, Ski, The Sporting News,* and much more.

This book does not attempt to range beyond the *Times* nor does it claim to be an encyclopedic reflection of every important person and every key event in the long-running drama of the newspaper; many people and many episodes have been omitted simply for space reasons.

In the account that follows, I have tried everywhere to be accurate, but I make no pretense of complete objectivity; I am a member of the *Los Angeles Times* family and cannot help being prejudiced about it. But I am going to show you the good and the bad, weakness and strength, shadow and substance. Like the newspaper itself, my aim is to get behind the scenes, to tell the story—indeed, wherever possible to let the participants tell the story—and to let you be the judge.

Part One

HARRISON GRAY OTIS
(1882 - 1917)

1

CRUSTY, choleric, cantankerous and quarrelsome, often narrowly partisan and too stubborn to admit that he or his paper could make mistakes, Harrison Gray Otis became a legend in his own time. He was a powerful, gutsy journalist who loudly advertised his triumphs and turned blinders to his shortcomings.

A strapping Civil War veteran, with hard blue eyes and a mustache that flowed down to meet his trim goatee, he stood six-foot-two and weighed well over two hundred pounds. When he strode into a dim and dusty adobe-brick printing shop on Temple Street in Los Angeles one hot morning in the summer of 1882 and began asking questions, his presence and booming voice were enough to make heads turn. What onlookers could not know was that the occasion marked a classic juncture of place and person, sparking a series of events that would ultimately have repercussions around the world.

The town itself had existed only a century, tracing its origin to a balmy night in September 1781, when a ragtag group of forty-four exhausted settlers, having traveled one thousand miles by boat and land from Mexico, gathered on the banks of a narrow river. Purpose of the gathering was to dedicate a pueblo: a farming community to grow grain and other foodstuffs to support Spanish soldiers who ventured north from Mexico.

The forty-four settlers gave the site the jawbreaking name of El Pueblo de Nuestra Señora la Reina de Los Angeles de Porciuncula—the town of Our Lady the Queen of the Angels of Porciuncula. It swiftly became known as El Pueblo and, almost abruptly, as Los Angeles.

Across the continent other events were in motion. America's War of Independence against England rushed toward a climax, and word traveled slowly through the colonies in a handful of paper-starved publications. With paper more available at the end of the war, newspapers sprang up. The *Pennsylvania Packet and General Advertiser* of Philadelphia, started in 1784, was the first daily newspaper to last more than a few weeks; and by 1789 more than eighty periodicals, including weeklies and biweeklies, were being published regularly.

Having lost trade with England, America demonstrated quick ingenuity in developing new avenues of business and commerce. There was no bank in the Thirteen Colonies—all borrowing took place between individuals—but in 1781 Robert Morris set up the Bank of North America at Philadelphia; New York and Boston followed with banks in 1784.

Trade with the Orient expanded—an eleven-month journey each way—and in time it included calls on the West Coast. In the pueblo of Los Angeles, and other California settlements where cattle had replaced foodstuffs as the main source of wealth, a new kind of commerce began: cattle hides —called "Yankee banknotes"—and tallow were traded in exchange for East Coast luxuries.

Yankee traders returned home carrying news of the coastal paradise, and gradually American adventurers began arriving on the scene. By 1846, when war erupted between the United States and Mexico, American soldiers had already infiltrated the province. Two years later the territory was ceded to the

United States by treaty, and Los Angeles became an American town.

Less than two weeks after the treaty had been signed, gold was discovered in Northern California. Not only drifters and desperadoes but respectable men, women and children left settled and fairly comfortable lives to rush into the unknown wilderness of the gold country. Farmers, doctors, lawyers, teachers, businessmen and even ministers abandoned their careers and set out, by any route known, to strike it rich.

San Francisco swelled in a few months from a tiny village to a city of twenty thousand. There and in nearby communities gambling, fighting, killing and claim-jumping became commonplace. Los Angeles, off the beaten path, grew at a lesser rate. Yet one year after the gold strike began, California became a state.

Gold brought regular passenger ships calling at California ports and, by 1869, the transcontinental railroad. A railway ticket from the Midwest to California cost only $1, and soon the Santa Fe Railroad was bringing hundreds of people to Los Angeles for its climate, crops and rich land. City ordinances were posted in both Spanish and English. The Chinese had emigrated to help build the railroads but later they turned to farming, especially planting citrus groves. Waves of new immigrants added customs and tongues to the scene. Italians, Greeks, Russians, Hungarians arrived by the trainload. A German-language newspaper, *Sued-Californische Post,* began as a weekly in 1874 and expanded to daily circulation in the 1880s, an era when the French began their own local daily, *Le Progrès.*

Among the town's newspapers was the *Los Angeles Daily Times.* A four-page, ink-spattered affair selling for a penny, its first issue—fewer than five hundred copies were printed— hit the streets at dawn on December 4, 1881, just as the city's gas lamps were being extinguished. Within thirty days of its debut, the paper's founders, Thomas Gardiner and Nathan Cole, Jr., fled when they were overwhelmed by bills. But three stubborn printers, occupying a tiny adobe-brick shop, clung to the task of publishing the paper. The outfit they inherited by default carried the grandiose name of Mirror Printing Office and Book Binder. Their funds were low.

The printers were searching desperately for someone who could lift the unwanted burden of ownership of the *Times* off their backs, at the precise moment when the imposing stranger, Harrison Gray Otis, entered the shop. They soon struck an agreement: he would become editor of the paper at a starting salary of $15 a week, and he would purchase one-fourth interest in the paper for $6,000, mostly secured by a bank loan. It was a tidy sum, for in that year porterhouse steaks were eighteen cents a pound and a five-bedroom house cost $1,200.

Who was this risk-taking character, eager to gamble his future on an apparently worthless newspaper? He gave some insights in a memoir he wrote many years later:

"1837: I was born February 10 in a hewed-log house on the hill in Adams Township, Washington County, Ohio. My father, Stephen Otis, was Vermont-born; my mother, a native of Nova Scotia. They were staunch, intelligent, God-fearing people of the Methodist faith, and neither rich nor poor. I was the youngest of my father's two families, which totaled sixteen children."

The youngster found considerable pride in his roots: "My paternal grandfather, James Otis of New Hampshire, was a renowned officer in the American Revolution. Another ancestor, the first Harrison Gray Otis, was an influential Federalist U.S. Senator from Massachusetts, and later mayor of Boston," he noted in his memoirs.

As a boy "I absorbed my first political sentiments from my father, who was active in the pre-Republican Liberty Party. Our house was a station on the Underground Railroad. Runaway slaves came our way, and were helped on their flight towards Canada."

After attending log-built schoolhouses, Otis left home at age fourteen to take a job as printer's apprentice on a country paper, the *Noble County Courier*. By 1856 he had become a printer in a Democratic newspaper office, where he was distinctly uncomfortable: "I was an enthusiastic champion of John C. Frémont in the presidential campaign, though I was not yet a voter. Democrat James Buchanan was elected, and his weakness was one of the primary causes that brought on the War of the Rebellion."

Following the election he quit the newspaper. Largely self-educated and eager to broaden his horizons, he signed up for a five-month course at a private academy in Lowell, Ohio. "There I met my future wife, Miss Eliza A. Wetherby, daughter of Mr. Charles T. Wetherby, woolen manufacturer. Three years later, in 1859, we were married, and I traveled to Cincinnati in search of employment."

He went alone, a twenty-two-year-old deeply in love and separated for the first time from his bride. In other circumstances throughout his life he would display dark outbursts of rage and a fiery temper that seared men's souls. But now, by candlelight in his hotel rom, he wrote letters:

Cincinnati, Oct. 15
Saturday Eve.

Dear Lizzie—*Darling Wife!*
I'm lonely without you, my Blessing. It is harder now to be away from you than ever before! All alone away from your woman's heart, the only home I have, it's a cheerless task. . . .

when I'm away out in the world, where we'll both be sometime, there I feel more than ever how much I ought to do, and yet how little I have ever yet done for you. It makes me almost ashamed that I yield to circumstances rather than make them yield to me. The fact is, I wish I didn't do a petty business in the world! You'll just remember that I've a young wife up among the Muskingum hills, and she's good and true, and it makes my poor heart tremble to leave her. I'll tell you, Lizzie, for you are an old friend, and intimate and confidential as ever I had friend, that she didn't like to part with me very well. She put her white arms around my neck and almost refused to let me go—and that dear embrace!

Sunday Morning—I'll go to church this morning, because I think a sermon will afford me food for pleasant and profitable reflection, and if that prove true, it may take the place of misanthropic and unprofitable musings.

Afternoon. What a glad surprise it was, Lizzie Darling, when your letter was handed me this morning at the office! It was my first visit to the Post Office since I reached the city, and need I tell my Wife that it was a joyful one? Heaven bless you, Dearest, for your loving remembrance and your more loving words!

And you too have felt with me how hard it is to be away! Lizzie, I can now speak for you and you can speak for me in whatever the heart would utter. The language of one is that of the other.

Cincinnati, Oct. 17
Monday Eve.

Dear, Darling Wife!

The rain might fall ever so fast and the night glow ever so dark, as they do tonight, but if you were close to my heart, no lonely feeling would be there.

Lizzie, it would never do for me to be a missionary, a sailor, or a fisherman, or if I were to turn my attention to any of those occupations you would most certainly have to prepare yourself to be a *voyageur* along with me: I couldn't get on without my wife. If at any future time I should chance to become the recipient of Presidential favors and be appointed *chargé d'affaires* to the Hottentot Country, or to the Unexplored Region where they converse in the unknown tongue, and live on dirt, I guess you would have to bundle up and *charge* with me: I couldn't treat with dirt eaters without the aid of my wife.

But while I must be away from my young wife, I will try to have the nerve that I believe rightly belongs to me, though I won't warrant the attempt to prove successful always. But there, it won't be long that I'll have to be alone and that thought does me good.

I don't find a demand for more than a million printers in Cincinnati. The daily newspapers furnish the most employment and the most opportunities for situations; I guess if I don't get something to do at Bradley's book office (who promised to send me a note if there should be any demand for additional compositors in his concern) I will try to get a little work on one of the morning papers, so as to earn enough to prevent my trip down here from being a losing one. That wouldn't do, you know.

Tuesday Morning—A happy, healthful "good morning" to you Lizzie. May these bright sun-risings find you well and strong.

I would not have you think, My Lizzie, brave good woman that you are, that I am devoid of "pluck" for I don't believe it is true. I know sometimes I evince something like a timid spirit, but you know it is more the shrinking from certain associations than from a hard task.

Cincinnati, Oct. 21
Friday Afternoon

Strange I don't hear again from you, Dearest Lizzie! A waiting heart *will* grow anxious, you know, sometimes, and mine is almost so because *five days* have come and gone without any word from my young wife. Don't smile at me, Lizzie, because I've a long face, which I fancy you may almost see when you read my letters, for it requires *fortitude* to brave all this waiting.

There must have been some delay in the mails, as you did most certainly write to me several days ago, perhaps on Sunday or Monday. The fault is not in *Lizzie; She* is always prompt.

But I hope to be greeted by a letter full of your sweet words,

conveying sweeter feelings and sentiments—sentiments right from
your heart, and feelings, that find their birthplace in your inner-
most soul—such a letter I hope will reach me tomorrow.

Saturday morning
Oct. 22

Must I pass by without reply all the sweet sayings that swell up
from your soul, and only tell you in brief that they are treasured
in my heart? Yes, I must do it, for I have three or four letters to
write today and then how can my poor pen do the office of the
heart's interpreter?

I will close now and hope to greet you very soon—don't your
heart *know* what that greeting will be?

Heaven bless you my best friend, My Love, My Angel-Wife!
and God guard you in safety to your husband.

Harrison Gray Otis found work finally in 1859 as a compositor on the *Louisville Journal,* across the river from
Cincinnati. "Lizzie and I were happy and hopeful on eight dollars a week," he reported in his memoirs. "The great presidential campaign of 1860 was on, and I was active, in an
apprentice sort of way, on the Republican side, having been
a delegate to the National Convention at Chicago in May
before, where Abraham Lincoln was nominated for the presidency (and won). Though the few Republicans of the state
worked under the handicap of being denounced as 'Lincoln
hirelings' in a slave state, I was proud to be a member of the
Republican state executive committee. I caused to be inserted
in the paper as an advertisement, the Republican electoral
ticket, headed by the great name of Abraham Lincoln. The
ad caused a lot of Secession editors to fly into a fury and
'holler their heads off' in denunciation."

Following Lincoln's election, Otis returned to Ohio. "An-
ticipating the early breaking of the storm of Civil War," he
enlisted in the Army and, during the next forty-nine months,

suffered wounds twice and rose in rank from private to lieutenant colonel.

At war's end he returned to newspapering, then landed a
job as compositor in the Government Printing Office in Washington, D.C. His interest in Republican politics burned
brightly, but he needed funds to support a growing family,
and he kept watch for opportunities. In 1874 he made his
first visit to California, to weigh the chances of a goat-raising
project. Discouraged, he returned to Washington, but two
years later he moved to Santa Barbara, where he published
the *Daily Press* and, with Eliza and three children, lived on
"not enough to keep a rabbit alive." Discouraged again—"the
sledding was extremely hard"—he wangled appointment as
U.S. Treasury Agent in charge of the Seal Islands of Alaska,
at $10 a day, "managing the important (100,000 seal furs a
year) industry for the government."

In 1882, Otis resigned his government job and, as he noted
in his memoirs, "returned once again to Santa Barbara, idle,
but with an eye on Los Angeles. Then I connected myself with
the *Daily Times*. Small beginnings, but great oaks, etc."

2

FROM the moment he became editor in 1882, Harrison Gray
Otis set his sights on ambitious goals: to increase his share
of ownership of the *Times*; to impose his own views and
standards on the paper; to heighten the quality and prestige
of the sheet; to enlarge its size (from four pages), its circulation
(fewer than four hundred copies were printed daily) and its
influence (not only in Los Angeles but throughout the region).

He dropped "Daily" from the name of the paper, doubled
the telegraphic news coverage, wrote livelier headlines and
made space for letters to the editor. Otis wrote in one of his
first editorials: "Los Angeles is in a transition state. She has
finally waked up from the dull lethargy of those old days when
she was one great sheep-walk and cattle range. All she needs
now is men of brawn and brains to grow up with her."

A fresh seriousness of purpose was appparent throughout
the paper. No longer would the *Times* say about itself, as it
had in a December 1881 issue, shortly before the ill-starred
founders departed: "A great deal of curiosity is being mani-
fested . . . as to the constituency of [our] editorial staff. [Our]
literary mentors include a temperance, political, religious and
real estate editor, plus a general scavenger and boss of the
devils." Still another, about to leave, helped "do all the loaf-

ing, take all the cussing, receive all the thrashings and drink all the whisky for the concern."

The paper's newly serious approach was underlined by a doughty motto, provided by the editor's wife, Eliza Otis, and later inscribed on a plaque on the building: "Stand Fast, Stand Firm, Stand Sure, Stand True."

Eliza worked closely with her husband. Indeed, she was virtually the entire editorial staff, the rest consisting of stringers paid meagerly by the inch for their contributions. Eliza handled two feature departments and invariably met her deadlines for the rickety old press. An early pressman described this machine many years later:

"Barring accidents, we were usually washed up and on the way home by 5:30 or 6:00 o'clock [a.m.] at the latest . . . after a couple of hours of running off the four-page paper." But mishaps occurred frequently, the most common of which would "come to us without warning . . . and against which it was impossible to guard. This was—a fish in the water-wheel!" Somebody then had to crawl down into the drenching chute to eliminate the "ill-advised carp" before the motor could start again.

Between writing editorials and proofreading, often at his cramped kitchen table at home, Otis munched sandwiches, prepared by his wife. His daughters took up duty as clerks in the business office when they came of age.

To increase his ownership of the *Times,* Otis sought ways to buy out the other partners, even though he had almost no cash. He found an answer, of sorts, when a flashy, wealthy character, Colonel H. H. Boyce, arrived from the East and announced his craving to be a publisher.

Teaming up to buy out the other three partners, Otis and Boyce in 1884 incorporated the Times Mirror Company for $40,000 divided into forty shares of a par value of $1,000 each. Where the money came from remained a puzzle, but it was no secret that in the midst of their dealings the two men disliked each other intensely.

Otis soon came to consider Boyce a financial buccaneer with minimal integrity, while Boyce detested Otis' hidebound ways and unflinching militancy as labor troubles developed.

Otis made up his mind to get rid of his partner, and within three years bought him out. Boyce promptly founded another paper, the *Los Angeles Tribune,* and their public feuding became an ugly exercise in mutual contempt.

In an article called "Boyce's Career" Otis wrote of his former associate:

" 'I like to get the better of people without their knowing it.'

"The notorious and devious career of the unfortunate man who is guided by the above quoted sentiment is familiar to scores of readers. . . . His perverted instincts and vicious training have from time to time involved him in a maze of difficulties.

"In an evil hour, he acquired an interest in this paper, and subsequently undertook the task of running the politics of the city, county and district."

When Boyce backed one Walter S. Moore as the Republican candidate for California secretary of state, Otis dealt with Moore in an editorial:

"The unsavory apartments over Bob Eckert's saloon on Court street were the scene of an orgie such as even the most salacious pen of ancient Rome never dared describe. . . . The actors were Walter S. Moore and three male companions . . . with four common prostitutes. Entering these rooms at 9 p.m., their orgie was not ended at 8 a.m. next day. At that hour, the scene was one of absolutely sickening bestiality. The four drunken male brutes and three of the four drunken female brutes were sprawled, almost nude, all in the most attrocious attitudes, about the front room. The negro waiter was stretched stupid upon the floor, surrounded with a halo of fifty-eight (empty) champagne bottles . . . while the man who now asks your suffrage for Secretary of State, almost nude, was endeavoring to arouse the waiter to go and get a photographer for an obscene purpose. . . . "

Otis concluded with mock piety: "That is one way to respect and honor one's family. These are bare, unmalicious facts."

Candidate Moore went crashing down to defeat.

Otis minced few words. Over the years in the *Times,* he denounced ex-partner Boyce as "a thief and a scoundrel," and Boyce's *Tribune* as "a bastard and lying sheet." E. T. Earl, the highest-ranking staffer at the *Tribune,* was identified in one *Times* editorial as "editor of the Morning Sodomite and the Evening Degenerate." When Otis discovered that E. T. Earl's middle name was Tobias, the *Times* referred to him as "Too-pious Earl."

Otis showed every sign of welcoming libel suits. Whenever charges of libel were threatened or filed against him, he would repeat in its entirety the original story, thus getting in another whack at the enemy.

Once, in 1888, Colonel Boyce won an award of one dollar, following a libel suit against Otis. The *Times* took note of it with a series of headlines on a page one story:

> $1—THE ASSESSED VALUE OF A SHATTERED
> REPUTATION—THE JURY CONCLUDE THAT
> 'SMOOTHY' HAS ACTUALLY SUFFERED—AND
> THEY ADJUDGE FULL COMPENSATION FOR
> HIS LOST CHARACTER

On its editorial page, under the heading "A LOW-PRICED CHARACTER," the *Times* reprinted the original stories.

Harrison Gray Otis, wrote a contemporary, "is a remarkably even-tempered man—his temper is always that of a hungry tiger."

* * *

Reluctant to admit errors, especially when news events collided with his political prejudices, Otis clung stubbornly to his sharply partisan views. On the morning of November 5, 1884, for example, the *Times* proclaimed its joy over the election of James G. Blaine to the presidency of the United States, even as other papers in Los Angeles and across the nation announced the election of Grover Cleveland. Not until November 16 did the *Times* concede that Cleveland had won the election.

Less than a year after Harrison Gray Otis became editor of the *Times,* a wan and sickly nineteen-year-old, Harry Chandler, reached Los Angeles by train at the end of a long, exhausting journey from Landaff, New Hampshire. Threatened with tuberculosis, he had come west seeking a warm climate to restore the health he had sacrificed in a reckless moment: on a foolish dare during his freshman year at Dartmouth College he had leaped into an ice-encrusted vat of starch and subsequently contracted pneumonia.

Coughing and wheezing, he found a room at a downtown flophouse. Next day, while looking for outdoor work to strengthen his weakened body, he trekked to the Cahuenga Pass and met a retired physician who offered him room and board in exchange for roustabout work in an orchard, plowing and harvesting orange and grapefruit trees. Because it was arduous labor, and fruit a superfluous item in much of that bountiful area, the elderly physician offered him the crop gratis.

Shrewdly, Chandler hauled wagonfuls of grapefruit to the Van Nuys ranch, in the arid San Fernando Valley, where grain-growing farmers and their work crews eagerly snapped it up. In this manner, charging $19 a load, Chandler amassed $3,000 within two years. The steady outdoor exercise restored his health; he had grown strong and husky. His manner was calm and controlled, his attitude one of all business and no play. He decided to invest his nest egg in *Times* delivery routes, available at that time to the highest bidder. He plowed his earnings into more and more routes, and he was conscientious: when the rains brought floods, Chandler serviced his clientele from a rowboat.

He was promoted and in 1887 at the age of twenty-three brought into work at the *Times* as a circulation clerk. Thrifty, calculating and aggressive, he continued to snap up not only *Times* routes with his earnings, but those of competing newspapers as well. Every day at dawn he parceled out papers to his carriers. He devised a bold plot to crowd one competitor, the *Tribune,* out of business. In the midst of a cold snap he arranged a picnic outing in the desert. Inviting a majority of the *Tribune*'s carriers, he kept them out there, happy, well fed and off the job, for almost a week.

When the *Tribune* folded in 1890, Harry Chandler quietly sent a third party to buy the *Tribune*'s production equipment for about five cents on the dollar.

The *Times'* business manager, Albert McFarland, learned of the sale, but not the purchaser's identity. Shortly after, McFarland went to Harrison Otis, complaining that the *Times* should have acquired the *Trib*'s equipment in order to cope with the expansion the *Times* was enjoying, now that one of its competitors had folded.

Otis called Harry Chandler and asked: "Can you find out who bought the *Tribune* equipment?"

"I think I can," Chandler answered. "The press, I understand, was taken back by the manufacturer, but the rest of the equipment was purchased by a speculator."

"Find him," Otis ordered, "and we'll make a deal with him."

"I won't have to go far. As a matter of fact, I bought it myself," Chandler admitted.

"Good!" Otis replied, reflecting both his characteristic dis-regard for business formalities and a conviction that any such action was made for the benefit of the company. "We'll move it right in!"

Harry Chandler was promoted to circulation manager and later made business manager of the *Times*. He married his boss' daughter, Marian Otis, in 1894 when he was thirty and she was twenty-six, but nepotism had little to do with his upward mobility. Hearty, hustling, recognized as a driving worker with few interests outside his paper, his family and a growing urge to acquire extensive property in Southern California, he was clearly a man of destiny.

Harrison Gray Otis had his own special brand of humor, and it blazed through his writing, particularly when he en-gaged in a vendetta. He feuded constantly with the owners of competing Los Angeles newspapers. A typical imbroglio occurred soon after a syndicate, led by one Wallace L. Hardi-son, took control of the struggling *Los Angeles Herald*. From the beginning, Otis labeled Hardison derisively as "Hardup-son," refusing to dignify him with his real name.

A climax of sorts took place when Hardison sent out by wire announcements of his impending marriage. The follow-ing day page one of the *Times* proclaimed:

KANSAS SINGER
TO MARRY HARDUPSON

*Telegraph Brings News That
He is "Wealthy"*

*Wonder if the Bride-elect Really
Thinks So—Nuptials Set for April—
And the Troubles of Mary Belle Will
Then Begin.*

Not surprisingly, the bridegroom-to-be was infuriated at this questioning of his intended bride, a Kansas singer named Mary Belle Daily. With his managing editor for support, Hardison paid a visit to the *Times,* only to learn that Otis was at a theater matinee. Hardison pursued him. While actors delivered lines onstage, there was a quick hushed colloquy between the two publishers, during which Otis refused to apologize, especially in view of Hardison's "notorious marital record."

Hardison lost his temper and pummeled Otis unmercifully, until police led him manacled to the nearby jail. With obvious calculation, Otis declined to press charges, and in a story he ran in the *Times* recounting the incident he informed his readers: "My injuries are trifling, and I am on duty at my desk, as usual."

But neither Otis nor Chandler found any redeeming humor in their dealings with labor unions. Otis had "surrendered to an invasion"—as he termed it—of unionized typographical workers in 1886, only four years after he became editor of the *Times.*

He recoiled, however, as union demands gradually "became more exacting and oppressive," he told his readers, and when unionists sought to deny the *Times* the right to hire or fire printers, Otis refused to go along.

His printers served notice that they would leave, and he bellowed: "Walk! I will get out the paper myself. I haven't forgotten how to set type."

He had, in fact, made up his mind to fight, and he imported from Kansas City a union-busting outfit known as the Printers' Protective Fraternity. He hired twenty of its members as replacements and summarily fired the unionists on the *Times.*

Later he wrote to M. H. DeYoung, owner of the *San Francisco Chronicle:* "In making the successful contest which we have made, the *Times* has aided in fighting the battle of every employer who claims the right to manage his own business in his own way; of every American citizen who cherishes the inalienable right to pursue his occupation under the protection of the Constitution and the laws; of every man opposed to socialism, anarchy and industrial despotism, and of every mechanic and laborer whether organized or unorganized, who is satisfied to do a fair day's work for a fair day's pay, without taking his employers by the throat."

Ultimately Otis became a fountainhead of anti-union sentiment in booming Los Angeles. With a group of businessmen, he set up an organization called the Merchants and Manufacturers Association under a banner of Industrial Freedom. The M&M, as it was dubbed, swiftly grew powerful. Its tactics were fully as brutal as those of the unions: one historian noted that whenever a contractor, merchant or firm hired a unionist, the employer was verbally browbeaten and even physically terrorized into line.

The *Times* led the way in encouraging the business community to resist the advance of the closed shop. In 1890 a *Times* poll of local merchants showed their adamantine resolve to resist unionizing and an astonishing willingness on their part to be quoted. One reported: "A [strike] delegation called on me [to say] they intended to boycott a competitor . . . and would throw business my way. I told them I would in such case assist [him, for] I did not approve of such measures."

Another said: "I have been a manufacturer in the East and know all about such labor troubles. I left the East on that account. . . ."

Another added: "I believe in running my own business to suit myself. I won't be dictated to."

Against a background of growing industrialization in Southern California, labor and management sped toward an inevitable, literal explosion. In the spring of 1910 a group of eight unionists slipped covertly into Los Angeles. Among them were two brothers, John J. and James B. McNamara, well versed in sabotage tactics and unafraid to use dynamite.

Although American Federation of Labor president Samuel Gompers insisted he was "unalterably opposed to violence and sabotage," the McNamaras had other ideas. They were members of the Ironworkers Union, an outfit that had survived a long-running storm of terror between labor and management. Historian Louis Adamic observed: "It is not difficult to explain, or even apologize for, the McNamaras. They were Irish, endowed with the same instincts that had produced the Molly Maguires; perhaps they were a bit more idealistic and social-minded than the Mollies. . . . Each was a kind of hero in the union. . . . They saved [it] at one of its darkest periods. Early in the current century every single union in the steel industry had been completely destroyed—except the Ironworkers, thanks to dynamite and the McNamaras. . . ."

At 1:07 a.m., October 1, 1910, the residents of Los Angeles were jarred by an explosive roar. Many thought it was an earthquake, but the shock and trembling were traceable to First and Broadway, where the *Times* building, now a three-story sturdy structure of granite and brick, had blown up. A series of blasts followed, knocking out walls, sparking additional explosions in tanks of flammable ink, housed in wooden barrels behind the building. Both Harrison Gray Otis and Harry Chandler, obvious targets, were absent from the building when the explosions occurred. Otis was due back that day from a visit to Mexico City, where he had spent a month as President William Howard Taft's envoy extraordinary during the centennial of Mexican independence. Chandler, who routinely remained in his office until 2:00 a.m. or later, had providentially decided to go home a bit earlier with his wife, Marian—for she, too, worked in the business office and might have been trapped in the holocaust.

The Chandlers were less than a block away when the first explosion, audible for ten miles around, battered their eardrums. Harry rushed back to the building while Marian Chandler stood transfixed in horror. Within seconds the headquarters of the *Times* was engulfed in flames and smoke. From beyond the collapsing walls there were cries of distress, followed by the groans and screams of those struggling to escape. Firefighting apparatus arrived on the scene minutes later, and many of the one hundred employees on duty were saved. When the smoke had cleared, twenty people had perished in the inferno, ranging from the night editor to an apprentice linotypist, and twenty-one others suffered injuries.

Harry Chandler's son, Norman, age eleven, was in bed at the family home on Fort Moore Hill when he heard the explosion. "I watched from my window a long, long time, and sometimes when I close my eyes now," he said decades later, "I can still see the building burning."

That night, with tears streaming down his cheeks, Harry Chandler took charge of aiding the stricken survivors. Later he led a group of employees to an emergency auxiliary printing plant. Within five hours the press was cranking out a four-page issue whose huge bannerlines minced no words concerning the identity of the malefactors:

UNIONIST BOMBS WRECK THE
TIMES: MANY SERIOUSLY INJURED

"The *Times* itself cannot be destroyed," wrote managing editor Harry Andrews in a page-one editorial. "It will be issued every day and will fight its battles to the end. . . . They can kill our men and wreck our buildings, but, by the God above! They cannot kill the *Times*."

Two days later Otis vented his soulful wrath on the bombers and printed this editorial:

"O you anarchic scum, you cowardly murders, you leeches

upon honest labor, you midnight assassins, you whose hands are dripping with the innocent blood of your victims. . . . look at the ruins wherein are buried the calcined remains of those whom you murdered."

Samuel Gompers declared it "inconceivable that a union man could have done this thing," and some militant unionists accused Otis of blowing up his own building; they claimed opponents of organized labor had much more to gain by the bombing, for in the aftermath of the *Times'* destruction a vast anti-union campaign got underway.

Few newspaper readers across the nation were uninformed of the crime. The *New York Times* ran its account as front-page news. Many large companies in major cities, especially where union-organizing activity was on the upsurge, increased their armed guards. In Los Angeles the police department expanded its ranks of patrolmen; officers were encouraged to investigate and jail all suspicious characters.

Shortly after the fatal explosions at the *Times,* a servant girl found a bomb alongside the home of F. J. Zeehandelaar, secretary of the union-hating Merchants and Manufacturers Association. Fifteen sticks of 80 percent nitro-gelatine were wired to a dry-cell battery and an eighty-nine-cent alarm clock. This improvised bomb failed to go off, but two hours later a suitcase full of high explosive was spotted by a gardener in the shrubbery against the facade of Harrison Gray Otis' home. When a policeman gingerly sought to pry it open, the valise blew up. Private detective William J. Burns and famed criminal lawyer Earl Rogers were engaged by the district attorney of Los Angeles to track down the culprits. Parts of the unexploded improvised bomb provided clues leading to a San Francisco factory which had sold the explosives to James McNamara.

Burns and Rogers also followed the trail of one of Mc-Namara's colleagues in the Ironworkers Union, Ortie McManigal. A recognized participant in dynamiting jobs directed against construction companies which employed nonunion labor, McManigal left behind an amazingly casual record of his journeys: wherever he went, he mailed tourist postcards and other souvenirs to his wife in Indianapolis.

Arrested in Detroit by Burns operatives, McManigal made a full confession of his activities and implicated both Mc-Namara brothers in a widespread dynamiting conspiracy against the construction industry. All three men were rushed under heavy guard to Los Angeles. Clarence Darrow, widely regarded as a brilliant defender of the rights of workers, was hired to represent the prisoners.

Following the jailing of the trio in April 1911, demonstrations were held throughout the United States. In Los Angeles twenty thousand men and women marched slowly in front of the jail, shouting and waving banners to protest the "frame-up."

Prosecution and defense planted spies in each other's camp: a prosecution deputy was later uncovered on Darrow's payroll, while a Darrow secretary turned out to be a Burns detective. "Before long," Irving Stone wrote in his classic biography *Clarence Darrow for the Defense,* "some of the private detectives were drawing three separate salaries, passing around their information in a daisy chain."

Behind the scenes Darrow searched in vain to find a flaw in Ortie McManigal's confession. Darrow sent teams of investigators across the nation to check on explosions described by McManigal; the investigators' findings confirmed his claims. In the second month of the trial, the McNamara brothers admitted their guilt. Darrow summed up the action: "They had it on us. They had a complete case. There was no loophole." The brothers were sent to San Quentin—James for life, and John for fifteen years.

Harrison Gray Otis stubbornly rebuilt the headquarters

of the *Times* into a larger and stronger edifice. Meantime there was no interruption in publishing the paper. It had occurred to him, following San Francisco's tragic earthquake of 1906, that a similar quake might strike Los Angeles, and he had taken the precaution of constructing an auxiliary printing plant one mile away. When existence of the auxiliary plant became public knowledge, there were renewed claims from organized labor that Otis had destroyed his own building. But the McNamaras' confession brought a convincing halt to suspicions that Otis might have been involved. On a frieze high on the glass-and-concrete headquarters of the *Times,* Otis fastened a bronze eagle with a plaque proclaiming anew the credo written by his wife, Eliza: "Stand Fast, Stand Firm, Stand Sure, Stand True."

Labor did not constitute the whole of the *Times'* preoccupations. Harrison Gray Otis entertained visions of greatness about Los Angeles and the West, and he used his editorial clout across the years to shape the destiny of the city and the region. He deemed it his responsibility to lead the community, and he never hesitated to use the paper as a platform for his views. Through the pages of the *Times* he demanded a "free harbor" for Los Angeles instead of one controlled by the then monopolistic Southern Pacific Railroad. His persistent agitation on behalf of a second railroad for the region led eventually to a rate war that sent ticket prices down sharply. At the same time he urged readers to alert their relatives in the East and Midwest to the benign climate, abundant land and ripe economic opportunities in Los Angeles. His relentless boosterism helped to set the stage for successive land booms.

Otis had no taste, however, for the "loose" life-style that befell boomtowns, and in the pages of the *Times* he thundered against gambling halls and the evils of booze. He implored his readers to clean up their own debris and to keep their horses tethered away from the main streets.

Otis regarded himself, not least, as a political kingmaker, and he fought bitterly with a vast array of politicians, especially those he deemed "liberal do-gooders."

Among the figures he scorned was Hiram Johnson, the Progressive party's candidate in 1910 for governor of California. Otis rated Johnson an upstart, unworthy of high office.

Johnson was, in fact, a reluctant candidate, largely because his wife abhorred public life, and preferred that he run for U.S. senator, if anything. But when he informed an audience that he was making a "sacrifice" by running, the *Times* heaped ridicule on him, declaring: "No one of this Johnson tribe was ever known to do anything for nothing." Conceding that voters at large held mixed opinions of him, the *Times* reported that "some say Johnson is pompous and conceited, others say that he has undoubted talents." The *Times,* however, rarely indicated what those undoubted talents might be.

The candidate was no less shrill and cantankerous than Otis. Needled mercilessly by the *Times,* Johnson retorted in a thundering denunciation that ran on the first page of the rival *Los Angeles Express* the next day:

"In the city of San Francisco we have drunk to the very dregs of infamy; we have had vile officials; we have had rotten newspapers. But we have nothing so vile, nothing so low, nothing so debased, nothing so infamous in San Francisco as Harrison Gray Otis. He sits there in senile dementia, with gangrened heart and rotting brain, grimacing at every reform, chattering impotently at all things that are decent; frothing, fuming, violently gibbering, going down to his grave in snarling infamy."

Otis' paper responded by running a story headlined: "JOHNSON IS VITUPERATIVE, Qualified as Circus Clown and a Rioter." One paragraph stated:

"His assault upon the *Times* and its editor was almost a frenzy of vituperation and was unspeakably abusive. Johnson is used to talking to San Francisco mobs where they like rough stuff. This tremendous tirade of foul abuse turned many of his auditors against him. Some cheered and many left the house."

Johnson won the election, but he had hardly warmed his gubernatorial chair when the *Times* resumed its attack, denouncing him as "bombastic, self-assertive, conceited, dominating." Throughout his career Johnson was stung by the *Times'* constant epithet: "Holy Hiram."

Otis' vision of political duty extended far beyond the borders of California. He spoke to his friend President William Howard Taft of a "World-Embracing Plan to End Wars," and when Taft urged him to put his ideas on paper, Otis devoted himself energetically to the task.

One evening, having decided to spend some time working on the Plan without interruption of other chores, he departed aboard his Locomobile for El Tejon, a 270,000-acre ranch located north of Los Angeles and acquired over the years by a group of businessmen, including Chandler and Otis. On this trip Otis was accompanied by Arnold Haskell, an eighteen-year-old "on loan" from a business associate to handle the secretarial work of committing the Peace Plan to paper.

Haskell described their approach to the ranch on a black, storm-tossed night:

"We had turned [off the old Ridge Route] at a stage center, and I could barely see the outline of the road. I eased up. Otis asked, 'Why are you slowing?' When I said, 'There's a gate here somewhere,' he replied, 'I know where the gate is. Step on it!' So I did, and pretty soon CRASH! BANG! We plowed right through the barricade. General Otis merely remarked, 'There was that damn gate!' We never stopped.

"He'd dictate mornings, and then we'd get in the car and travel around to the most impossible places till we got stuck and a team had to drag us loose. It seemed he was never happier than when he was in physical difficulty.

"We stayed at El Tejon for a whole month while he dictated his Peace Plan. One morning I spelled General Grant's name 'Useless' instead of 'Ulysses.' We stopped working, while I got a five-hour lecture on the Civil War and Grant."

Otis drafted six revisions of his Peace Plan and submitted it to Taft in hopes that it would exert a measure of influence on creation of the League of Nations. The *Times* fought stubbornly for the League and took its defeat bitterly.

In sharp contrast to his setback on the world scene, Otis hit a remarkable streak of luck at home.

Part Two

Part Two

HARRY CHANDLER
(1917 - 1944)

3

THE luck of Harrison Gray Otis was traceable, in a profound way, to his relationship with Harry Chandler.

Otis gloried in the taste of power and sweep of personal journalism. A writer and perfectionist, throughout his career he remained closely involved in the editorial process; he wrote voluminously and he required others to rewrite their copy extensively before it satisfied him.

Words were his ammunition, and he devoted countless hours to firing fusillades at his enemies. He also thrived on a heavy emotional attachment to the military. Much earlier, following the outbreak of war with Spain, in 1898, he took leave of absence from the *Times* to accept appointment as brigadier general of United States Volunteers. The appointment was tendered personally by President William McKinley, who had served as a major under Colonel Otis during the Civil War. Otis was assigned in 1898 to command the Fourth Brigade of the Philippine Islands Expeditionary Forces, and during the winter of 1899 the *Times* carried stories of the general's "fighting brigade" at Manila, including first-person dispatches from Otis. Following his return to civilian life in 1899 he was promoted to major general, and forever after he chose to be addressed as General Otis.

His attachment to the military colored his vocabulary. He

built one large house and called it the Bivouac. A second was the Outpost. The staff of the paper was known as the Phalanx and the *Times* building itself was known as the Fortress.

But Otis had only limited skills in the world of business. Harry Chandler, on the other hand, was an astute, complex and marvelously subtle businessman, described by a contemporary as "really a statesman in the way he could handle people." He seldom relaxed, spending long hours working alongside Otis. Moreover, the younger man's zealous fervor left Otis free to wield his formidable pen.

Chandler had a lively sense of humor and a tolerance of human frailty, but no patience at all with sycophants. He took a particularly dim view of one member of the staff who kept finding fault with the business and editorial departments while lavishly praising Chandler. When Chandler could stand it no longer, he called the man into his office and said: "I notice that you criticize practically everyone, but I have waited in vain for you to tell me what is the matter with me. I assume that I am perfection and make no mistakes." Chandler then sacked the troublemaker.

Unlike his father-in-law, Chandler never outgrew his distaste for public appearances. He could devise huge business ventures, and bring them to golden fruition, but he did not like to talk about his outside affairs, except in semiprivate chats with a few associates.

Sometimes mischievous, he once focused his cool attention on an editorial dude who regularly wore fancy top boots to the shop, then sneakily doffed them in favor of carpet slippers in his private office. One night, when this dandy was readying himself for a civic banquet, all hell broke loose: Chandler had nailed the Beau Brummell's boots to the floor.

By the turn of the century, to observers inside and outside the *Times*, it was clear that the enterprise, less than twenty years after Chandler joined up, had become a joint venture of the two strong-willed men, with their duties clearly divided: business for Chandler and policy for Otis. One scholar of the era noted, "The subtle mind and manner of Chandler consistently affected the decisions of Otis and the course of the *Times*. Their complementary combination proved formidable. Niccolò Machiavelli once observed that the ideal ruler is half-lion and half-fox. The composite of Otis and Chandler met this standard." That view of bombastic Otis, the roaring lion, and shrewd Chandler, the fox operating behind the scenes, was shared by many acquaintances of the two men.

The bond between Otis and Chandler grew stronger year by year. When Otis, in failing health, sensed his own mortality, he took pen in gnarled fist and scrawled a "Declaratory" to son-in-law Harry and daughter Marian Otis Chandler. Dated November 12, 1914, the missive embodied a deed to the *Times* and "fundamental injunctions" on how the co-heirs should assume the "high trust and valuable property":

You know, and will always bear in mind, the paramount fact that this journal is, and must continue to be, first of all a *newspaper*— a vehicle for the dissemination of current news reports and information; a faithful recorder of contemporaneous history and public affairs, of new knowledge of the tremendous daily happenings of the mighty Present around all the globe, no matter of what nature or complexion the occurrences may be, provided they possess human interest. Moreover, the *Times*, being a proper medium for thinkers, they will be given, as always in the past, impartial hearings in its broad columns whenever they are able to enlighten the world, or contribute to those transcendent problems of human life, human living and human government which, if they are to be wisely solved, will always require the best thought and effort of the best men and women upon earth. In the columns of the *Times* will be found, I doubt not, in the future as in the past, graphic accounts of the doings of the far-flung human race; absorbing narratives of adventure and achievement; of research and investigation; of travel and discovery; of progress in the arts, sciences and invention; of toil and triumph; of hardship, endurance and ultimate success; of everything, indeed, that is new to men and of living interest. The press is a colossal surveyor of the worldwide news field, scanning the entire civilized globe and faithfully purveying to an ever-waiting public the luminous record of daily and mighty happenings among men and nations.

Marian and Harry Chandler published the document after the death of Otis in 1917, pledging their adherence to "the sacred trust and grave responsibilities conveyed to us, the faithful carrying out of which is dearer than life itself."

Chandler, however, also followed his own complex impulses and independent nature. He devoted considerable time and attention to the growth of Los Angeles and the West; and within that large endeavor he pursued a goal of achieving financial independence for himself and his family. He fixed his sights on the acquisition of "solid" land, amply watered and broadly cultivated, or divided into profitable tracts. Some of these far-outlying spreads would include oil. Yet what lay beneath the surface was almost incidental. May Goodan, Chandler's second daughter, recalled many years later how her father foresaw a jam-packed San Fernando Valley "before you girls die." The population explosion he predicted came to pass, but he lost an even more lucrative opportunity by paying so little attention to oil beneath the land. "He was offered Signal Hill [site of one of the greatest U.S. oil strikes of the early 1920s] for $500, and turned it down."

Chandler's appetite for land development was whetted early, in a curious sequel to a series of land booms in Los Angeles. Housing lots—some on grazing lands as far as fifty miles from City Hall, others on mountaintops and still others under the sea—changed hands rapidly, passing from one owner to another with neither buyers nor sellers taking time to look at their holdings. "It has been a subject of regret," wrote Charles Dudley Warner in the *Atlantic,* "that I did not buy Southern California when I was there last March and sell it the same month. I should have had enough left to pay my railroad fare back . . . and had money left to negotiate for one of the little states on the Atlantic Coast."

The *Times* grew fat with real estate advertising. But whenever a land boom burst, speculators hurried away, and the *Times* found itself with hundreds of advertising accounts payable only in deeds to worthless lots. It then became Harry Chandler's problem, as business manager of the *Times,* to turn large parcels of land into money to meet the *Times'* payroll. He sold some lots at bargain prices and held onto other acreage for long-term appreciation. Overall, in the realm of real estate, he was shrewd indeed. He formed a syndicate and wisely invested its money in broadly separated areas that sprawled from Mexico's Baja California to El Tejon, a mountain pass gateway ranch of 270,000 acres linking California's southern and central sectors.

A Chandler son-in-law, Earle Crowe, onetime financial editor of the *Times,* made a detailed study in 1957 of the syndicate's "empire-buying complex" and observed that Chandler himself was "land crazy," regarding the good earth as the finest investment a man could make: better than gold, silver, stocks or bonds. At its peak the syndicate held approximately 1,500,000 acres, but the group often found itself land-poor, borrowing money repeatedly from banks to meet payments.

Wheeling and dealing in a grand pageant, Chandler made acquisitions that became notorious in some instances for violence and skulduggery. Across the Mexican line, in Baja California, he found 860,000 acres of desert, lying below the riverbed, and partially underwater at flood time, a sort of miniature Nile Valley, with nobody using it. Negotiating a deal with Porfirio Díaz, then dictator of Mexico, Chandler organized the California-Mexico Land Company, which built 2,500 miles of canals and turned the acreage into one of the largest cotton plantations on earth.

But Mexico's strongman governor of Baja California confiscated the ranch, leaving Chandler's syndicate out in the cold. In turn, Chandler made bold moves to regain the ranch. He and six others were indicted by a United States federal grand jury in 1915 on charges of plotting to arm an expeditionary force that would overthrow the strongman. (Chandler himself was not intimidated by the indictment. A key aide, Kyle Palmer, quoted him as saying: "You're not a man until you've been indicted at least once.") Although he was exonerated two years later, suspicion ran deep that one of Chandler's employees, the foreman of the ranch, was involved in the expeditionary force.

Closer to home, especially in the San Fernando Valley, just across the Santa Monica Mountains from thirsty Los Angeles, the syndicate's land acquisitions were hotly disputed for another cause, summed up in a word: *water*. It needed water desperately because it was a desert surrounded by mountains and ocean.

For a desert its growth had already been extraordinary. Its population climbed from 12,000 in 1882, the year Harrison Gray Otis arrived in town, to 100,000 at the turn of the century. Historian Carey McWilliams observed that "by 1900 Los Angeles was the best advertised city in America." The Chamber of Commerce circulated more than two million brochures extolling the bright sunshine and year-round flowers. A special train, bearing the painted name *California on Wheels,* whistled across the Midwest and the South, and wherever it stopped porters emerged bearing baskets of fruit and neat packets of photographs of life in Los Angeles.

By 1910 the city's population had trebled, to nearly 320,000. A transit system operated by Pacific Electric Railway—and identified simply as the Red Cars—ran all the way to Long Beach, twenty-four miles south of Los Angeles. The Red Cars provided all the interurban rail traffic needed for decades.

Among newcomers to the city in 1910 was a theatrical director named D. W. Griffith. He brought with him a company of players including Mary Pickford, then sixteen years old. He found the climate "just right" for winter filming, and he shot one movie after another in the San Fernando Valley, including *The Birth of a Nation,* an effort which moved President Woodrow Wilson to comment: "He's writing history with lightning."

Harry Chandler later took an active part in encouraging the movie industry to make its headquarters in Los Angeles, but his priorities, in the first decade of the century, dealt with other matters. Los Angeles and its surrounding area, always in need of water, had depended for more than a century upon streams of varying sizes that flowed down from the San Gabriel Mountains, sometimes raging spring torrents, more often a slow but steady underground push. Recurring droughts sharply curtailed urban life and brought severe hardships to farmers. A growing city—and Harry Chandler had nothing less ambitious on his mind—would require a vast new source of water. "If you don't get the water," the city's chief engineer, William Mulholland, often remarked to civic leaders, "you won't need it."

All the water Los Angeles required was found in the heart of the Sierra Nevada, 240 miles to the northeast, in a green valley of orchards and farms fed by the Owens River. Thanks to a land development program initiated by the United States Congress and the Federal Bureau of Land Reclamation, farmers in the Owens Valley gained the impression that a major

project was underway to capture the spill from the Owens
River for the purpose of developing thousands of acres of
land. Most farmers, seeing direct benefits ahead, relinquished
their water rights.

Complications developed, however, when the Federal Reclamation Bureau changed its mind about developing the Owens
Valley. The water rights, up for grabs, were quickly purchased by a Los Angeles syndicate led by General Otis and
Harry Chandler, E. H. Harriman of the Southern Pacific and
assorted bankers. At the same time the *Los Angeles Times*
thumped enthusiastically for a mighty aqueduct to carry water
from the Owens Valley to the San Fernando Valley, which
offered a natural underground reservoir from which the city
could pump water as it was needed. There was a legal obstacle,
easily overcome by Los Angeles annexing the San Fernando
Valley. Los Angeles voters approved a bond issue to pay for
the long aqueduct, which was built at a cost of $23 million.

When in 1913 the 240-mile aqueduct was completed and
water gushed forth, chief engineer William Mulholland delivered a curt, classic comment: "There it is; take it." As the
Los Angeles desert grew lush, other nearby towns eagerly
annexed themselves to the city in order to get water.

"You and the *Los Angeles Times* have been so conspicu-
ously devoted to the successful upbuilding of Southern California," wrote one of Harry Chandler's business colleagues
to the *Times* publisher, "that with an adequate water supply
—and having the climate, electric power, oil and gas—all the
fundamentals are at hand to create in Los Angeles County the
largest center of population which the world has ever known."

Whether the Los Angeles–based syndicate sought mainly
growth for a city in need of water or wealth for the members
of the syndicate—or whether those two goals were inseparably
interwoven—has never been documented. But some critics

from the beginning were sure they knew the answers. The aqueduct became a cannon in a water war that still rages on in the twentieth century, with recurring claims that water was obtained for Los Angeles by "the rape of the Owens Valley."

What really happened? Dr. Abraham Hoffman, a specialist in environmental history and a teacher at Los Angeles Valley College, made a searching examination of the evidence and in 1981 published a landmark study (*Vision or Villainy: Origins of the Owens Valley–Los Angeles Water Controversy,* Texas A&M University Press). In it he unveiled some fresh insights into the long-running drama:

From the diatribes of hostile critics in the 1930s to the motion picture *Chinatown* and the PBS television program *California Dreams: Thirsty City,* virtually everything available to the public dealing with the Owens Valley–Los Angeles water controversy derives from a long-forgotten civic reformer named Andrae B. Nordskog. Although his name is barely remembered today, Nordskog had a tremendous influence on the writers who in a long historiographical chain have made familiar the conspiratorial idea that Los Angeles stole the water of Owens River from the people of Owens Valley.

Andrae Nordskog was one of these rare people who put an astonishing amount of activity into one lifetime. A native of Iowa who came to Los Angeles around 1920, Nordskog was at one time or another a professional concert tenor, a teacher of voice, an author, publisher, record producer, candidate for vice president on a minor political party ticket, and a newspaper editor. He named his weekly gadfly newspaper the *Gridiron,* a title that had nothing to do with football. Nordskog aimed to put the heat on local politics.

At first the *Gridiron* took on such targets as telephone rates and graft in street paving, but before long . . . the water dispute attracted Nordskog's attention, and he became converted to the

Owens Valley's cause. In 1927 he began featuring headlines and editorials in the *Gridiron* that severely criticized the city's position in the controversy. He obtained radio time on station KGEF and baited Los Angeles Department of Water and Power officials with charges of corruption and incompetence. His campaign ended abruptly, however, in November 1927. Wilfred and Mark Watterson, leading Inyo County bankers who had organized the fight against the city, were found to have embezzled funds from their own banks. With the failure of the banks, resistance against the city collapsed. In the investigation that followed, DWP representatives discovered documents which showed clearly that the Wattersons had paid several thousand dollars to subsidize Nordskog's newspaper. The Los Angeles Municipal League, a pro-aqueduct civic organization, gleefully published the incriminating letters and challenged Nordskog's integrity.

Although subjected to exposure and ridicule, Nordskog remained firmly convinced of the rightness of the Owens Valley's grievances. Brushing off criticism of his acceptance of the subsidy, he began to look further into the motives behind the city's aggressive water policies.

Early in 1928 Nordskog went to Washington, D.C., and visited the Bureau of Reclamation offices. He secured permission to transcribe documents and was in fact able to remove letters from the files. Nordskog used this material to fashion a 540-page manuscript which he titled *Boulder Dam in the light of the Owens Valley fraud*. This remarkable effort linked the then pending construction of Boulder Dam with the Owens River Aqueduct as a seamless conspiratorial plot dating back to 1904. The scheme involved leading Los Angeles entrepreneurs who had enriched themselves at the expense of California taxpayers. In charge of this plot was the "Mulholland political crowd," a somewhat amorphous group that linked [chief water engineer] William Mulholland, the Harrison Gray Otis–Harry Chandler Los Angeles Times dynasty, and other city leaders together in a scheme to make their city and themselves all-powerful in the development of Los Angeles' potential urban influence. . . .

Nordskog's *Boulder Dam* manuscript seemed destined for oblivion despite its sensational charges. [But] in March 1931 a state senate committee was investigating Los Angeles' actions in Inyo county. Nordskog boiled his manuscript down to a lengthy letter which he sent to the committee as a "communication," summarizing his charges against the city and the aqueduct supporters. Nordskog's letter did not affect the committee's recommendations. . . . But its content did impress the committee. The letter was ordered read into the legislative journal, and 1,500 copies were printed as a twenty-eight-page pamphlet: *Communication to the California Legislature Relating to the Owens Valley Water Situation.*

This pamphlet has come to be of lasting influence in the history of the water controversy. Published by the state printing office, it carried the state seal on its title page, which to the uncritical eye gave it the appearance of an official state document. Copies were placed in every major public and school library in the state. . . . [The pamphlet and a series of books based on it] formed a seedbed of influence for later writers, from Carey McWilliams in his 1946 *Southern California Country* down to David Halberstam's 1979 *The Powers That Be*. Professional historians, including the authors of leading textbooks on the state's history, have accepted Nordskog's findings at face value. . . . Nordskog died in 1962, his legacy a viewpoint of the water controversy that has kept the fires of alleged conspiracy alive until and beyond *Chinatown*.

Throughout his life Harry Chandler pushed hard for the growth of the city. He accepted wholeheartedly his father-in-law's dictum that it was a publisher's privilege to be a community booster and he kept vigilant watch for opportunities to lure new industries to Southern California. He took careful notice when M. H. DeYoung, publisher of the *San Francisco Chronicle,* induced the Christie Brothers, creators of custard-pie comedies, to locate their film-making activities near San Francisco, even providing them with a studio.

The Christies were large vivid figures in the infant film industry, and if they took root in San Francisco, DeYoung knew that other studios would follow.

Harry Chandler swiftly arrived at the same conclusion. He had made it his business to know how movies were shot and understood that artificial lighting had not reached the intensity required to photograph interior scenes, and therefore cameramen had to rely on the sun. Indoor scenes were shot against three walls with an open ceiling. When the sun went behind a cloud, shooting stopped. Through the *Times* correspondent in San Francisco, he kept track of the weather, and when a period of fog settled over the bay, Chandler urged the Los Angeles Chamber of Commerce to send a mission north with a message that the sun was shining in Los Angeles. Finding the Christie company idle and disgruntled, the Los Angeles expeditionary forces loaded them—cast, cameras and custard pies—on a southbound train. That ended San Francisco's movie aspirations.

As additional moviemakers settled in Los Angeles, Chandler sent reporters to observe their activities. He became so impressed with the possibilities of film that in 1913 the *Times* elevated cinema to a place of equality in the performing arts. Shortly after, the paper launched the first motion-picture page in American journalism.

Constantly alert to the possibility of enticing other industries to Southern California, Chandler urged the Chamber of Commerce to beat the drum hard for tourists, and to promote the area's climatic advantages as invaluable to the task of plane-making, much of which had to be accomplished outdoors in the final test stages. World War I had emphasized the potential of aircraft in daily life as well as over the battlefield.

Donald Douglas, a thirty-eight-year-old aircraft engineer,

arrived in Los Angeles with a $600 grubstake in 1920. He carried an order from the U.S. Navy for three experimental torpedo planes and he also carried letters of introduction to Californians of substance who were charmed to meet him but not interested in financing the production of aircraft.

He used part of his minuscule bankroll to rent the back-room of a downtown barbershop as a base for pursuing capital, and he enlisted the aid of a friend, William M. (Bill) Henry, to put him in touch with potential backers.

Bill Henry, who later became a widely known columnist for the *Times,* brought Douglas in to talk with Harry Chandler. The engineer figured he needed $15,000.

"I am not sure whether you know anything about building airplanes or not," said Chandler, "but Los Angeles needs more business enterprises." On a scrap of paper he wrote the names of the nine largest financial investors in town. "If each of these men will guarantee one tenth of the loan, I'll guarantee a tenth," he said.

Surmising that Douglas was too shy for the task, Chandler urged genial-mannered Bill Henry to accompany the aircraft engineer. They had four days in which to qualify for the Navy contract. The last name on the list was that of Joseph Sartori, head of the huge Security Bank. When he signed, Henry asked if the banker would consider it a good loan.

"I guess it's all right," said Sartori. "You have at least a hundred million dollars' worth of guaranty behind the fifteen-thousand-dollar loan."

The three planes were finished in a tool shed downtown. As soon as the Navy tried them, it placed an order for twenty-five more. Whereupon engineer Donald Douglas rented an abandoned movie studio in Santa Monica and began building planes in a big way, a move that led ultimately to making the region a major center of aerospace activity.

Interviewed many years later about his early plane-making experience, Donald Douglas recalled that Harry Chandler never asked for a share of the company. "He in those days was really the chap who made the town progress. He was many, many things. When you got in [to see him], you'd sit down and discuss your problem with him. He was a very kindly chap. Of course, I'm sure that in certain sectors he had the reputation of being a money-grabber, but that was not my experience."

In the privacy of his office, however, Harry Chandler was not entirely uncritical of plane maker Douglas. When the aircraft firm made plans in 1940 to celebrate its twentieth anniversary, Chandler sent a note to *Times* editor Loyal Hotchkiss complaining about all the publicity given to the plane-making company.

"Of course," wrote Chandler, "it will make altogether a sensational story of progress and achievement." But he objected to the pressure tactics of Douglas press agents who sent along "a mass of material." He added: "Douglas, I assume, must have grown very wealthy, but when it comes to money matters he is as 'tight' as they make them. He never does any advertising, and because his progress has been so rapid as to make it sensational, he has naturally had an enormous amount of free advertising in the form of news."

Awed by the marvels of aviation, Harry Chandler possessed no basic comprehension of nor trust in mechanical devices. He disdained motor cars, and never really mastered the driving art. One *Times* editor, Harry Carr, related in a privately printed memoir how Chandler first ventured out on his own: "He couldn't remember how to stop the first car he drove, and yelled 'whoa' at it. But he learned. He finally emerged with a 1910 Franklin which he drove until he wore the thing out.

"Those who [traveled] with him would hear a crack and a pop and some of the machinery would bounce out in the middle of the floor. 'Wonder what that was?' he would say mildly. 'Well, seems to go all right without it.' "

Chandler usually read *Times* editorials after they were in print, for such was the faith he placed in his appointees in key positions. Only if an issue was especially sensitive would his top editor show him the copy beforehand.

Letters of complaint occasionally reached Chandler's desk. He would scan them quickly, digest their content, then scrawl across the top: "What's this all about? H.C." He backed his troops to the hilt when the facts jibed, but his wrath rang loud if his precious paper was found wrong.

When community-wide complaints came to his attention, Chandler could without hesitation involve himself personally, as he did in the booming Twenties when a widespread demand for business loans sent interest rates skyrocketing. Numerous readers wrote to the *Times* to protest that bankers were taking unfair advantage of the boom and charging usurious rates, and Chandler soon teamed up with an influential attorney, Marshall Stimson, to explore ways of enacting an anti-usury law. Stimson, who had been a political enemy of General Otis', recorded in his memoirs a "very close friendship" with Chandler.

Of their collaboration on the project Stimson wrote: "Chandler said the practices carried on by some of the money lenders were an outrage. . . . He gave a check for $1,000 [to a senatorial control advocate] and told him that the *Times* would support the campaign [to stop the banks] to the fullest extent, which was done, and greatly aided in the successful effort to put the [anti-usury] law on the statute books." When a group of bankers protested, claiming it would hamper ex-

pansion, Chandler replied: "Gentlemen! If your business success is dependent on such practices as usury, you had better
go out of business."

Chandler involved himself energetically in community
causes. When a worthy project came to his attention, it was
his practice to invite a group of wealthy acquaintances to
lunch, in a private dining room above his office in the *Times*
building, and there he would tap each guest for a contribution
of $1,000 to help put the project across.

One participant later recalled a typical telephone invitation
to lunch:

"Fred, I'm giving a luncheon Tuesday and I want you to
come."

"Is there going to be a touch, Harry?"

"No touch, Fred—that is, unless the majority wills it."

It became axiomatic among Los Angeles businessmen that
it cost $1,000 to have lunch with Harry Chandler. He per-
suaded his luncheon guests in 1920 to join him in building
the California Institute of Technology. The following year
he pressed them to support the construction of a mammoth
coliseum, so that the city might eventually play host to the
Olympic Games (and the Olympics went to Los Angeles in
1932). Another time he put the touch on his friends to help
build the Hollywood Bowl. He took the lead in replacing
scattered multiple railroad points-of-entry with a single, elaborate Union Station, opened in 1939.

Harry Chandler attributed his considerable energy to an
alert and abiding interest in good health. In fact, he was a
health faddist dating back to his arrival in Southern California
and his earliest efforts to overcome illness. In his sixties he
grew hugely interested in so-called "goat gland transplants"
which were presumed to rejuvenate the male sex drive. As
a result the *Times* featured frequent stories on this procedure
and made much of a "world-famous surgeon" who claimed he

had performed more than eight thousand such transplants in a valiant "battle against old age."

The *Times* backed gingerly away several years later, however, after Dr. Philip M. Lovell, the paper's "Care of the Body" columnist, wrote business manager Jacob Baum that "there is about one-tenth of one percent merit in this endocrinology stuff. . . . Confidentially, this fellow [the "world-famous surgeon"] is the biggest hokum peddler of them all."

There was an ironic side to Harry Chandler's keen interest in health. He failed to notice that the *Times* itself was not in hale and hearty condition, nor vigorous enough to cope with serious problems on the horizon.

4

From the eagle-encrusted turret of his granite headquarters at First and Broadway, Harry Chandler's agate brown eyes surveyed the world with dignity. Unlike his father-in-law, he did not enjoy a scrap for its own sake. He had infused the paper with an air of congeniality that pleased and surprised many readers grown inured to Otis' thunder. It was not hard for Harry Chandler to feel congenial. He had inherited a rapidly expanding concern, one that owed much of its predominance in Southern California to his thrust and ambition; it was he who had kept his New England nose to the grindstone while Otis busied himself with editorial wrangles.

His appealing good nature proved challenging to the editors of the fiercely rival *Los Angeles Record*. They embarked on an acerbic portrait of the *Times* and its owner in 1924, calling him and his paper "the greatest power of darkness in Los Angeles." Yet the *Record* editors were moved to a few kind words, with slight reservations, about his work habits and home life:

Even though his "unflagging activity makes him dangerous to all progressive projects . . . he hasn't a lazy bone in his body." The *Record* noted that he was a multimillionaire, yet drove himself harder than any of his employees. An early riser, he ate a large breakfast, but no lunch. He often carried a large apple in his pocket and munched on that, even at business luncheons. He would hurry home for a 6:30 p.m. dinner, then return to the office to work until 2:00 a.m., always "putting the paper to bed." In short, his was an eighteen-hour day.

The *Record* sketch continued: "In one sense Chandler is extremely democratic. There he sits, with all the doors to his office always open, for anyone who wishes to come and go. . . . He receives more people every day than all the rest of the Los Angeles publishers combined. . . .

"At sixty he is hale and hearty as a nut, with still a fairish amount of greying hair, with a twinkle still in his clear keen eyes, his cheeks rosy as a girl's, his smile ready and winning. . . .

"His family life is almost his sole recreation. He seldom has opportunity, with his hours, to step into a playhouse, whether for grand opera or for vaudeville. He has eight children, ranging in age from Frances, 33, to the twins Philip and Helen, who are 17. They are still at Hollywood High School."

Harry's eldest son, Norman, was far from a spoiled heir. He labored summers as a farmhand on the 270,000-acre Tejon Ranch, seventy-five miles north of Los Angeles, punching cattle and picking fruit, learning from high school age on that he would be expected to perform specific chores in exchange for a regular allowance, however meager a sum it might be. "Father never gave us money to spend foolishly, on the theory that if we didn't earn it, the gift would spoil us."

Courtly and charming, dashingly handsome, coppered by the sun, Norman cut a striking figure on the campus of Stanford University, where he enrolled in 1919. He majored in economics, and while he was not a brilliant student, he performed his academic assignments tolerably enough to stay abreast of the tide.

During his sophomore year he whistled at a pretty girl and soon learned that her name was Dorothy Buffum. She was called Buff, and her father was mayor of Long Beach and proprietor of a department store. They began dating, and Norman chafed under the restrictions of a miserly allowance. "Whatever we did," Buff recalled later, "banana splits, dinners, anything like that, I would usually have to pay at least half the bill, because he was always broke."

When dating led to love, Norman took a bold step. "I decided I would rather go to work and get married than continue my studies. I was anxious to start a career at the *Times*, and the courses I was taking didn't look like preparation for the newspaper business. I had two more semesters remaining when I asked my mother if I could quit. When I told her why, she gave me her blessing."

In 1922, the year they were married, much of the populace was feeling prosperous, but Buff and Norman were strapped. As a trainee Norman worked in various business departments of the *Times*, including circulation, where he delivered and collected papers for a salary of $16 a week. Living on this and the proceeds of a small trust fund, they drove a Model T and rented an upstairs flat at a fractionated address. Years later Buff remarked: "I remember being so embarrassed when I charged things, to have to list that half."

Quiet and cautious, tackling a variety of chores as his father's untitled aide, Norman had no literary pretensions. "I didn't see myself as a writer, but I was fascinated by writers and the way they worked."

Norman noted carefully that his father delegated editorial authority to subordinates, and Norman never altered that relationship. Norman did not demand that his top editors devote excessively long hours to the job, but he grew accustomed to seeing them do so. Ralph Waldo Trueblood, a short, squarish, solemn-faced man, was the prototypical editorial executive. City editor Loyal Hotchkiss claimed Trueblood could put in a twenty-four-hour day, including working during the time he spent commuting aboard the big red trolley car from central Los Angeles to his Brentwood home, nearly twenty miles away. Those who shared his bench on the trolley "still bear scissor marks from sitting too close to him on those daily trips," as he bent over the paper with his bespectacled eyes alert for clippable items.

Stanley Gordon, an employee of the era, recalled of Trueblood: "Both his steely-eyed glance and resonant voice were penetrating, and this was because of his deafness. In conversation he had to watch the other speaker's lips to aid his hearing, and he spoke a bit louder than normal because he wanted to make sure you heard him.

"I worked in the editorial library for four years and Trueblood was our most indefatigable 'customer' in search of accurate facts and figures. He seemed to be personally checking out every statement of fact made by the *Times*." If a reporter was right, Trueblood would fight to the last ditch for him, Gordon noted, whereas "proof of error" by a writer resulted in "the guillotine."

During the Twenties and Thirties, Los Angeles grew rapidly. A young air-mail pilot, Charles Lindbergh, in 1927 picked up a $25,000 prize for his feat of making the first transatlantic flight from New York to Paris, an achievement that helped to stimulate activity in Southern California's aircraft industry. That same year Ralph Bunche—a twenty-two-year-old political science major—delivered the commencement address at the University of California's Los Angeles campus, then located near the center of the city. "The world is periodically scourged and scarred by fiendish wars," said Bunche, who would later win the Nobel Prize. "The future peace and harmony of the world are contingent upon the ability—yours and mine—to effect a remedy." That same year William Mulholland, the engineer in charge of bringing water by aqueduct from the Owens Valley to the San Fernando Valley, was guest of honor at a banquet given by the Los Angeles Department of Water and Power. Someone suggested that Mulholland run for mayor, but he rejected the idea instantly, saying: "I'd rather give birth to a porcupine backwards." Across town the movie industry was experimenting with motion pictures in which, a *Times* reporter noted, "you can actually hear what the actors and actresses are saying."

The growth of the area advanced rapidly, stimulated not only by activity in the movie and aircraft industries but by relentless advertising campaigns in Midwestern and Eastern publications extolling the benign climate of Southern California. Businesses sprang up across the city, attracted in part by a surface calm in labor relations. Many business investors, searching for a location, were appalled and frightened by the spectacle of San Francisco—a vivid example of a municipality held in thrall by unions, with periodic general strikes, waterfront violence, hiring halls and all the other accouterments of Big Labor. To keep Los Angeles free of labor strife was an article of faith for the *Times,* and for the powerful Merchant & Manufacturers Association.

The Los Angeles Police Department formed an "antisubversive" squad which grew to impressive proportions under the reign of three consecutive mayors. The squad devoted most of its time to defusing union picket lines and keeping strike action to a minimum, much to the *Times'* pleasure. Vice and gambling flourished across the city, but the Establishment—legal big business—was too preoccupied with its own expansive affairs to worry about little things like clandestine amusements, even when underworld tentacles began reaching into the area's nonpartisan government. Los Angeles' "good name" remained important. So when early crusades raised their voices against these evils, the Establishment responded: Stop denigrating our fair city; criticism hampers development of Southern California.

When a 1928 grand jury indicted four police officers for prostitution and gambling payoffs, the *Times* referred to the jurors as "busybodies" and played the incident down.

In 1933, Los Angeles chose Frank Shaw as its mayor, and one historian of the era wrote: "From his immediate predecessor . . . Frank Shaw inherited a load of mischief—a compound of impudent knaveries imposed by a group of political shysters, petty bosses, vice barons, and business cliques whose main idea was to keep open for themselves the avenues of graft and privilege at City Hall. Shaw never seemed to view his inheritance as uncongenial. Rather, he worked energetically to improve its potentialities."

Times political reporter Carl Greenberg wrote about Frank Shaw in a retrospective four decades later: "Shaw announced that the 'era of snooping' in and out of the police department was over as far as he was concerned. Yet houses of prostitution were all over town. So were gambling joints. Slot machines could be found in the rear of many restaurants. Pinball machines that paid off in cash helped pay the rent in many small business establishments. Bookies were tripping over each other. Neither public nor press had raised an alarm."

A fledgling *Times* reporter late in 1934 accompanied a police prowl car, one of the first equipped with two-way radio, on a nightlong tour of the city. In the small hours, Commanding Officer Bradford J. St. Charles asked whether the newsman and his photographer would "like to visit a whorehouse." This was too tempting an offer to decline.

So the police car parked in front of a moldering two-story frame house. All four occupants debarked. They pounded up an outside stairway, rang the doorbell and were greeted by a flustered madam who shouted angrily, "Officer St. Charles,

I paid you last week." This incident never saw print. It was deemed too inconsequential by Editor Hotchkiss, a solid *status quo* journalist.

Three months later, Commanding Officer St. Charles, a dapper, pencil-mustached hero of "many gun battles with bandits," was summarily arrested as the fingerman for a bank robbery gang, and accorded a fifteen-year prison term at McNeil's Island.

Corruption on a massive scale became a hallmark of the Shaw regime. A citizen group of reformers, dedicated to the mission of recalling Mayor Shaw from office, went before a grand jury and brought accusations of well-financed underworld influence over Los Angeles County officialdom; use of vice profits to help elect the district attorney, sheriff, various mayors, councilmen and judges; public ignorance through cover-ups; terror campaigns against concerned citizens; the subsidizing of newspapermen; special "honors" for civic and religious leaders.

The *Times* itself was termed derelict in its duty to print all the news about the quickening scandals. Inside the paper, when Harry Chandler asked for an explanation, editor Hotchkiss sent him a defensive memorandum: "We have carried all of [the citizen-group's] statements that are newsworthy and in no instance have we ever side-stepped news of vice in Los Angeles."

But if Hotchkiss failed to see the scandals, the voters did not, and Mayor Shaw was recalled from office by an almost two-to-one margin.

The *Times* itself harbored a nest of colorful characters. Tim Turner, a tall, lean, skin-bald newsman who had covered Pancho Villa's Mexican rebellion for the Associated Press, joined the *Times* in the mid-Twenties and worked the hotel beat: based at the Biltmore, he fanned out from that golden hostelry to other places where the famous stayed during their visits to Los Angeles.

With Turner arrived one Major Gaston da Prida, who had been a correspondents' aide in the revolution south of the border. A self-assured, pint-sized character, he nominally worked for *La Opinión,* the local Mexican newspaper. He visited the *Times* regularly to swipe photographic electroplates, borrow sawbucks from an amiable Harry Chandler at odd hours and accept Hotchkiss' hand-me-down suits. Da Prida's most notorious foray into the city room occurred late one night when he brought with him a tall redhaired girl clad in an ankle-length mink coat. Swept back, it revealed total nakedness beneath. The diminutive major provided a congenial respite for the staff, and a sizable wad for himself, by parceling out her favors at $2 per fifteen minutes in the darkroom.

Enter the Great Depression. By 1934, Upton Sinclair, a fiery social reformer, had written forty-seven books and dramas advancing conclusions about the country's errors and his theories of how to set things right. His final book, before he plunged into the gubernatorial campaign that year as a Socialist-turned-Democrat against a united Republican party and a broad assortment of disgruntled Democrats, was *The EPIC Plan for California,* which outlined an anti-Depression program.

"To me," Sinclair wrote in his autobiography, "the remedy was obvious. The factories were idle, and the workers had no money. Let them be put to work on the state's credit and produce goods for their own use, and set up a system of exchange by which the goods could be distributed. 'Production for use' was the slogan."

EPIC, which stood for End Poverty in California, was hotly denounced across the political spectrum. At one end Norman Thomas, the preeminent U.S. Socialist, called the plan a "tin-can economy" and Sinclair "a renegade to the Socialist movement." At the other end, the conservative press, led by the *Times,* attacked EPIC and dismissed Sinclair as "a visionary, a consorter with radicals, a theorist."

When Sinclair won the primary, the *Times,* which then had a circulation of 175,000, stepped up its attack. It carried stories predicting that hordes of unemployed in other states would immediately hop freights for California if Sinclair was elected. It climaxed these alarms by dispatching Guy Stafford, an ardent Chandler loyalist and future city editor, to the Yuma, Arizona, and Needles, California, border to interview the oncoming jobless. His story, appearing less than two weeks before the November election, leaves scant doubt that he handpicked his subjects with finesse:

Steam sizzled from a capless radiator. Screeching brakes died with a whine and the bedlam of rattles and bangs stopped as a dilapidated truck came to a sudden halt at the State border. . . .

"We're part of a crowd of folks that started from Oklahomie and Texas early in September and we air just gettin' to Californey," the head of the family announced. . . .

Discreet inquiries brought out the information that the caravan contains some 200 cars and trucks with about 1,000 passengers.

"Yeah, we're comin' to Californey to get some of that free land when this feller Sinclair is elected Governor. We been told that he is goin' to give an acre to every married man and that the youngens can work. . . . "

Multiply these scenes by almost every hour in the day, each day in the week, and one gets a picture of the great migration of "end poverty" that has been pouring into California since the first week in September.

Upton Sinclair was defeated in the November election by Republican Frank Merriam, a colorless transplanted Iowan who had the staunch support of the *Times*.

Norman Chandler had complete faith in the goals of the Republican party, but his gentle and kindly nature stood in sharp contrast to the sometimes excessively harsh and narrow editorial policies of the *Times*.

Not that he ever entertained doubts about the correctness of the paper's refusal to recognize the closed shop. Throughout his life he carried vivid memories of the 1910 bombing. But while he had little sympathy for unions, he also had a keen sense of the need to establish enlightened personnel policies, and, in the early 1940s, when his father eventually gave him sufficient authority to make improvements in the paper, Norman proceeded to hire a personnel manager, set up a personnel department and establish such unheard-of benefits as pension and medical plans, a bonus and an annual salary review to keep *Times'* pay levels abreast of prevalent rates.

Norman was made distinctly uneasy by some of the candidates the *Times* chose to support. He held serious misgivings about Mayor Frank Shaw, who was "a bad egg. We went overboard in supporting him. We were wrong."

But Norman was never a boatrocker. At age thirty-five he was still his father's untitled aide, and he possessed neither the time nor the intimate knowledge of public affairs to raise many questions about the paper's news and editorial coverage. He was almost totally preoccupied, from the moment he joined the staff, with the health and welfare of the *Times*.

He was astonished by the paradoxes in his father's nature. For a man possessed of extraordinary business acumen, Harry Chandler was an easy mark for those who had fallen onto hard

times or simply needed a break. "He was always helping someone in trouble," Norman said, "and he held more worthless
IOUs than anyone else in town."

Harry Chandler fit the image of a wealthy eccentric who
paid less attention to money than to land. Family grocery
bills frequently went unpaid. His children were unsure
whether the cause lay in absentmindedness or in land acquisitions that left him short of cash.

Even more astonishing was his approach to the *Times*. Often
engrossed with wheeling and dealing on a larger stage, chan-
neling his energies toward building an empire and a city,
Harry neglected to pay close attention to the financial condition of the newspaper. Management procedures ranged from
nonexistent to breathtakingly casual. An easygoing paternal-
ism kept the paper heavily staffed with deadwood; few were
let go even when the stock-market crash of 1929 foreshadowed
hard times and a dwindling of newspaper revenues.

Devoted to his father and yet privately dismayed at his
benign approach to the details of *Times'* business, Norman
waged a lonely battle to check the drift of the paper. In time
he concluded that nothing less than a major shakeup was
needed, from top to bottom. He told an interviewer years
later: "We were not in good shape financially, and things were
getting worse. By the early Thirties, with depression all
around us, both Hearst papers, the *Examiner* and *Herald,*
had passed us in circulation. We held a slight lead in advertising volume, but they were gradually overtaking us."

Norman was essentially a transition man, very different in
important ways from his grandfather Otis (Norman had no
time for choleric anger, no taste for squabbling and feuding)
and very different from his father (Norman frowned on ruth-
less behavior, sidestepped the tumult and roughness of political and economic warfare in an open arena).

He obtained his father's permission in 1933 to hire an efficiency expert, Colonel Guy T. Visknisski, to make a detailed survey of the entire company, and to produce "concrete recommendations" for cutting costs and boosting revenues. A grim-faced bantam who specialized in doctoring ailing newspapers, Visknisski drew up a book-length blueprint of steps to be taken, and he personally took charge of hiring and firing. Despised, branded a mercenary interloper, he ignored the scorn heaped upon him by employees who nervously asked each other: "Have you been Visknisskied yet?"

One of Visknisski's important early actions was to name Norman assistant general manager of the *Times*. This step, taken in 1934, relieved Harry Chandler, then general manager, of "details of his functions" by making sure all top-level orders were "carried out in the spirit as well as in the letter." The new title also made Norman the executive to whom the advertising and circulation managers reported; it was a long-needed tightening up of the key revenue-producing departments of the paper.

Norman's reputation as a conscientious scion was not lost on rival publishers, including William Randolph Hearst. Although there was never a close relationship between the Hearsts and the Chandlers, they inevitably ran into each other occasionally at social functions. One time Harry, Norman and Buff were invited by Marion Davies to spend a weekend at Hearst's San Simeon castle. The reason for the invitation, Buff later learned, was to present Norman as role model to young George Hearst, whose life up to that point consisted almost entirely of playboy escapades.

Although respectful and deferential toward his father, Norman approached his newly defined responsibilities by carefully asking Harry's advice as each important business decision arose. "But my father's standard reply was: 'Well, you're running the paper, you do what you want.' So I stopped inquiring and just went ahead."

The downward drift of the *Times* could not be reversed easily, however, especially during the Depression. One Christmas in the late Thirties, addressing his assembled employees, Norman wept openly when he had to announce that the customary annual bonus was canceled for lack of funds.

Part Three

NORMAN CHANDLER
(1944 - 1960)

5

B ENEATH his gentle, kindly manner Norman had a steely determination, a keen sense of dynasty, an intuitive responsibility to family and family interests and the community at large. He never let his attention stray from the affairs of the company or from the condition of Southern California's economy—the *Times* and the West were linked inextricably.

The dark clouds of the Depression, lifting gradually over Los Angeles in the late Thirties, vanished completely as defense orders poured into West Coast factories. With Germany's Luftwaffe pounding one European country after another in a furious crescendo of air assaults, the United States in 1941 adopted the Lend-Lease Act, which authorized the President to "sell, transfer, exchange, lease, lend" any defense articles "to the government of any country whose defense the President deems vital to the defense of the United States."

Demand for war equipment, especially aircraft, brought about a swift transformation in Los Angeles. *Fortune* magazine in 1941 noted the changes: "They are making dive bombers in the Land of Oz. . . . Here is the airplane industry, depending on metals, an industry that belongs in Detroit or Gary, mushrooming up in the richest agricultural county in the U.S. . . . Here is an industry, attracting masses of labor, springing up in a city that is supposed to hate labor's guts. . . .

There is no precedent in incongruity for what is happening in Los Angeles in 1941—except the eternal incongruities of Los Angeles itself."

The city's population had passed the 1,500,000 mark in the 1940 census, and in that same year a new $5 million limited-access concrete road was completed, connecting city and suburb. It was called the Pasadena Freeway and became a prototype of express roads in the future. One British architectural critic later called the Los Angeles freeway system "one of the greater works of man."

Artists were borrowed from movie studios to camouflage Los Angeles area defense plants; the massive roofs of aircraft factories, including Lockheed at Burbank and Douglas at Santa Monica, were painted with cows and trees.

Inside the aircraft industry another kind of change took place. Large production orders, coupled with the departure of men to military service, created a labor shortage. Women applied for assembly-line jobs, but at first, industry management resisted the idea of women and men working together. Vultee Aircraft produced a document claiming that it lost $250 in worktime whenever a woman walked through the plant because men stopped to look.

As the labor shortage intensified, factory doors were gradually opened to women: by 1943 there were 113,000 women working in aircraft production, representing 40 percent of the labor force. But patronizing attitudes persisted. Douglas forbade women to wear tight-fitting sweaters with bare midriffs. In one corner of a North American factory a sign was posted: "No Profanity. Women Working Inside." When one company's bomb shelter was rumored to be a trysting place, heavy paper was tacked over the entrance with a sign: "To be broken only in case of a real air raid." Another company, in its house publication, offered helpful hints with an article

"Beauty Tips for Planeswomen," assuring that even work-stained hands can be made "soft and white as ever."

Not only aerospace but a wide range of industries boomed in Los Angeles during the war, from electronics to photographic equipment, from metalworking machinery to plastic and rubber products. Scientists, engineers, technicians arrived in the city, as many as five thousand a week, in search of jobs, and their presence created an extraordinary demand for housing, furniture, appliances, streets, autos, schools, shopping centers.

The changes taking place at nearly every level of society were immediately apparent to Norman Chandler. He had learned even as a young man that the paper's classified ads functioned as a barometer of things to come, foretelling the needs and desires of the population.

Frequently, after an evening of studying the ads for the next day's *Times,* he would remark to his wife Buff that the transformation of Los Angeles—in the rising tide of population, the humming economy and new houses springing up rapidly across an ever-widening landscape, and not least in the emergence of women in the ranks of labor—was happening almost too swiftly to be seen and understood.

Buff agreed, and her reaction encompassed a personal drama in the saga of consciousness-raising. She was restless. A person of extraordinary drive and ambition, she was destined to become the most celebrated of the Chandler women, to gain world fame as an achiever, to make an unprecedented mark on Los Angeles and the West. This was not foreseen, however, in Norman Chandler's family, where enthusiasm for Buff was noticeably restrained. The family—a sister here, a brother and sister-in-law there—did not see Buff, the daughter of a dry-goods merchant, as quite good enough for the Chandlers.

They were wrong. Trim, intense and imaginative, her green eyes shining with vitality, she was the perfect complement to Norman. Where he was inclined to be shy, even introverted, she was outgoing and outspoken. Dashingly handsome, elegantly mannered, Norman did not need the limelight because, beneath his shy manner, he was very sure of himself, a strong-willed man with a gentle and courtly demeanor. Buff *wanted* the limelight, needing acclaim and approval, and in her competitive and ambitious way she became more Chandler-like than many of the Chandlers.

Not that her politics were conservative. She felt comfortable always as a middle-of-the-roader, preferring Dwight Eisenhower to Robert Taft, Nelson Rockefeller to Barry Goldwater.

But her need to achieve, to make a mark, to leave her footprints for others to see—these qualities were there from the start. Even in her teen years she had had a sense of time running out. "Many times I'd wake up with an anxious feeling that there was much for me to do, would I ever be able to get it done?"

From childhood she carried into adult life an active interest in the performing arts. The Buffum house in Long Beach had been filled with music and the family had a special enthusiasm for the legitimate theater. Whenever a good play or a first-rate concert opened in Los Angeles, the Buffums climbed aboard a big red electric trolley car for the twenty-four-mile ride to the city.

Buff's own family always seemed openly expressive, warm and caring. But when she married, she found a disturbingly distant attitude among several of Norman's family. Buff did not help matters by avoiding what they looked upon as "the right things"—the Junior League and other social groups. "It was important to me to help Norman in his work, to travel with him to newspaper meetings, to broaden my interests, but it didn't seem important at all to get involved with the family's garden clubs."

When outsiders inquired about coolness within the family, there were usually denials. But not from Buff. The distant attitude troubled her. She told an interviewer:

"I didn't feel they were trying to be difficult, but I felt lost because they didn't communicate. No matter how hard I tried to please them, or win their approval, they remained withdrawn, never offering a kind word or a compliment. It was terribly hard for me, because my own mother surrounded people with outgoing love. She communicated, she told people if they were pretty, or looked well, or had done something with excellence. 'How are they going to know if I don't tell them?' she often asked. So when I came into a nonexpressive family, I began to feel that something was wrong with me. I began to doubt myself, and question myself, and most of all to find faults with myself, especially when I was tired."

With two growing youngsters—Camilla, born in 1925, and Otis, born in 1927—Buff was often tired, and she found increasing fault with herself. Abruptly, at age thirty-one, she went off to live in a private psychiatric clinic in Pasadena run by Dr. Josephine Jackson. Buff stayed there for six months, coming home for a visit about once a week.

The therapeutic interlude was an unqualified success. "Dr. Jackson taught me that I had a place to fill as Norman's wife, a place of major importance in the future of the city and at the *Times* as well. She persuaded me that Norman needed me very much, and when she explained his family to me, it reversed the situation for me. She taught me to accept them as they were and, in a large sense, to bend my desire for communication and kindness, which were assets, to their weaknesses. She taught me how important it is to get the most from your assets and not to find fault with things that maybe aren't even there. She helped me to see Norman's family was not going to change or destroy me, nor was I going to change or destroy them."

With her new base of confidence, Buff grew restless. "I became more and more desirous of doing something beyond just the housewifely things that every mother does."

She went to work as a volunteer at Childrens Hospital, and on the side she raised funds for it. But during World War II she turned to a new endeavor, this time at the newspaper. The impetus came from Norman, who asked her to lend a hand. She had no specific charter; she was given the vague title of "special assistant," and, as a first step, she decided it was essential to learn more about the actual operations of the paper.

The timing was right: their children, Camilla and Otis, were away at school, and Norman was traveling frequently, undertaking periodic survey trips of Europe and Asia at the request of the U.S. government. During his absences Buff moved into the *Times* building, where she fixed up a penthouse apartment for herself, consisting of bedroom, kitchenette and bath, in what had been a loft.

She also signed up at the University of Southern California's School of Journalism, where she took courses in headline writing, copy reading, feature writing and women's sections. She studied at USC for a year, taking classes during the day, and nights she occasionally invited staff editors to visit with her in the penthouse apartment at the *Times*. Talking with them about their living and working conditions, she grew interested in personnel policies. When the company later added a new ten-story building adjacent to its headquarters, Norman placed her in charge, as management's representative, of supervising the architects and decorators.

Buff had an instinctive feel for the comforts, colors and interior design that would please staffers, but she also began to sense some staff resentment. "I'm sure people thought, 'Well, there is the boss's wife. What's she doing here? What's she sticking her nose into these things for? She doesn't really have any authority.' So I went over and applied for my social security number and went on the payroll. I noticed a change immediately."

Later she took charge of renovating and redecorating offices within the *Times* building itself, and she paid particular attention to the needs of women reporters. "I asked myself, what if I were pounding out copy all day, and then I had to go out at night to cover a concert or some social event—what facilities would I wish to have, to make myself happy and more comfortable?" She arrived at a sensible answer, and the *Times* installed a special lounge for women reporters and editors, complete with showers, ample closets for long dresses and racks for high-heeled shoes, a kitchen for refreshments, a chaise longue for taking a rest.

The challenge and fascination of discovering a new outlet for her considerable energy in the world of journalism kept her busier than she had ever been, and her clear-minded approach opened Norman's eyes wide to her executive ability. When he faced difficult decisions, he would unhesitatingly turn to Buff for advice. He disliked gambling, but during World War II he took a big chance—after discussing it with Buff—and it paid off handsomely. Amid a serious shortage of newsprint, with papers reduced to twelve or fourteen pages, Norman chose to ration advertising and to give overwhelming priority to publishing the news. The tactic stunned competitors and won a large following among readers; the *Times* emerged from the war as the only Western daily where substantial news coverage could be found.

Taking chances, however, went against the grain. The Depression era, when advertisers could not pay their bills and readers hesitated to spend a nickel for a copy, had drummed

caution into him. He knew the graveyard of history was lit-
tered with the tombstones of failed publications, and throughout his career Norman remained mindful of risks inherent
in the newspaper business.

But he gambled again in 1948 when he launched a breezy
tabloid, the *Mirror,* to attract a postwar influx of industrial
workers who were scattering into fast-growing suburbs. Norman believed that the creation of a rapid transit system was
inevitable, and that commuters—freed from their cars—would
constitute a new large market of afternoon readers. Thus
Norman could see room, he told an interviewer, "for a *good*
afternoon newspaper," meaning that Hearst's *Herald-Express*
was vulnerable to competition.

Buff gave him reinforcement by agreeing enthusiastically.
Her sources were the newcomers to Los Angeles. She became
aware of their viewpoints because she traveled among them,
raising money for cultural projects. Her involvement with
fundraising had begun on a small scale. Ever since those
childhood journeys from Long Beach on the red trolley cars,
she had been particularly alert to the ferment of artistic
change, a condition some sociologists identified as a cultural
explosion. She could see, even in the immediate postwar years,
that the once parochial community of Los Angeles was becoming a very modern city. She enlisted in a civic effort to save
the Hollywood Bowl from closing in 1951, and she discovered
that it was the newcomers to Los Angeles, not the older es-
tablished families, who cared enough about culture to support
the performing arts.

After the Hollywood Bowl, a cultural "summer house," was
saved, she followed up with another fundraising project for
a year-round home for the Los Angeles Philharmonic Orches-
tra. She persuaded the Los Angeles County Board of Super-
visors, the most powerful governmental agency in Southern
California, to set aside seven and one-half acres in the central

city (down the street from the *Los Angeles Times*) as a site for development of a Music Center.

She set an early goal of raising $4 million to build a concert hall, and she approached her prospects with a strategy that included appeals to civic pride and civic duty. When the projected costs climbed to $6 million, she raised the additional sum singlehandedly. Afterward, to celebrate, she flew to London with Norman for a ten-day vacation. Most of the ten days were spent at London's great theaters, where her attention was diverted from the onstage performances to the physical environments.

She returned from London convinced that two more buildings were needed for the Music Center—a large theater for drama, perhaps two thousand seats, and a much smaller amphitheater with perhaps seven hundred seats. Cost estimates doubled immediately, to $12 million, then rose sharply again when Buff added to the plans two restaurants and private dining rooms, additional rehearsal halls and studios.

She decided that high-ranking business executives ought to help the fundraising effort. She contacted forty-two industrialists and gave them an imposing organization title: Executive Committee of the Building Fund for the Music Center. She filled their pockets with pledge cards and prospect lists and detailed instructions on how to proceed efficiently. Their results, however, were negligible. Buff found that she had to do the job herself.

She created another group, an elite outfit known as the Blue Ribbon, whose members paid $1,000 annually for the privilege of belonging. Together they helped raise a minimum of $400,000 a year. She went much further, causing some of the city's wealthy citizens to wonder if, after all, her late father-in-law Harry Chandler had been comparatively modest with his $1,000 luncheons. Buff invited well-heeled acquaintances to a meal and unhesitatingly put the touch on them for individual contributions of $25,000, $50,000 and on some occasions $100,000.

She had raised $18 million dollars by 1964 to put up the buildings and then, to her dismay, discovered that her task had only begun. A pavilion of culture was one thing, but the performances inside carried their own steep price tag. Year after year she found it necessary to raise additional millions to cover the recurring annual deficit between the high cost of the performing arts and the much lower income from admission tickets. If actual costs were passed along to the public, as she often explained the situation to prospective donors, only the wealthy could afford to buy tickets, and this would defeat the very purpose of the Music Center: to make the performing arts available to the widest possible audience.

6

BUFF Chandler's marathon effort on behalf of the Music Center became one of the great virtuoso performances in the history of private fundraising. In her explorations across the vast Los Angeles basin she sought out more and more well-heeled newcomers, the legions of younger entrepreneurs who had arrived in town after World War II and were energetically creating new industries.

Touching base among them, constantly alert for new donors, probing, listening always with great care when others voiced their concerns, she perceived clearly that the swiftly changing population of the city required and even demanded more than a conservative, provincial newspaper. She and Norman arrived at the same conclusion. What she had put her finger on was a continuation and an outgrowth of the metropolitan stirrings that had led him to launch the tabloid *Mirror*.

By any measure Norman was less aggressive than Buff, but in his quietly cautious way he recognized in the Fifties that improvements were needed at the *Times*. Measured against the best newspapers of the East and Midwest, it was arguably a narrow, parochial, self-serving paper, boosting its friends and denouncing its enemies. Narrow in viewpoint and erratic in coverage, its reporting and editing had a distinctly small-town quality. There was no fine-arts section, no Sunday opinion or business section, no wide-open window on Washington or the world. The best items in the paper were wire-service stories and canned features bought from syndicates.

Its politics were too much the mirror reflection of one man, Kyle Palmer, who had joined the paper in 1919, at age twenty-eight, with the initial assignment of covering Washington, D.C., for the *Times*. Devoted to Harry Chandler and to his kind of conservative Republican principles, Palmer had become Harry Chandler's alter ego and a person of unsurpassed influence in political affairs. He carried the title "political editor" and during four decades gradually acquired power that no other subordinate on the *Times* ever possessed, before or since. Gladwin Hill, *New York Times* bureau chief in Los Angeles after World War II, made an exhaustive study of California politics and concluded that Palmer "was probably the top strategist of California's Republican party."

Short and stocky, with a head of wiry gray curls, Palmer had a delightfully ingratiating manner and beneath it a ruthlessly cynical nature. He spent his early years as Harry Chandler's ambassador to politics, and later he continued in the ambassadorial role on Norman's behalf. Palmer enjoyed giving large political dinners, always inviting Buff and Norman as well as important officeholders, from governor and senators and congressmen to members of the state legislature. He told candidates when to seek office and when to step aside, advised incumbents how to vote on specific issues. He plotted strategies and dealt in intrigue hour after hour.

Palmer loved the excitement of politics. He was always at the center of decision-making. It was a vantage point from which, beyond wheeling and dealing in the rarefied atmosphere of power, he picked up morsels of gossip, tantalizing items that never reached print but gave his closest associates and especially the Chandlers a feeling of being on the inside.

Some power brokers referred to Kyle Palmer as the Little Governor while others identified him merely as Mr. Republican. He made no secret of his influence, and he was, for a long time, the political boss of California. It was Palmer, of course, who brought a young lawyer, Richard Nixon, freshly mustered out of the Navy, to the attention of the Chandlers in 1946. Palmer treated Nixon like a long-lost son and guided his career with a steady hand. When at the 1952 Republican convention California's delegation failed to hold steady for its favorite son, Governor Earl Warren, and instead put thrust behind Richard Nixon to become vice-presidential candidate on the Eisenhower ticket, the liveliest topic among delegates consisted of informed speculation that it was the handiwork of Kyle Palmer.

But Palmer's manipulation of the paper's political coverage—boosting friends and denouncing enemies—was clearly an anachronism, and the most obvious symptom by the Fifties of a need to upgrade the editorial quality of the *Times*.

So when Buff relayed the complaints of influential newcomers to Norman, he was ready. In his quiet way he had already turned the switch of change; he set in motion an electric current of improvement in 1958 by tapping an uncommonly gifted staffer, Nick Williams, to become managing editor.

There was nothing radical about Nick. Like Norman, he was a gradualist, sensitive, quiet and keenly intuitive about people. Nick had been itching to strengthen the editorial staff, and while it was not his style to make waves—he had an instinctive feeling for the past and tradition—he was aware of many ways in which the paper could be changed for the better. He also knew that change did not occur quickly or lightly at the *Times*.

He had been employed at the paper since 1931, when he was twenty-five, but he had been introduced much earlier to the dash and excitment of the press. "I had my first job on a newspaper when I was eleven years of age, in Texas, where I worked nights after school as an office boy at the *Dallas News*."

Nick found that learning was sometimes painful. After graduating from the University of Texas with a prelaw degree and a minor in Greek, he landed a job as a reporter at the *Nashville Tennessean*. "But I couldn't make the grade. I could describe an event but I was simply too shy to ask questions. A well-known novelist came through town and the paper sent me over to do a piece on him. I told him it was my first interview and I wasn't going to be very good at it, but I'd like to try. Without any probing on my part, he talked a blue streak for forty-five minutes and gave me enough for a story. But I could see it would be impossible to throw myself on the mercy of whomever I interviewed." The understaffed *Tennessean* reassigned him to the telegraph desk.

Amid the unfolding Depression, however, Nick grew fearful that the *Tennessean* would sink financially, and he traveled to Los Angeles, where he found an opening on the copy desk of the *Times*. The salary was modest, but he had begun writing short fiction—first for the pulp magazines, later for *Collier's, The Saturday Evening Post* and *Liberty*—and he continued writing fiction for other publications during his years at the *Times*, using a pseudonym not only to spare the paper any possible embarrassment but also to avoid confrontation with Loyal Hotchkiss.

A crusty tyrannical editor of the old school, Hotch vented anger regularly on his staff, often turning explosively toward Nick. During two decades Nick rose to become senior deskman in charge of producing the daily paper, a role equivalent to managing editor but without the title or pay, and whenever Hotch spied an item that displeased him, he would hurl barbs directly at Nick. Indeed, even when Norman Chandler sought to begin improvements, Hotch was slow to respond.

Beyond the need to initiate a gradual upgrading of editorial quality, Norman knew that it was essential to modernize the business practices of the newspaper. Norman had seen how narrowly the *Times* had survived the Depression, how precarious was the cash flow. Norman knew the paper was vulnerable not only to ill winds in the economy but to a determined onslaught by organized labor, if, for example, a powerful union chose to start a competitive publication unhampered by the need to make a profit, with the single goal of bringing the nonunion *Times* to its knees.

But Norman did not take lightly to change; he was not swift to make bold and daring moves. On one occasion *Newsweek* was quietly offered to him, as an acquisition for the Times Mirror Company. *Newsweek* was not making a large profit at the time, however, and Norman found the idea of buying a national news weekly just a bit overwhelming, especially as *Time* magazine appeared to have a commanding lead. Consequently he backed away from the *Newsweek* offer.

Norman's closest associates were quick to understand his caution and, importantly, to respect his strengths. He was neither a raging editor in the image of his hot-tempered grandfather nor a bold financial dreamer in the steps of his empire-building father. Norman was the steward of a family business, and the uncomplaining heir to all the problems and crises which, like barnacles, form around family businesses.

All too often, when he perceived the need to make improvements, Norman was held in check, partly by his own conservative nature, partly by members of his family. Harry Chandler held the keys to power much too long, not relinquishing full authority until his death at the age of eighty, in 1944.

During the next fifteen years Norman embarked on a program of gradual improvements. But his sisters and brothers, comfortable with a family-owned company, resisted each innovation as if it might contain the seeds of a dangerous alien force.

Norman's task was made more difficult because it was not in his temperament to be rebellious or to make waves. Respectful and affectionate toward his sisters and brothers, he made every effort to avoid conflicts over the direction of the paper. But conflicts were inevitable.

7

THE outside world knew nothing of the struggle taking place behind the scenes in the Chandler dynasty during the late Fifties.

Norman and Buff were at the center of it. She, always outspoken, suggested to Norman, from time to time, that he give some thought to the next level of the dynasty, meaning the succession of their son Otis to the publisher's job. Norman was close to sixty, enjoying vigorous health, certainly not an old man, and he was reluctant to step aside as publisher. The office was much more than a job; it was his inheritance, his identity, his place in the world. He ignored Buff's suggestions at first, but he changed his mind when, by coincidence, McKinsey & Company, the management consultants he had hired periodically for guidance, recommended splitting corporate responsibility between two top executives in 1959. McKinsey's notion was that the *Times* needed the undivided attention of its publisher while the parent company could expand best if it was led by a separate boss, freed of distractions at the paper.

McKinsey's advice made sense to Norman, but as a recipe for growth it contained a bitter ingredient for the Chandler family. With Norman slated to take the job of leading the parent company, his younger brother Philip, who was fifty-one and had been a vice-president and general manager of the paper for seventeen years, expected to become publisher. The rest of the family backed Philip and argued that he deserved the job. They did not want Otis, who was only thirty-two and considered to be too young and too inexperienced, to be named publisher.

The family was not swayed easily. The rancor against Buff had built for a long time, and everyone suspected that she was the sponsor, the prime mover, behind Otis. Norman was caught painfully in making a choice between his brother and his son.

Much later Norman told Otis in confidence about another dimension to the conflict. Several outside directors of the company, led by Litton Industries' chairman Charles B. "Tex" Thornton, urged Norman and other members of the family to choose Otis. Norman did not, however, rush into a decision. He had not been appointed publisher until he reached forty-five. He was a traditionalist. He did, in fact, consider thirty-two as somewhat *young* for the job.

But Norman, in private moments, regarded Philip as something of a lightweight, not entirely competent to take an aggressive leadership role at the *Times,* while Otis had been trained immaculately, had worked hard and conscientiously, had demonstrated that he was far better qualified to become publisher. In the end, Norman had his way and named Otis to be his successor in 1960.

What shaped Otis? Born to wealth in an influential family, surrounded by prestige and power, enveloped by limelight, he had countless opportunities to become a pathetic case history in the lost legion of dynastic offspring—a bored heir, lacking challenge, squandering his time and energy in an endless summer, his aimless life chronicled on the tabloid pages in a melancholy montage of dissipation.

He learned, even as a five-year-old, that limelight and afflu-
ence meant a certain amount of personal vulnerability. Soon
after the infant son of famed aviator Charles Lindbergh was
kidnapped and slain, a bungled attempt was made to abduct
young Otis, who had been playing on the front lawn of the
Chandler house.

Buff and Norman were protective and watchful. Camilla
(two years older than Otis, and breathtakingly pretty even as
a child) had taken early to riding horseback and in a short
time amassed enough winner's ribbons to cover one wall of
her room. Otis, in turn, was given riding lessons. One day as
the riding master led him around a ring, teaching him to
jump, seven-year-old Otis was thrown. He landed on his head.

Buff reported later: "I rushed him to one doctor who said
it was too late—a fatal concussion. But I drove us to Huntington hospital and, luckily, right inside the emergency entrance
I met a doctor who happened to be an old friend. He gave
Otis a shot of adrenaline and then there was pulse activity.
It was just good fortune and good timing, a mother's persistence and a doctor's knowing what to do. They kept Otis in
the hospital for two months.

"His grandfather Harry had lots of grandchildren but Otis
was his favorite; they somehow communicated well with each
other, and there was a distinct physical resemblance. Harry
had tremendous responsibilities, he was a really busy man,
but he rushed over to the hospital when he learned Otis had
been hurt, and he stayed there all night with Norman and me.
He visited often during the next two months, and throughout
his life the grandchild Harry always inquired about was Otis.
Without putting it into words Harry somehow conveyed the
idea that he was counting on Otis—as the son of his own
oldest son, Norman—to carry on the Chandler tradition."

Yet Buff and Norman were also careful not to goad their

son toward triumph or conquest; they deemed it prudent to let him develop at his own pace. They sent him at the age of eight to summer camp, where he awakened to the romance of outdoor adventure. He learned how to canoe, kayak, sail, fish, aquaplane, water ski, backpack. He learned how to shoot a rifle and to use a bow and arrow.

"I became aware at camp," Otis said years later, "I'd been blessed with good coordination and could do well in sports. Nobody pushed me to achieve—certainly not my parents— but I made up my mind to do better each time, to win all the awards at the end of summer camp, to pile up the most points. I didn't realize it at the time, but afterward, looking back, I knew it was an early sign of a competitive nature. I simply had to be the best."

Quiet and shy, especially among elders, he would let his head droop, a tendency that provoked his mother to lose her restraint and to remind him: "Stand up straight, Otis, put your head up." He was distinctly uncomfortable delivering recitations to his classmates at Polytechnic, a private elementary school in Pasadena, and once when a teacher summoned him before the class to speak, he was overcome by a wave of fright and nausea.

Where he excelled was at physical activity. Many days he rode a bicycle from school in Pasadena to home in Sierra Madre, a journey of ten miles, much of it uphill, and he found great satisfaction in the physical challenge as he gradually developed powerful muscles in his legs. He acquired a taste for speed, and one day when he pumped along at thirty-five miles an hour in a twenty-five-mile-an-hour zone, a motorcycle cop waved him over to the curb and gave the boy a ticket for speeding, an offense that required him to attend traffic school on Saturdays.

The distance to Sierra Madre presented a special social

barrier that would affect his personality: the Chandler house stood too far away from the center of residential life in Pasadena, where his classmates spent their hours after school and on weekends, for him to socialize much. Years later Otis told an interviewer: "There was nothing antisocial about it. I had plenty of friends when I was at school, and it was always fun to be with them. But I found I didn't have to be with them constantly. Then, growing up, there came another stage of personality development. I found it was crucially important to have moments of privacy, moments in my own space.

"This is one reason why I could never run for public office. It would mean a total loss of privacy. Some people love being 'on' all the time, but it's not my idea of life."

Norman had labored in the fields of the Tejon Ranch as a boy, and in time he shared his work ethic with Otis, enlisting the youngster to spend weekends in the family orchard, among rows of trees bearing apricots, plums, pears, peaches and avocados, cultivating and fertilizing and watering the acreage.

Otis put up a basketball backboard and hoop and, usually alone, practiced sinking baskets. He also set up crossbars and a high-jump pit with sawdust, and he leaped over the bars time after time. The solitary practice paid off in excellence and increasing self-confidence, a positive reinforcement that stood him well as he encountered hurdles across the years.

His parents sent him first to Cate, a prep school eighty miles away, in the seaside community of Carpinteria, where many of his former classmates from Pasadena had been enrolled, but soon Buff and Norman suspected that he was not sufficiently challenged in the affluent but insulated atmosphere of Cate. They guessed that he would gain larger perspective at an Eastern prep school, and they arranged a transfer to Andover.

"I was ill equipped," Otis said later, "going from a small, sheltered school and suddenly being tossed in with eight hundred fifty boys from all over the world, kids from many different economic levels and social backgrounds. It was a brutal adjustment for me academically. For the first time in my life I had to learn to study. I wasn't accustomed to classroom discipline and I was strictly on my own as a person. Nobody was impressed by the family name. Nobody had ever heard of the Chandlers. I was strictly a tall, skinny blond kid from California."

Nor, to help ease the shock, was there a generous allowance. Buff and Norman took a dim view of parents who lavished money on their youngsters. "I was always broke," Otis said.

What made the adjustment possible at Andover was Otis' skill at sports. When he arrived at the school he promptly found a place on the varsity soccer team, and that immediately "put me over the hump in terms of dealing with people."

Following his senior year at Andover, Otis grew interested in weight lifting and throwing the shot put and discus. With a mere 155 pounds on his six-foot-three frame, "I was intrigued with the idea of becoming strong and husky." He embarked on an intensive weight-lifting, shot-putting program, and three months later, when he entered Stanford University, he had built his body to a solidly muscular 190 pounds and had equaled the world's record in the twelve-pound shot put.

There was never any question that he would attend Stanford—it was the school where his parents had met. "When I arrived at Stanford, everybody was way ahead of me in dating, because I'd come out of a very strict prep school. I began making up for lost time. Suddenly life was a great big cookie jar of women—girls at Stanford, girls at San Jose, airline stewardesses. I was part hellion and playboy, part serious athlete, and not much of a student."

What remained unchanged was his modest financial status. Many classmates received funds from home for clothes, cars, dates, "but if I wanted anything I had to work for it. During the football season I'd park cars and at other times I'd hash food in the fraternity house. When I took a girl on a date, it was usually Dutch treat. The most lavish transportation I could afford was half interest in a secondhand motorcycle."

He was mildly annoyed but not deeply troubled by his own financial limitations. "The one thing I always had going for me was athletic ability. Thanks to those long hours of solitary practice, I always made the teams at school—basketball, soccer, track and so forth—and in so doing, I felt I could accomplish whatever I chose to do."

During his first year at Stanford Otis made the varsity track team and broke all freshman collegiate records for the shot put. He won one honor after another, setting new records in the Pacific coast conference and national collegiate competition. By the time he graduated from Stanford he had put the 16-pound shot a distance of fifty-seven feet, five and one-half inches, an achievement only six and one-half inches short of a world's record, the second best mark in track history.

His skill as an athlete routinely put him "on the inside with upperclassmen. I was accepted by my elders, and found I could verbalize and get along with them. Athletics also gave me a leadership role, big jock on the campus and all that. At Stanford I became captain of the track team and president of my fraternity, Delta Kappa Epsilon.

"The sense of leadership, and feeling comfortable with older people, stayed with me and became a tremendous help when I went to work at the *Times,* where I had to become a leader of people who in most cases were considerably older."

He could also see corollary influences shaping his character —competitiveness coupled with fanatical dedication to a goal.

"The goal was not to be an academic star but physically fit. Athletics had become terribly important because it was the one thing I did well. I didn't write poetry and I didn't play the violin, and I wasn't an outstanding scholar. Even when I cut back on hell-raising and spent more time studying, my grades were just average. I'd put in a full day at classes, practice for two or three hours in the afternoon with the shot and discus, study, occasionally go to a movie with a girlfriend, return at midnight and lift weights for an hour or so."

He trained systematically at Stanford for the 1952 Olympics and he pursued a strict exercise routine when, following graduation from Stanford, he signed up for an Air Force flight training program. Told to lose seventeen pounds because he exceeded the weight limit for pilots, he starved himself for days, making the grade at the last moment, afterward gaining back all seventeen pounds and immediately converting it back into solid muscle.

But he was rejected for flight training because of his large frame. Assigned to duty as a ground officer in charge of athletics, he became co-captain of the Air Force track team and traveled around the world to compete in track events. He had set his sights on taking part in the Olympics and his Air Force duty enabled him to keep training toward that goal.

He missed out only when he sprained a wrist at the last minute. Disappointment ran deep, but of far greater importance, he had begun a lifetime pattern: he could set his sights on a distant achievement and work toward it with the dedication of a champion, making it not because of wealth or family connections but because he found a powerful exhilaration in the sweet sense of competition.

During his Air Force hitch he gave the first signs of becoming a shrewd, tough entrepreneur who knew how to buy low and sell high, and it was a characteristic that stuck with him over the years. He had married his college sweetheart, Marilyn "Missy" Brant, bright, lively, athletic, singularly outspoken, and with an infant son, Norman, they occupied a rented house near Camp Stoneman, a base in Northern California where servicemen awaited orders to be shipped overseas during the Korean War.

"It was standard practice," Chandler recalled years later, "for a man to wait there in a holding pattern for months, and then suddenly receive shipping orders. This meant, among other things, he'd have to sell his car within a matter of hours or at most a couple days.

"I passed the word that I was in the market for cars, and a regular routine developed. A man would bring in a car. I'd offer him a ridiculously low price. He'd storm away, insulted by the offer. But he'd received shipping orders, you see, so he had no chance to travel around to nearby towns and test the used-car market. He'd come back in about an hour, after he had cooled off somewhat. I'd then up my offer a little bit, but I was still 'stealing' the car, in effect. Then I'd turn around and sell it at a much better price. Every night I'd drive home in a different car. I knew the used-car market very well, and while I was at the camp it became a helluva business for me."

Near the end of his Air Force term he considered his prospects in the world. During undergraduate days he had spent occasional summers at the *Times,* carrying heavy metal plates from the pressroom, enjoying the weight-lifting exercise but not regarding the work as more than a brief interlude, not sure whether he would make a career out of the newspaper business. Years later he said: "When I was a boy I dreamed about being a doctor. I was always fascinated with medicine. If publishing hadn't been a tradition in the family, I'd probably have pursued medicine in a serious way. But even with a publishing tradition, I wasn't sure which way to go when I got out of the Air Force."

He turned toward the *Times* again, not from a clear-cut sense of duty but because he did not know where else to go, and he had a wife and child to support. "I had to have a job, and I just didn't see any other options. I knew my father expected me to go to work at the *Times,* but I had no idea what the job was going to be."

Mustered out of the Air Force in 1953, Otis gathered up Missy and the child, loaded their possessions into a station wagon and rented trailer, and drove to his parents' house in Sierra Madre, arriving on a Friday night.

After a round of warm greetings, "my father stood there grinning like a Cheshire cat and he handed me a sheet of paper. It was a typed outline of a seven-year executive training program—to begin the following Monday. I protested about not having a vacation, I'd hoped to get a week off, but there was no reaction, no sympathy, I was expected to start Monday —on the graveyard shift, midnight to eight in the morning— and that was that."

Otis began with little sense of family history; his father had seldom talked with him about the past. Once, when Otis was twelve, Norman had taken him to an annual memorial service conducted in memory of *Times* employees killed during the 1910 bombing. Otis was not impressed. "My father told me I should hate unions because they were bad. But I didn't really have that same hatred for unions. I didn't love them, but I didn't feel one way or the other."

He went to work in the pressroom as an apprentice at a weekly salary of $48, thus beginning a carefully designed journey through the major departments of the *Times,* mechanical, circulation, advertising, editorial.

Coincidentally, during Otis' training program, Norman Chandler had brought in McKinsey & Company, the management consultants, to take a periodic overview of efficiency at the *Times*. Amid a study of personnel and payroll practices, McKinsey's Jack Vance called Norman's attention to an oddity: every time Otis was assigned to a new department, he reverted to the status of apprentice at $48 weekly, with the result that after several years' work he remained at a beginner's salary. (Otis had mentioned the problem several times to his father, and Norman had nodded sympathetically but taken no corrective action. In time Otis learned the reason. "My father wanted to protect me against charges of favoritism," Otis later told an interviewer. "An executive training program was a new concept to him, and he was afraid I'd be resented by others, every time I entered a new department, if I'd been paid more than a starting apprentice was worth." But after Jack Vance called attention to it, and explained the acceptable compensation standards of an executive training program, Otis was given salary increases commensurate with other employees.)

He found it stern duty to tour the various departments. "Some jobs amounted to a grinding routine, just functions that I had to experience, pushing around some heavy piece of equipment. But my father was very smart about this. He wanted me to learn all about everything, the boring parts and the much more interesting phases as well. He also wanted me to be seen and to meet everyone, and as a result my working hours kept changing. I'd spend a week on the graveyard shift, a week on the swing shift, a week on the day shift, and in this way I met practically the entire staff. But my biological clock was all screwed up, my sleeping habits were unraveled because I kept changing shifts."

Some tasks left him numb, but when he entered training

in the editorial department Otis gradually acquired a sense of drama and excitement about the paper. "Up until I reached editorial I could have been talked out of making a career at the *Times*. But during my hitch as a reporter there was a definite crossover in my thinking: this was the business for me."

He wrote clearly and carefully, turning out painstakingly researched features on mental hospitals and on a large-scale governmental effort to apprehend dope smugglers, and numerous other stories.

Chandler made no effort to conceal his anxiety about performance, his determination to do well. "I knew people were looking at me, in effect, to set an example for others. I wanted to be accepted as 'one of the boys,' but at the same time I was functioning in a glass house, in full view of the staff. I simply had to outperform everybody."

Throughout his executive training period Otis filled up notebooks with observations, and occasionally he shared his findings with his father. One tour of duty led Otis to a trainee-reporter's job on the afternoon *Mirror,* the breezy tabloid owned by the *Times*. When Norman launched it a decade earlier, with the goal of attracting legions of post–World War II newcomers who were settling into rapidly growing suburbs, his idea was to make the *Mirror* very different from the *Times*—in effect, to reach an entirely new audience. At the outset Norman hired Virgil Pinkley, then general manager of the United Press in Europe, as publisher, and J. Edward Murray, a firecracker of a newspaperman, as managing editor. They put together a lively, entertaining, tightly edited paper which carried a parade of colorful features including a page of "personals" in which singles could advertise for dates and mates.

The *Mirror* added plenty of zest to booming Los Angeles and grabbed a large audience; by the late Fifties the *Mirror*'s hefty circulation was neck and neck with Hearst's rival tabloid, the *Herald-Express*.

But the *Mirror*'s business ledgers reflected financial disaster. Although he was classified merely as a reporter, Otis knew a great deal about the *Mirror*'s problems, and he made a deliberate effort to learn more. Eventually he sent a confidential report to his father outlining the extent of the *Mirror*'s money troubles; and it was instantly apparent that Norman's lessons in thrift across the years had made a deep impression on the son.

Noting that publisher Pinkley and editor Murray were often absent on "global junkets" and promotional appearances while the *Mirror* was "losing money at the rate of nearly $30,000 a week," Otis recommended as top priority the hiring of a business manager with enough clout to attack the deficit. He wrote: "Never do [Pinkley and Murray] examine their weekly budget and try to come up with new ways to cut the deficit. Instead they always find new ways to spend money. They remind me of the proverbial spoiled son at college with the unlimited checking account and no idea of where the money is coming from."

Impressed with his son's hardheaded critique, Norman promptly sent the confidential report along to Pinkley. "I was horrified," Otis said later, "at my father's naiveté about how people react to criticism. He thought my recommendations were right on target and just what Pinkley needed to be told. I said to myself: 'If he should have known these things, why didn't you simply tell him verbally that these were your own observations?' My father's candor absolutely ruined my relationship with Pinkley. After all, I was just an executive trainee, working as a reporter on a paper of which Pinkley was publisher, so it was a terribly uncomfortable experience for me."

Indeed, Pinkley wrote a forty-page report rejecting Otis' findings "because of his lack of experience, his presentation of half-truths." But the *Mirror*'s deficits kept piling up. To make matters worse, the market outlook for an afternoon paper, hemmed in on deliveries by traffic congestion and curtailed in readership by an increase in television news shows, held out little reason for advancement.

Otis approached each new responsibility as if he were lifting weights in a gymnasium—cautiously, firmly, never rushing in without preparation but rather advancing in tiny stages, thrusting forward in millimeters of progress. His father appointed him to be marketing manager of the *Times,* a role requiring close supervision and direction of the advertising and circulation departments, the two key areas from which revenues flowed into the paper. Otis' grasp and thrust was evident from the start, and within a year the two departments rang up new records.

Thus when the time arrived for Norman to remove himself from the publisher's role and to devote himself instead to the affairs of the parent company, the winds of logic mounted to a gale force on behalf of Otis to be his successor. Otis had been groomed for the job as no one in the family before him. During seven years of executive training, commencing in 1953, he had tackled one difficult assignment after another. There was no other candidate with comparable qualifications.

The climactic scene took place on April 11, 1960, in the Biltmore Bowl, where more than seven hundred guests, including government officials, community leaders, business executives and key employees, had been invited to a special luncheon. Norman, silvery-haired and smiling, stepped to a microphone and said: "A newspaper must be the image of one man, whether you agree with him or not. I now inform you that there is to be a new image of the *Times,* but not a radically different one. My successor is younger, serious, competent, well trained, creative, possessing character and integrity; of sound judgment, with an appreciation and warmth for his fellow man.

"I hereby appoint, effective as of this moment, Otis Chandler as publisher of the *Times,* the fourth publisher in its seventy-nine-year history."

Otis smiled boyishly and exclaimed: "Wow." But there was certainly nothing boyish about his approach to his new job.

Part Four

OTIS CHANDLER
(1960 - 1980)

8

IT was an eventful era for the press. Nikita Khrushchev, the first Soviet Premier to visit the United States, expressed a wish to see Disneyland, twenty-five miles south of Los Angeles. That request was turned down by the U.S. government with the explanation that adequate security could not be provided at the mammoth amusement park. He seized the occasion to needle his hosts: "Have gangsters taken over the place?" But he settled happily for a tour of Twentieth Century–Fox movie studios.

Not only Disneyland and the film studios but all of California faced an onrush of tourists. Many chose to stay. The 1960 census showed that new residents were arriving at the rate of 4,000 a week, 200,000 a year, creating a continental tilt by which California soon surpassed New York as the nation's most populous state.

The Democratic National Convention took over the Los Angeles Sports Arena in 1960 and handed the Presidential nomination to Massachusetts Senator John F. Kennedy. That same year Otis Chandler moved into the publisher's office. Fiercely ambitious, he immediately set his sights on a *Los Angeles Times* to rank high among the best newspapers in the world, by employing topflight writers and editors, a network of talented staff correspondents, a stable of influential critics and columnists. He intended the *Times* to become a total journalistic enterprise characterized by prestige and quality.

It was axiomatic that this would require spending money on a gigantic scale—a scale never before contemplated at the *Times.* As Otis gradually unfolded a series of costly steps to boost the quality of the paper in the early Sixties, there were anxious questions from his father. Norman had no quarrel with making improvements; he agreed that changes were long overdue. But Norman was also reluctant to tamper with success, and he warned his son against assuming a heavy financial burden that could prove—in a bad year—to be too much, could overwhelm the paper, perhaps even shatter it on the rocks of insolvency.

Why, argued Norman, take unnecessary risks when the *Times* was already a substantial moneymaker? It carried more advertising linage than any other newspaper. And if it was not a glittering jewel in the crown of American journalism, it was nevertheless making a gradual effort toward becoming a better paper. It was Norman, after all, who had begun changing the *Times* several years earlier, instructing his gifted managing editor Nick Williams to "push." He elaborated, "I want some investigative reporting. I want reporters to go out there and dig. And above all I want the paper to be fair. . . ."

But Otis was stubborn. He had not the slightest intention of taking unnecessary risks or tampering with success. He intended to be *more* successful than any of his predecessors. The paper he envisioned must be not merely a moderately better *Times;* it must rank with the best in editorial achievement. To do this he knew he would have to develop and increase profitability, on a scale equal to or in excess of his editorial goals.

Otis was a champion of editorial independence inside and outside the paper, and he understood deeply and intuitively that an essential ingredient of editorial independence was a hefty level of profits. A publication in trouble might exchange its editorial independence for a chance at economic survival. His passion for profitability reached, in an ironic thrust, beyond his father's cautious ways: it was Otis who ultimately persuaded Norman that the afternoon tabloid *Mirror* had to be abandoned. The *Mirror* had been Norman's baby, *his* invention, and Otis was respectful, but it had become a nightmare of losses, and there was no sign of reversing the trend.

Norman was proud of the *Mirror,* but in the end he listened to Otis' arguments. On January 5, 1962, Norman stood before a hushed gathering of staffers in the *Mirror*'s city room. With tears in his eyes he informed the staff that they were at work on the burial edition, and he added: "This is to me the most difficult, heart-rending statement I have ever had to make. The *Mirror* was my dream—this paper was conceived by me."

It was not, however, an unmitigated disaster. Otis used it as the occasion to forge a deal involving a shrewd exchange: the *Mirror* was folded, leaving the afternoon market clear for the Hearst paper, the *Herald-Express,* and in return the Hearsts closed their morning paper, the *Examiner.* This move left the morning market to the *Times.* It was a staggeringly simple arrangement between two publishing companies, one making money on its morning paper and losing money in the afternoon, the other doing well with its afternoon paper but losing out in the morning.

Traditionally the Justice Department frowned on such arrangements. But the chief of the Antitrust Division had himself suggested it, as a way out of an unfortunate economic fact of life, and subsequently Otis made it central to any plan for closing the *Mirror.* The Hearsts failed to realize until too late that they had grabbed the wrong end of the stick: the afternoon market was disappearing, and they had given the Chandlers an exclusive franchise, in effect, on morning readers. Many years later, when an interviewer asked him about the important milestones of his career, Norman referred with considerable pride to the founding of the *Mirror* because—indirectly but effectively—it resulted in tying up the morning market in a neat package for the *Times*.

Bargaining was a competitive expression for Otis Chandler, not much different in its essentials from weight lifting or throwing the shot put—where he competed against himself—and he competed against others, in bargaining situations, to triumph over opponents.

He expressed his need to triumph in countless ways. He became a big-game hunter and, not surprisingly, his drive made him a celebrity among other sportsmen. In later years, he collected classic cars. In time his painstakingly assembled collection—including rare and extremely valuable Duesenberg, Ferrari, Mercedes, and Rolls-Royce models and even a 1927 Isotta-Fraschini roadster once owned by Rudolph Valentino—was recognized by connoisseurs as one of the best in the world.

In middle age he took up auto racing and collected rare sports cars. He welcomed excuses to spend a day at the ocean, where he competed with himself to improve his skill at surfing. But nowhere was the big push, the reach for achievement, more visible than in his approach to the *Times*. He began with the premise that quality, of itself, is a sound investment. A second-rate newspaper carrying only wire-service stories and canned features could be profitable (and hundreds of newspapers were daily proof of the point). But he felt not the least temptation to continue with the second-rate; his built-in pride dismissed anything but the best.

Gradually he found additional reasons to reach hard for quality: newspapers were facing increasingly stiff rivalry from television and radio news, which offered the advantage of instantaneous bulletins and brief news highlights; and another kind of rivalry from the national newsmagazines, where technology had made possible a highly sophisticated system of "zoning" cities for advertisers, thus enabling a company to aim its advertising message at local areas, which traditionally had been the special preserve of newspapers.

Perceiving the broad outlines of this threat, Otis reasoned that newspapers of the future would have to provide much more, giving their readers interpretive and analytical stories, plus practical service-type, consumer-oriented features that would prove useful in coping with the increasingly complex challenges of daily life.

Quality had other important connotations for him, not least an end to shrill political partisanship, a balanced and fair approach to the issues, an aggressive run at discovering and reporting the important news—locally, nationally and around the world.

All this, in the gradual raising of his consciousness, could have been dismissed as a totally unrealistic ambition, for it presented a circular and domino-like arrangement of formidable problems. To produce a quality newspaper he would have to lure topflight people. Yet to attract such people (especially when many serious journalists regarded the *Times* as something of a joke) he would have to pay salaries and staff benefits at levels comparable to the largest Eastern-based papers and newsmagazines.

To earmark larger sums for the payroll, he would have to generate steadily larger revenues and introduce much greater efficiencies than the paper had known before. Some efficiencies, such as bigger and faster printing presses, would require a vast initial investment. Other efficiencies would result from actually participating in advancing technology, and to do this he would first have to make a substantial investment in research and development. He could not depend on other papers to lead the way in introducing technological improvements. Most newspapers, especially the metropolitan dailies, were hobbled by the encrusted practices of labor unions; every labor-saving device was stubbornly resisted. As a result, Chandler encouraged his staff to pioneer numerous technological advancements, and in later years executives of the *New York Times,* the *Washington Post* and other large newspapers would make pilgrimages to the *Los Angeles Times* to eyeball its efficiencies. And all this was only a beginning; the massive spending on staff and on modern plant and equipment was not to be a one-shot affair but a continual outpouring of gigantic sums.

To make a beginning, Otis told an interviewer later, "I set up a blackboard in my office, drawing columns and figures with chalk. The columns and figures represented the inner life of the *Times,* on a daily basis: the number of lines of classified ads actually sold versus the number of lines needed to meet budget estimates versus the number of lines sold on the same day one year earlier versus the all-time record. Another column showed the same breakdown in dollar revenues for classified ads. Other columns gave the breakdowns for display ads, numbers of papers sold, numbers of stops and starts in the pressroom, numbers of late papers, and so forth.

"It was a utilitarian method of self-education, somewhat crude at first, but I kept refining it. I set my goals competitively against the publicly reported figures of other papers.

"It was simply one kind of management control, but I wanted much more and much better controls. The *Times* had been on a weekly budget system, when I became publisher, and it consisted of taking a full year's revenue and spending and then dividing it into fifty-two weeks. That was okay, but it didn't tell me as much as I wanted to know. I recognized that each week had its own significance, and the only way to judge a trend was to know exactly what was happening each week. When you develop a budget system you cannot cut expenses dramatically week to week, because there are large fixed costs—newsprint and labor. So what do you do? You begin watching trends. If there is a bus strike which would affect retail shopping, or a strike by auto workers which would affect car-buying, or a newsprint strike which would restrict our ability to produce the paper—any of these developments can add up to a trend. Seeing a downtrend, I would tell each department head to cut, for example, ten percent out of his budget for the rest of the year.

"How do you cut ten percent when you are dealing with large fixed costs? You begin to not hire replacements when there are openings. You put a freeze on all new hiring and you don't replace people who leave. Then you add to this the smaller items that cumulatively trim expenses. You don't send your fashion editor to Europe for the latest show. You send fewer reporters on the political campaign trail.

"By attacking all these fronts, very early whenever I saw the economy starting to turn down, we were able always to come up with substantial savings. It was a matter of moving in quickly, calling in the department heads and saying, 'Look, we're in for a tough year,' and they would take action quickly to minimize the impact.

"At the same time we developed an operational plan for five-year budgets, giving each department head the responsibility of demonstrating how revenues would be achieved for the next five years, how capital expenditures would be justified for the same period.

"It might have appeared to each top-ranking executive—editorial, advertising, circulation and so forth—that I was badgering him alone." But in fact Chandler dealt with his departmental chiefs as if he were a musician surrounded by instruments in a one-man band.

"And while the pounding was going on, I had to make some very tough decisions. I'd been filling up notebooks for seven years, jotting down what I'd do if and when I became publisher. When I got the job, I had to make the toughest decision of all: to fire or retire or somehow move aside a great many high-ranking executives. It was terrible to have some young kid take over and tell them they weren't good enough to do the job. It was *extremely* tough for me, but it had to be done. There was no incentive to lead a mediocre team. I wanted the best of everything."

Years later a managing editor, Frank Haven, recalled: "When Otis took over, he found that not one of his top executives had a number-two man—not one of them. That's the best way to keep your job, for Christ's sake, but damn poor management. So, when Otis came in he gave orders that every executive had to groom two assistants who could take his place. This was essential, because in practically every department the top men were in their sixties, and not one of them had developed a potential successor."

Chandler's aggressive approach sent new shock waves through the company. His insistence on developing subordinate talent for possible succession brought about striking changes in the management structure. As younger men were admitted to the decision-making process, they—like Otis himself—began to question past practices. Otis took pains, however, to temper his aggressive approach with a cautious managerial style. He said later: "I realized that the fastest way to disrupt an organization is for the top man to keep diving in at various levels, short-circuiting the chain of command, trying to make everybody believe he's a good Joe. It mucks up the organization."

The risks were instantly apparent to him. He wanted to increase the editorial budget substantially. But if the bigger expenditures were not transferable and translatable into advertising and circulation gains and thus into profitability, the result would be to add to the editorial payroll and carry nothing to the bottom line.

He continued: "Now, if substantial improvement is made in a paper and everybody sees the improvement, you might imagine there's an immediate recognition and an immediate payoff—but it isn't so. People become aware *gradually* of an improved appearance, of better graphics, or increased coverage of many different categories of news, of additional sections, of the unmistakable fact a paper is getting bigger and better. A publisher cannot just wait and hope everything works out well. What he must do, as the editorial changes are made, is reduce the lag time as much as possible by developing good promotion and advertising campaigns and dealer contests and circulation drives by trying to get the paper into non-*Times* homes.

"The risk, in short, is enormous. The challenge is to make editorial improvements in just the right way, at just the right speed, picking up circulation and advertising gains to pay for the improvements. Unless it's all done with great care and precision, the whole venture can bomb out disastrously and might very well sink the ship."

Otis received no specific instruction, no restriction, no written document, no list of priorities from his father. Much later Otis recalled: "I'm sure he monitored me closely. He didn't attend the meetings I held with my staff, but he saw the weekly budget and of course he watched the performance of the paper."

Otis knew well, after the long period of executive training, that one important challenge would be to improve productivity. The technology of publishing a newspaper had changed little for more than fifty years. He set up a research and development committee (R&D), consisting of engineers and management experts and mechanical efficiencies arrived gradually but steadily.

"We set a policy that encouraged workers to cooperate with the installation and use of new equipment. On many papers the unions fight bitterly against labor-saving devices, but we told our employees, in effect: 'Look, we are not going to terminate any permanent, full-time people. Whenever we develop a machine that enables us to perform tasks more efficiently, we'll put a freeze on hiring, and we'll take only part-time, temporary help until the new machinery is put into place. Meantime, our permanent employees will be retrained to other crafts, acquiring more skills and earning more money than previously.' "

A typical device developed at the *Times* was called the counter-stacker. Before it was introduced, the slow process of taking freshly printed newspapers and preparing them for delivery required the services of groups of four men. Each quartet put together a stack of fifty papers, tied a bottom wrap and top wrap on the bundle, then lifted the bundle onto a conveyor belt to carry it toward a loading dock. The counter-stacker, however, automatically put together a fifty-paper bundle, tied it and fed it onto a conveyor.

Out of the R&D committee came other advancements, including a process called photocomposition that made obsolete the practice of setting metal type by man-operated machines; and a device called satellite printing whereby the paper could be reproduced electronically, via microwave transmission, in multiple locations. The purpose of satellite printing, as Chandler viewed it, was twofold: to have an alternative plant in the event of an earthquake or other catastrophe at the main publishing facility, and to bring the paper at great speed to the rapidly growing, wealthy suburban areas of Orange County, south of Los Angeles.

The purchasing power of *Times* readers was always on his mind. "There is no future for the *Times,*" Chandler remarked soon after he became publisher, "in trying to be a paper primarily for low-income audiences. If our readers can't buy the products offered by our advertisers, then in a short time we won't have advertisers and we won't have a paper. So, to survive and grow, we have to be both a mass and a class paper, aiming at the middle-class and upper-middle-class market."

Otis made no secret of his ambition to move the *Times* light-years ahead on multiple fronts, not least as an editorial vehicle. He had observed Nick Williams carefully, and he was not put off by the older man's squeaky voice or shy manner. Otis had considered it a great stroke of luck when Loyal Hotchkiss, the editor of the *Times,* had retired and Nick had been named to take over the job. The timing had coincided with the elevation of Otis to the role of marketing manager in 1958, a final two-year grooming stage before becoming publisher.

Working in close collaboration, Otis and Nick cut away at the unproductive traditional core of big-city journalism, known as the "beat." Reporters on the beat were stationed protectively at police departments and government buildings waiting for large stories to break. This waiting game required a huge investment in time and money.

Far better use could be made of the *Times'* resources, the publisher and editor decided, by redeploying reporters to general assignment chores. Subordinate editors were instructed to send reporters out in aggressive search of important stories, instead of waiting idly in pressrooms for routine happenings on a beat.

Redeployment was only a first step. Otis gradually chose to bolster the science and financial staffs, to expand metropolitan coverage, to renovate old-hat fashion and society pages with a broader "Family" section that reflected the swift-changing demographics of the city and aimed at male as well as female readership.

"Otis was a little more specific than just indicating he wanted the *Times* to be among the top U.S. newspapers," Nick Williams recalled later of a huddle with the newly designated publisher in April 1960. "He said, 'I want it to be the number-one newspaper in America.' When I pointed out this would involve spending a tremendous amount of money, he was undeterred. We could both see many, many weaknesses, but he had made up his mind to revitalize the *Times* into a modern national newspaper. As we agreed on projects we would like to undertake for each successive year, Otis would ask me to place a price tag on them, I would send him a shopping list, putting a dollar sign on specifics, X amount for staff in Los Angeles, and so forth.

"If he took something off the shopping list, but still believed in the expansion, we would delay it until the ensuing budget. His dual objective was to increase profitability while creating a better paper. He underscored his approach with the realistic recognition that rising profitability was the key element, for it made increased editorial spending possible."

In his earliest moves toward investing the *Times* with quality, Nick Williams explained that the kind of person he sought for the staff was someone "whose work everyone in town *must* read every day."

With Chandler's blessing, Nick began a massive recruitment of new talent into the editorial offices, luring from national magazines and other newspapers prestigious editors and writers whose presence would directly enhance the pages of the paper and at the same time signal a serious intent, thereby serving as a magnet to attract still others of quality.

Aggressive reporting turned up important stories. The

unmasking of the John Birch Society and its right-wing extremist activities was typical of the era. The Birchers, organizing busily throughout the nation, were pillars of the community. They made no secret of their beliefs about the roots of all the trouble in America: left-wingers were leading the country out of control, and among the most dangerous elements were Communists, Socialists, Negroes, and the United Nations. The Birchers were eager to impeach U.S. Supreme Court Chief Justice Earl Warren for his opinions advocating racial desegration.

Bundles of hate mail arrived in the offices of the *Times*. Nick Williams recalled later: "I'd never even heard of the John Birch Society. But after I got the gist of their message, I asked Norman Chandler if he thought Earl Warren was a Communist, or even a radical. He said, 'No, of course not.' "

Williams assigned Gene Blake, a slim, quiet veteran journalist who specialized in legal affairs. He spent a month looking into the Birchers and then he wrote a five-part series on the society. It was low-key, almost deadpan reporting, quoting the Birchers at great length and allowing them to incriminate themselves with their own statements.

Nick Williams carried the five-part series into Otis Chandler's office. The young publisher was shocked. His uncle Philip Chandler and Philip's wife Alberta were big wheels among the Birchers; Alberta was an officer of the society and she had played hostess at a reception honoring Robert Welch, a Boston candymaker who was president of the society.

Otis told Nick: "I didn't realize there was something as dangerous as this in our midst."

Nick suggested winding up the five-part series with an editorial, and Otis said: "Why don't we play it on the front page?"

Reaction was swift and emotional: more than five thousand readers canceled subscriptions to the *Times*. Otis observed, however, that newsstand sales increased, leading him to suspect that irate subscribers were still eager to read the paper and, having vented their protest, they were buying it over the counter.

Inside the Chandler family, tempers flared. Norman took pride in his son's increasing independence, but Norman's brothers and sisters did not. Philip Chandler, who resigned from the paper shortly after Otis became publisher, protested bitterly against editorial changes taking place under Otis' direction.

Uneasy about the *Times'* increasing political independence, critics of the paper frequently channeled their complaints through Norman's brothers and sisters. Sam Yorty, Los Angeles mayor from 1961 to 1969, a peppery, short-tempered man of towering ambition, feuded constantly with the paper; one recurring claim was that the *Times* refused to print his statements on foreign policy, and on one occasion he sent a sheaf of his press clippings to Norman's brother Harrison, with a note: "Some excellent examples of stories skipped by the *Los Angeles Times*—WHY?"

Harrison Chandler relayed the material to his nephew Otis, with a covering memo: "The mayor seems to have a good point here. Why?"

Otis penned a swift response: "The mayor does *not* have a point. The truth of the matter is that we cover on a daily basis his conduct of the office of Mayor of Los Angeles, including his criticisms, when made, of the *Times*. We do not cover as a general rule his views on foreign affairs. He was not elected mayor to develop his own foreign policy."

Years later Otis said: "In my relationship to all members of the Chandler family, there was no way to keep everybody happy. I made an effort to be polite, courteous, considerate. But there was no point to pussyfooting around on the direction of the *Times*. The paper was published every day and they could see it. They disagreed endlessly with my editorial policies. But they never disagreed with the financial results."

News of large-scale improvements in the *Times* traveled east slowly, and even the usually observant management of the *New York Times* failed to pay attention. Deluded into believing that a vast audience awaited it on the West Coast, the Eastern paper made plans to launch a Western edition. It began October 1, 1962, and egregious mistakes dogged the venture from the outset. One *New York Times*man later confided what went wrong. Or rather, how nothing ever went right.

Area representatives of the Manhattan journal were never consulted, whereas "small teams" came out, hastily checked the terrain, and decided upon a mail delivery service. "This flopped, and by then it was too late to establish proper dealerships."

The Western edition "never penetrated the public's consciousness," developing instead into a pale carbon copy of the New York original, with its promised thirty-four pages straggling down to twelve before its anguished sixteen months of life petered out.

Consequently the Western edition could not compete with the *Los Angeles Times* either in advertising or in local reporting, and in January 1964, "Punch" Sulzberger decided to abandon the project. That decision came as no surprise to Chandler, who had perceived almost from the outset that the venture was doomed. He held a brief celebration with members of his staff, and afterward he rolled up his sleeves to prepare for new challenges ahead.

9

LIKE the *New York Times,* many East Coast publications were slow to become aware of the changes taking place in the West. By 1963, however, *Time* magazine included the *Times* in a list of the nation's ten best newspapers, and two years later the *Wall Street Journal* wrote: "The [L.A.] *Times* has been converted from a newspaper of dubious reputation to one of the more respected and complete papers in the country. And one of the most lucrative. . . . While many big-city newspapers elsewhere have been slow and indecisive in facing up to increased competition from television and suburban papers, the *Times* has moved vigorously to meet it. Otis has also beefed up news coverage, both in quality and quantity, and, largely under his aegis, the paper has shucked its traditional image as a spokesman for arch-conservatism."

The process of shucking the image, having begun with an exposé of the John Birch Society, continued to unfold at a rapid pace—too rapid for Richard Nixon to comprehend the changes taking place behind the scenes at the *Times.* Nixon had been invented by the paper—counseled by Kyle Palmer, befriended by Norman Chandler and supported editorially in his election campaigns.

But Nixon encountered puzzling changes following his defeat by John Kennedy for the Presidency. He returned to

Los Angeles and began weighing the possibilities of a run for the governorship of California. One evening, accompanied by his wife, Pat, he dined with Buff and Norman Chandler at their elegantly furnished Hancock Park mansion.

Nixon raised the prospect of challenging Pat Brown, the incumbent Democratic governor. His words and manner made it clear that he anticipated encouragement. But the Chandlers pointed out carefully that Pat Brown was popular and well entrenched; Norman (diplomatically) and Buff (bluntly) told Nixon that it would be a mistake.

Years later Buff recalled the evening: "He simply refused to listen. Pat was very uncomfortable and wanted to go home but he ignored her. He drank too much and he kept talking, delivering a monologue. He went on much too long, insisting Pat Brown was just a clown who was headed for certain defeat. The monologue was so intense that we didn't even attempt to inject one other important reality: the *Times* was now in the hands of a new publisher, Otis, a very independent man, and Nixon would err seriously if he expected to be helped by one-sided coverage."

Nixon was given a sharp lesson in the new independence on the morning after he announced his candidacy for governor. Instead of welcoming him enthusiastically to the race, the *Times* stated: "If, for example, Mr. Nixon had merely been searching for a mechanism to keep him floating until he could have another fling at the Presidency, he might have found one with a more reliable safety factor. Getting elected governor of California will not be easy. . . ."

The *Times* put tough, aggressive reporters onto the campaign, and they asked hard questions. Nixon was stunned. He regarded the Eastern press corps in general as his enemies, but he had expected a better shake from the *Times*.

Unaccustomed to balanced coverage by the *Times*, Nixon decided that he was the victim of a conspiracy by the

Chandlers. If he needed any further evidence, it was soon forthcoming.

Preoccupied with raising millions of dollars for culture, Buff Chandler cast her sights across the horizon for a large national figure whose presence would lend prestige and renown to the formal dedication of a building site for the Music Center. Her ambitious gaze fixed on Washington, and she sent a telegram inviting President John Kennedy to attend and deliver the dedication speech on October 27, 1962.

Kennedy accepted promptly. Dick Nixon construed the invitation and timing as still another cruel blow from the Chandlers, for the event would give Kennedy an excuse to visit California and to campaign for Pat Brown within ten days of the election.

Despite a last-minute cancellation of the Kennedy visit—he was detained in Washington by the Cuban missile crisis—Nixon remained furious with the *Times* and the Chandlers. When Pat Brown won the election, Nixon seemed to snap under the strain. His press secretary, mild-mannered Herbert Klein, stood before reporters in the Beverly Hilton ballroom, preparing to issue a statement of concession. It had been agreed in advance that Nixon would not make an appearance, but in the end he could not stay away.

Bleary-eyed, suffering from lack of sleep and general exhaustion, slightly incoherent from late-night drinks, twisting in self-pity, the defeated candidate mounted the podium, launched into a rambling invective against the press and promised: "You won't have Nixon to kick around any more, because, gentlemen, this is my last press conference. . . ."

Insiders at the *Times* knew his remarks were aimed at them. Nixon underlined his feelings next day by canceling his subscription to the paper.

The process of shucking the *Times'* traditional image took another great leap forward in 1964, the year Barry Goldwater and Nelson Rockefeller, standing at opposite ends of Republicanism, both sought the Presidential nomination.

Otis preferred the liberal Rockefeller, and, as the California primary election drew near, he discussed the editorial-page situation with his parents. "I feel," Otis said, "the *Times* should endorse Rockefeller."

Buff and Norman both shared their son's preference for the liberal New York governor, but Norman raised a second-stage question: if Goldwater won the primary, what editorial position would the *Times* take in the general election?

"I don't want to endorse him," Otis replied. "I don't think he should be President."

Norman was visibly distressed. Regardless of who won primaries, the *Times* traditionally supported Republican candidates in November. In the event Rockefeller lost the nomination to Goldwater, Otis had in mind an endorsement of the incumbent Democrat Johnson.

Norman could be pushed only so far. Otis sensed somehow that it would be unfair to press his father beyond the point of reasonable change. Reluctantly Otis agreed to adopt the paper's customary pledge of allegiance; he wrote an editorial backing Rockefeller but promising that the paper would stand behind the GOP primary winner in California, regardless.

Otis eventually decided, however, that the traditional practice was obsolete, and in 1973 he announced an end to *all* endorsement of Presidential candidates. He prepared the groundwork for that decision with a confidential memo to his father and other members of the Chandler family, explaining the rationale: "Newspapers no longer can wall off or ignore large segments of the community simply because they differ in political beliefs and points of view. A metropolitan newspaper cannot survive as the voice of a small minority. The newspaper of the past, with its narrow point of view, one-sided presentation of the news and provincial outlook cannot succeed against the competition of more sophisticated media in today's society. Newspapers cannot close their eyes to change and progress.

"If in our news report or editorial pages we demonstrate an automatic political bias in favor of a particular cause or group, we thereby relinquish forever our single most important asset—the integrity and credibility of the *Times,* our only real value to this community and therefore our only reason for existence."

The massive changes Otis was making at the *Times* caught the attention of Philip Graham, the brilliantly erratic publisher of the *Washington Post.* They had met at sessions of the American Newspaper Publishers Association. They were temperamentally very different. Graham, who drank too much, did not know how to pace himself with people, with work, with life itself. Chandler, who drank little, paced himself like an athlete who knew that pauses could be fully as critical as bursts of speed.

But they had important attributes in common: a powerful drive to succeed, a rising curve of influence, a "hot" newspaper. They fell quite naturally into discussing the possibilities of a common venture.

"We both wanted to build up our foreign coverage," Otis said, "and our first idea was to divide up key cities and avoid the expense of duplication. 'You could take Brussels and we could take Tokyo,' was the way it began, 'or you take Lisbon and we'll take Hong Kong.' But the divisions quickly proved impractical. We both wanted our own man in Tokyo, our own man in Hong Kong and so forth.

"Gradually, however, we discovered it was possible to pool our stories without, so to speak, dividing up the world. We cautiously began exchanging copy from overseas as well as national stories. We assigned subordinates to work out the details, and in fairly quick order the parts began to mesh. We called it the Los Angeles Times–Washington Post News Service, and we sent a salesman around the country to pick up a sampling of reaction from the major papers. The product brought a positive response." Some two dozen papers signed up immediately, and eventually more than 350 subscribers bought the service.

The arrangement was characterized, however, by signs of strain behind the scenes, like a marriage where tightly drawn curtains conceal tensions from the neighbors. One point of friction arose over accounting practices. The *Post,* never as successful financially as the *Times,* rebelled against the *Times'* supercautious system of pinpointing and allocating all costs on a pro rata basis. *Post* accountants claimed their paper was being overcharged; *Times* accountants denied it, and among themselves the *Times*men were dismayed at the *Post*'s financial procedures, which seemed neither modern nor efficient.

Another recurring problem lay in local pride. The *Post* regarded Washington as its special preserve. Battling constantly with the *New York Times* for prestige and influence in the nation's capital, the *Post*'s editors did not adjust gracefully to scoops by out-of-town papers. The *Post* was even more embarrassed when the faraway—and once lowly esteemed—*Los Angeles Times* scored a clear "beat" on the news. But as Otis Chandler beefed up his paper's Washington bureau, hiring better and more aggressive reporters, more and more clear beats became inevitable. The *Post* was reluctant to use the stories but now and then it would rewrite a piece without giving credit to the *Times.*

Chandler paid scant attention to squirming by the *Post*'s bosses. His goal was to push the *Times* into an ever-rising orbit of influence and power. Making his wishes known via his own top editors, Otis encouraged the Washington bureau to try hardest for stories that neither the *Washington Post* nor any other publication was getting. The results were impressive:

—The Washington bureau detailed two reporters, Stuart Loory and David Kraslow, to explore the possibility that America had missed opportunities to make peace in Vietnam. They traveled overseas and spent eight months of 1967–68 on the project, pulling together highly classified information and eventually producing an award-winning story.

—Washington bureau chief Robert Donovan filed a piece in 1969 on the first withdrawal of U.S. troops from Vietnam before Richard Nixon announced it, thereby spurring the President to shout expletives at Secretary of State Henry Kissinger and to begin hot pursuit of the source of the leak.

—Following up on a story first uncovered by *Life* magazine, *Times* Washington correspondents Ron Ostrow and Robert Jackson obtained the details in 1969 of an elaborate arrangement whereby Supreme Court Justice Abe Fortas had agreed to accept $20,000 annually for life from the foundation of Louis Wolfson, a freewheeling entrepreneur who subsequently was sent to prison for selling unregistered stock. Fortas resigned from the court.

—Intrigued by such goings-on in the highest court of the land, the Washington bureau kept digging and struck another rich vein, learning in 1970 that U.S. Supreme Court Justice William O. Douglas was the recipient of $12,000 a year as the president of a foundation whose income was partly derived from gambling casinos in Las Vegas, and that the foundation's chief sponsor was involved up to his armpits in the gambling business. Douglas managed to ride out the scandal and hold onto his Court seat, but he resigned from the outside foundation and returned his previous salary.

10

Otis Chandler seized on marketing research as another challenge. It had been around for years as a somewhat primitive device to gain modest amounts of information about readers for the benefit of advertisers; in its crudest form, the goal was to learn whether the newspaper's readers were poor or middle-class, and the information was gathered by a routine glance at a neighborhood: if the housing appeared somewhat respectable, subscribers in that area were designated as middle-class, and the word was subsequently passed along to advertisers that another pocket of purchasing power had opened up.

But Otis Chandler took command of the *Times* at a singular moment: Los Angeles had begun to reflect in major ways the West's rising leadership and influence in the nation. A condition some writers chose to call the "continental tilt" was in full swing. Not only did the East-to-West tilt encompass the greatest voluntary migration in history but also, within the space of a few years, it included the most dynamic explosion of educational, cultural and scientific exploration that America had ever seen.

"The time was right," Otis said later, "to aim our newspaper at an audience of better-educated men and women with greater purchasing power, and to bring our readers and advertisers together in a fast-growing marketplace on a scale much larger than ever before."

The marketplace snowballed with media during the next twenty years. By 1980 the metropolitan Los Angeles area contained, in addition to the *Times* and the *Herald-Examiner*, nineteen daily community papers, more than three hundred weekly and semiweekly shopping papers including ethnic and religious publications, more than one hundred regional editions of national magazines or locally edited magazines, twelve commercial and three noncommercial television stations, twenty-five cable television companies, thirty-two AM and fifty FM radio stations, dozens of direct-mail advertising services, and a variety of outdoor advertising facilities.

The many media took aim at a metropolitan population of 9 million, occupying 3.5 million households scattered across 4,800 square miles. (The Los Angeles metropolitan area is 153 times larger than Manhattan.) It was a population with buying power—there were 4.1 million jobs within the marketplace; and a population in motion—there were 4.5 million autos registered in the area, or one for every two persons.

Numbers fascinated Chandler. Day after day he pulled up close to his massive walnut desk, stacked high with thick folders of material. One stack dealt with his roles outside the *Times* as a member of the board of directors of news-related organizations, including the Associated Press and the American Newspaper Publishers Association; as an adviser to Stanford and Columbia universities on their journalism schools' programs; as a speaker and lecturer to newspaper-connected audiences.

Another stack of folders dealt with other outside activities: he was a member of the board of directors of California Institute of Technology; of Pan American Airways; of TRW, Inc., a giant in the electronics and aerospace industry; of Unionamerica, a bank holding company; of the Tejon Ranch.

Other stacks of folders dealt with his role as a director and trustee of Chandler family trusts; with managing business interests for himself, his wife Missy and their five children; with management and maintenance of his material possessions, including three houses, a collection of classic cars and a separate collection of sports cars; with personal recreation ranging from hunting trips to auto racing to weight lifting to surfing to riding motorbikes; to community and civic responsibilities that rested on his shoulders because he happened to be a Chandler, the publisher of the *Times* and the vice-chairman of the parent company.

He avoided none of it, but he rejoiced in numbers. Each new batch of data brought new discoveries, as he directed his research staff to unravel and analyze the complex and densely interwoven threads of the metropolitan area. He found the dimensions of the marketplace truly awesome. For example, the Marketing Research department assembled estimates based on data collected by various governmental agencies and concluded that buying power in metropolitan Los Angeles amounted to $70 billion, a sum larger than the combined totals of five other major metropolitan areas—Houston, Minneapolis–St. Paul, Miami and Cincinnati.

Hardly less astonishing was a study of comparative populations. The market researchers found there were more people in scattered sections of metropolitan Los Angeles than in entire U.S. cities. For example, the San Fernando Valley had a larger population than Dallas. The San Gabriel Valley had more people than Des Moines; East Los Angeles more than Salt Lake City; Central Los Angeles more than Wilmington; the Santa Monica/South Bay district more than Atlanta; the Southeast section of the city more than St. Louis; and Orange County more than Philadelphia.

The challenge, as perceived by Chandler and marketing vice-president Vance Stickell, a courtly and strikingly handsome senior colleague, was not only to gather first-class information on the marketplace but to translate the research into compelling reasons why advertisers should hawk their wares in the *Times* over and above all other media.

Refined and polished over the years, the Marketing Research department today is organized into four main sections, each with distinct and unique functions. One section specializes in advertising sales presentations. A second group, Consumer Survey Research, produces primary research on consumers and consumer trends. Studies may be done on a one-time basis, and samples may represent groups such as airline travelers, discount-store shoppers, new-car buyers, and so forth. Various research techniques are used to meet specific needs. These include telephone interviews, personal interviews, mail questionnaires and group interviews.

A third division of Marketing Research specializes in economic and statistical data, ranging over a multitude of product and brand categories. A fourth division of Marketing Research is graphic arts, which takes responsibility for the layout and visual appearance of all presentations, surveys and reports.

Still another service performed for advertisers is a series of maps that illustrate the competition. Virtually everything is sold through a retail outlet. Otis Chandler says: "We prepare maps showing all the home-improvement centers, all the places you can buy a dress shirt or a pair of shoes, all the drugstores, all the shopping centers, all the department stores and so forth.

"All this information becomes tremendously important to our advertisers. A manufacturer based, say, on the East Coast would like to develop distribution for his product in the Los Angeles marketing area. The manufacturer's representative could spend months driving around our forty-eight hundred square miles to explore the shopping centers, or he could save a great deal of time by consulting our advertising department."

Early in his career it became clear to Otis that the knowledge gleaned from marketing research paid exceedingly well. For, by serving its audience, in effect, as an information and marketing center, by bringing advertisers and customers together meaningfully in the marketplace, the *Times* followed a steady path toward financial success.

On the sixth year of Otis' publishership, 1966, Norman Chandler reached his sixty-sixth birthday. He began hinting, subtly but unmistakably, that perhaps the hour had arrived for Otis to allocate more attention to non-newspaper activities and thus prepare to become chief executive of the parent company, Times Mirror, at such time as Norman moved upstairs to become chairman of the executive committee.

Otis, however, held a different view. Beyond his role as publisher, he carried the title of senior vice-president of the parent company. But corporate activities often interfered with and rarely matched the excitement of the publisher's office. He preferred to give less attention to the parent company and more to the *Times*. He had made significant accomplishments in his six years as publisher, but he believed that his achievements had only begun. He drafted a memo to his father, outlining some of the challenges, present and future, along with his reasons for allocating a larger proportion of his waking hours to the newspaper; and thus, in effect, he waived any immediate desire to follow in his father's footsteps. Otis concluded: "All of this means only one thing to me: the present publisher either runs the *Times* or you get a new publisher. I feel that I can be of more benefit to the company as publisher of the *Times* than moving into non-newspaper activities. I realize this desire to specialize on the *Times* is possibly incompatible with certain other requirements that you might have for me in the future. The one thing that I do know is that the strength of the *Times* must be maintained and enhanced; and in these critical years ahead I suggest that I can be of most benefit to the Times Mirror Company by playing the role I have indicated here rather than splitting my time, as I have been."

Norman Chandler found the arguments persuasive, and with the help of Buff and Otis, he began casting for a successor to lead the parent company. The man they chose was UCLA chancellor Franklin David Murphy, fifty-two, an inquiring, restless, chain-smoking, clear-talking man, known widely in intellectual and government circles as a dynamo of ideas.

A physician by training, Murphy had become an educator, and he remained a challenger, an innovator, a man tuned in on the world but constantly sending off messages of his own. He had served on so many government committees that he carried the intellectual hash marks of government service: he knew the inner workings of bureaucracy (a most useful piece of knowledge for a top decision-maker in a major corporation). He also understood people problems, and he had a keen sense of social responsibility. But most of all, he was an educator moving at full tilt into the knowledge industry, looking for connections between education and government and business.

When a *Time* magazine correspondent asked forty-year-old Otis Chandler why he, as son and heir, had not been named chairman, Otis replied that there was still plenty of time. Otis pointed out that Murphy, at fifty-two, could be chairman for thirteen years before reaching retirement age. At that point Otis himself would reach fifty-two and thus become eligible for a thirteen-year hitch as chairman. Meantime, he noted, there were too many items on his agenda as publisher of the

Times, more than enough to keep him fully engaged in the years ahead. One of the largest, thorniest items was the difficult problem of press responsibility.

He worried constantly about it—or the lack of it. "Are we doing our job as well as it can be done?" he asked himself every time he glanced at the newspaper.

The question encapsulated a long list of concerns, reaching back in the web of memory to the shadows of his grandfather and great-grandfather, and then spanning the years to his own era. The question had many meanings, adapted each time to conditions of the moment. Were journalists too often above reproach? Did the *Times* readily admit mistakes? Did it make every effort to maintain credibility? Was news coverage balanced? Were the police—who obviously had a difficult and dangerous job to do—covered fairly in their encounters with blacks, Chicanos, anti–Vietnam War demonstrators, campus activists? At the opposite end, did the *Times* deal fairly with civilians who ran afoul of overzealous police officers?

The press, Chandler wrote to a friend, "has great power, as we are often reminded, but we need to keep in mind there is no more difficult achievement than to exercise great power wisely and well. Nothing is easier than to dissipate power by exerting it for unfair purposes. The power of the press is linked directly to its sense of responsibility."

Chandler shared his concerns with Nick Williams, and Nick himself held definite opinions on editorial responsibility. Beyond his everyday, ongoing duties, Nick conducted a vast correspondence, peppering the staff with memos and replying to letters from readers.

To a subscriber complaining about the "slant" of a story: "I just don't know what you are talking about when you counsel us to resist the 'political pressures which so obviously influence your reporting policies,' " Nick wrote. "We have no political pressures of any kind, as I think you too will conclude when you read the very wide range of opinion on our editorial pages. We encourage our reporters to write exactly what they see and hear regardless of any *Times* editorial position."

To a reader protesting the "subliminal" content of political messages in the Dick Tracy comic strip, Nick wrote: "I doubt that many people's political opinions are formed by comic strips—and if, in fact, they are, I suspect that they would have pretty absurd political points of view anyway."

A memo to a desk editor: "To an extent that it is consistent with good journalism, we ought to think about this and talk about it some time. Rather frequently when we report the murder of a woman, we include a statement that 'it was not immediately determined whether she had been raped.' If rape is an essential part of the story, we're stuck with including it, but I don't know that it is necessary for us to speculate on what we don't know."

To a book publisher soliciting advance reaction about a possible cookbook: "If you publish it, I'll buy a copy. Once I get a couple of martinis in me, I get to be a very devoted amateur chef with a record of success that you would expect from any chef who has prepared himself primarily by taking a couple of martinis."

To a reader who complained about the "sympathetic" tone of an interview by Jack Smith with a prominent Communist, Nick wrote: "I don't think Jack Smith's article on Dorothy Healy did very much to glorify her. It was rather a sad story. He quoted her as a 'poor unfortunate victim of her own very strange but very strong delusions.' It might be a good idea for readers in general to know just how one working and vigorously regimented Communist looks back on her own life."

To a reader who complained that the newspaper was trying to boss the metropolis: "The last thing in the world the *Los Angeles Times* wants to do is run the city of Los Angeles. We do have, however, an obligation, as a newspaper of both opinion and news, to comment upon it when we believe the city is not being run in the best interests of all its citizens."

A letter to a reader dealing with the personality cult of television news: "Despite the many magnificent things that it does, TV is a curse. What bugs me is TV's unavoidable tendency to make all issues demagogic and to persuade people of every age that a provocative personality means that the man is one of the good guys, which just ain't so."

Otis Chandler savored the wit, grace and wisdom of Nick Williams. But the editor's rare qualities produced an additional effect. Like a recurrent rapping at the door, Nick's overall excellence became of itself a nagging reminder to the publisher of a difficult task ahead.

Part Five

A NEW NEWSPAPER

11

HIGH on Otis Chandler's agenda loomed the challenge in 1970 of finding a "practical egghead" to succeed Nick Williams, who was scheduled to retire the following year. Chandler sifted through a number of possibilities, inside and outside the staff, and ultimately fixed his gaze on the *Times'* own Washington bureau chief, Robert Donovan, a well-liked, widely respected journalist. An author of Presidential biographies and a veteran of the *New York Herald Tribune*, Donovan earlier had been a prize catch for the *Times*; his presence helped to lure other gifted correspondents to the staff in Washington and overseas.

A reflective man, whose soothing manner put sources at ease even as he probed hard, Donovan wrote with style and unmistakable authority.

His ability and reputation were highly regarded in the home office. After careful inquiry, Otis Chandler offered him an opportunity to move to Los Angeles with the title of associate editor, to sit at Nick Williams' side for a year, and then to become editor when Nick retired.

Donovan declined at first. He was honored and flattered, he said, but he considered himself essentially a Washington reporter, as he had worked that "turf" for a quarter of a century. He was on intimate terms with the high and mighty of the Washington establishment. In contrast, he had no sense of place and no feeling for Los Angeles or its people.

But Chandler and Williams courted him persistently, and in time Donovan changed his mind. He and his wife, Martha, moved to Los Angeles, and, to his surprise, he grew outright enthusiastic about the idea of building a new life in the West. The city's reputation, he discovered immediately, was in need of revision.

Easterners, who frequently continued to ridicule it as Tinseltown, were sadly out of touch with the new Los Angeles—a glittering center of higher education, finance and economic power, as well as an extensive complex of culture that challenged New York's long-running dominance in the arts. The continental tilt and the ferment of change had produced a cultural explosion. University and college campuses were crowded day and night with scores of lectures, dance recitals, concerts, and plays and art films. Art galleries flourished.

Highly visible in the center of the city, two short blocks from the *Los Angeles Times,* was the Music Center. When Buff and Norman Chandler invited Martha and Bob Donovan to be their special guests, Donovan felt a glow of civic pride for his newly adopted city. His gaze encompassed the tapered white columns, honey-colored onyx walls, massive chandeliers. Yet, dazzled as he was by the glitter and vigor of Los Angeles, to his continuing dismay he found that he had little comprehension of its complexities and subtleties. He took part in numerous meetings where the verbal exchanges were often conducted in elliptical code. Afterward he would worry aloud to colleagues: "I shouldn't be editor of this paper—I don't know what they're talking about."

Otis Chandler was touched by Donovan's candor, and in time he, too, grew uneasy. He recalled later: "Gradually I developed a gut feeling that Bob was correct: he was *not* the right person for the job. But it was too early to make a final judgment and I didn't even mention my unease to Nick.

"Finally I told Nick it just wasn't going to work out. Nick objected strenuously, reminding me that I had, in effect, promised Donovan the job. I said: 'I know, but I'm not going to do it if it's not right.' I tried to be nice and polite, but when I gave the news to Bob it was an enormous blow. It was bloody awful, but it just had to be said and done."

Donovan returned to the *Times* Washington bureau, where, as associate editor, he wrote special features and books until he retired seven years later. When the news broke at the paper that Donovan would not be editor, the staff was stunned. What few detected was the personal anguish for Chandler. No decision had been more troubling, and, ironically, no other personnel decision brought on as much shrill denunciation by media critics, who called Chandler's action callous.

Chandler's ultimate choice, William Thomas, surprised many observers. "Some senior executives regarded him as perhaps too brash or too rough around the edges. But I had a good feeling for Bill," Chandler said afterward. "I liked his style. He had a solid grasp of the paper and plenty of savvy about the local scene. As metropolitan editor he'd hired a lot of talented people, and they worked hard for him."

Bill Thomas proved quite different from his predecessor, Nick Williams, yet rapidly became precisely the right editor at the right moment in the life of the *Times*.

The Michigan-born son of a small-town banker and concert pianist, Thomas had been encouraged by a friend to major in journalism at Northwestern University, and there, for the first time, he grew seriously interested in newspapers. He stayed on for a master's degree, then landed a job on the copy desk of the *Buffalo Evening News*.

In time he moved to California, to join a colleague in launching a small weekly paper, "but I discovered that a small weekly doesn't produce enough revenue to support two families."

He went to work as a reporter on the *Mirror,* and later moved to the copy desk. When the *Mirror* folded he was brought aboard the *Times* as an assistant city editor. A senior colleague characterizes his style as "unassuming and hardworking. He doesn't do a lot of backslapping, but he has a vibrant quality, a fire that he transmits to the reporters working under his direction."

Named city editor, Thomas was quick to grasp the changing responsibilities of the *Times.* Looking back years later, he told an interviewer: "Otis and Nick and Frank Haven had developed a strategy of regional news coverage. The days were long gone when the paper could limit itself to a big crime in the central city or some action by the city council. Naturally, we couldn't ignore any sensational, fast-breaking stories, but we had to seek out deeper stories that illuminated the essential character of the region."

Following the lead of his superiors, Thomas reduced the number of beat reporters and shifted them into specialized areas. "We needed to search out reasons and causes and trends, to spend time on worthwhile investigative stories."

Even so, the *Times* did not anticipate the Watts riots of 1965. Editor Nick Williams later admitted: "We knew things were tough in Watts—very acutely, because our circulators were having one hell of a time there. It was very hard to keep men on the job, black or white. It was the poorest section of Los Angeles, with the exception of Skid Row, but we didn't foresee an explosion. Hell, we didn't even have a single black reporter on the staff."

But Bill Thomas rallied the metropolitan staff to extraordinary coverage after the riots broke, and the effort brought the

Times a Pulitzer Prize in 1966 for local reporting.

The following year the paper turned its back on a tradition of civic boosterism. Bill Thomas set in motion an investigation of cozy dealings on the part of public officials who were supposed to be responsible for protection of the urban environment. Trickling into the *Times* were rumors of influence peddling and allegations of questionable zoning decisions. Assigned by Bill Thomas, a seasoned investigative reporter, George Reasons, and a team of staffers followed leads for six months.

In one series, reporter Reasons and his colleagues unfolded the story of a city commissioner who had recommended a $302,000 contract for the design of three city golf courses to a firm with no business license, no office, no background in such projects. The commissioner resigned and was later convicted of taking a kickback on the contract. Still another commissioner withdrew from office after a story in the *Times* pointed out that he had advanced his wife's acting career by taking a municipal theater away from one drama group—which she had just quit—and giving it to another—which she had just joined.

When the investigative series was over, five city commissioners and a city councilman were indicted on criminal charges, and four other commissioners resigned under pressure. The city charter underwent major revision.

Managing editor Frank Haven entered the entire series in the 1968 Pulitzer competition. The entry, sent by air freight, was delivered to the wrong building at Columbia University, where the awards are judged. The package sat on an empty shelf, unconsidered by the committee. During a phone conversation with a representative of the Pulitzer panel, Haven learned that the entry had not been received. In a fury he called the president of the air freight firm and galvanized him into remedial action. The package was located in time to be considered—and won another Pulitzer, this time a gold medal "for disinterested and meritorious public service."

During six years on the city desk, Bill Thomas led his reporters to more than thirty awards, including a series of citations from Sigma Delta Chi saluting the *Times* as outstanding among the nation's newspapers in the field of investigative reporting. In recognition of his efforts to transform a once-provincial city news department into a regional news-gathering group, Thomas' title was changed from city editor to metropolitan editor.

One day in 1971 he received a message that Otis Chandler wanted to see him. Thomas was "simply astounded" when he heard that he was to be appointed editor when Nick Williams retired. He quickly grew comfortable with the news and moved into his new role eagerly and energetically. Prodded constantly by Otis Chandler, whose competitive spirit towered over the total enterprise, Thomas led the staff toward broader coverage of the news. He demanded sharper writing and more critical editing, and encouraged regular in-depth coverage of subjects largely ignored by newspapers, including a critical examination of the press itself.

He was both passionate about the news and clear-minded about the people who made it. He met with them at breakfast, lunch or dinner in the handsome private dining rooms of the *Times,* but he was scrupulously careful to avoid personal involvement or to build a social life around newsmakers.

He was quick to grasp situations, quick to make decisions, quick to speak. He knew that he was often excessively blunt, particularly in defense of the *Times.* When *Time* magazine press critic Tom Griffith suggested in an essay published in 1977 that the *New York Times* and the *Washington Post* ranked in a class above all other newspapers, Thomas flew into a rage. For a moment he considered drafting a letter to

the effect that a person who read only the East Coast press
could not be expected to know better, but the hard truth was
that the *Los Angles Times,* much bigger and more successful
than any other paper in the country, carried fully twice as
many columns of news as the *New York Times* and infinitely
more than the *Washington Post.* Then, on second thought,
Thomas dismissed the idea of a long letter and sent Griffith a
briefer message: "Parochial bullshit."

A magazine veteran with a well-deserved reputation for
honesty, Griffith had based his judgment on regular reading
of newspapers published in the East and Midwest. But in response to the terse message from Bill Thomas, he added the
Times to his reading list and made inquiry about it among
other newspaper and magazine editors. He revised his earlier
assessment and in *Time*'s May 4, 1981, issue he wrote: "Journalists generally rank the *New York Times,* the *Washington
Post* and the *Los Angeles Times* as the three best papers in
the country."

Nor did Thomas soften his tone when the youthful governor of California, Jerry Brown, went public with an oddly
uninformed view of the contents of the *Times.* "Dear Jerry,"
Thomas wrote to the governor, "I'm told that at a recent
Washington dinner party you pleaded ignorance on the general topic of Uganda and Idi Amin, among other reasons
because you read only the local (Sacramento) papers and the
Los Angeles Times, and did not have time to read the *New
York Times* and the *Washington Post.*

"I am enclosing only some of the stories you could have
read in the *Los Angeles Times* about Amin and Uganda in
the past two weeks alone. Not only that, these are stories you
would have read in the *Washington Post,* too, because they
have no African bureau and rely on much of our coverage
there."

Thomas was no less blunt toward his associates on the *Times*. He was the first to confess that he might never qualify for the job of Secretary of State. But the staff responded well to his candor and his strict emphasis on integrity and credibility.

Between Chandler and Thomas there developed a close comfortable relationship. Their interpersonal communications were sparklingly clear, without laborious explanations; a word, a sigh, a glance could speak volumes.

Both men were quietly determined to continue building on the foundation of responsibility that had begun when Otis first became publisher. Repeatedly they gave full coverage to stories that provoked criticism from readers. A storm of protest arose, for example, in 1975 when the *Times* carried a lengthy story on extramarital affairs. In reply to a reader's criticism, Thomas wrote: "Why the story? Because it's our job to try to report as accurately as we can the real world, not the one we wish we lived in."

Mindful of the need for credibility and responsibility, Bill Thomas addressed himself day by day to the task of establishing the reliability and dependability of the *Times*. He ordered departmental editors and their deputies and deskmen to take every reasonable measure toward authenticating and verifying the basis for all stories written by the staff of the *Times*.

Nor did he neglect other major suppliers of editorial material, especially those who relayed controversial material without checking independently on the reliability of the sources. "The wire services," Thomas wrote to the highest-ranking editorial executives of Associated Press and United Press International, "are giving us more and more stories based on those published by other media, especially by *Rolling Stone, Penthouse* and similar publications.

"Would it be too difficult for you to provide our readers with some idea of the substance underlying the central points of such stories? Could you tell us, for instance, whether sources or documentation were provided in the original version, and what they were? And, if they are absent, could you tell us that, too?

"You see what I'm after. I don't think we should repeat allegations simply because they were published elsewhere without giving our readers some idea of the weight they should attach to them."

In his effort to strengthen the quality of the *Times*, Bill Thomas invented an extraordinary forum. Identified first as Senior Writers and later renamed Senior Group (because it included editors), it consisted of fewer than a dozen staff members who served rotating terms and held informal meetings monthly.

At each session the participants raised searching questions about the *Times* itself; questions relating to the staff, to promotions, to the quality of writing and editing, to salaries, to frustrations. At one level, each meeting of the Senior Group could be considered mass therapy, for it enabled the participants to ventilate their worries, anxieties and grievances. At a second level, by calling attention to problems, the meetings often produced solid improvements.

Among the questions pinpointed and discussed at typical group sessions and afterward weighed for further action by the paper's top management were these:

• Are our existing standards on reporter conflicts of interest sufficiently clear and up-to-date? Do all editorial staffers, including management, understand what can and cannot be done without compromising the *Times* news columns?

• Should we ever publish stories that say "Mr. High-Ranking Public Official is being investigated by the Department of Justice,

it was learned today," but produce no evidence of wrongdoing?
If there are times that we should, under what conditions?

• Are we getting too sensitive about the feminist movement when
it comes to editing? Two minor recent examples: "Baryshnikov
dropped the ballerina on her pretty head"—an editor wanted to
kill the word "pretty"; "A lady asked me" was changed to "A
woman asked me . . . " Is "lady" a dirty word?

• Should we give our photographers guidelines on invasion of
privacy to avoid the grieving-widow or people-in-distress photograph?

• Do we need a policy on tape recording? One staff writer routinely tapes telephone interviews and regards it as consistent with
his role to report accurately what people tell him. He says he
informs those on the other end of the line. What are our liabili-
ties? Is it ever appropriate to use a concealed tape in face-to-face
encounters?

The Senior Group became, in effect, a special device for
challenging at every step the actions of the *Times.*

Serving as an eye-opener to management and staff, it has a
singular ongoing role in the life of the newspaper. But no
single device could pretend to cope with all the problems of
daily journalism.

12

IN pursuit of press responsibility, Chandler was troubled most often by newspaper coverage of business subjects. He heard criticism on the one hand from businesspeople who complained about biased, incompetent reporters and editors who did not understand the judgments involved in the financial world. He heard complaints on the other hand from writers and editors about the difficulty of getting candid responses from the business community and about the self-serving selectivity of information made available to the press.

The problem, Chandler knew, was not peculiar to the *Times;* every publication faced it. But he mentioned it at intervals to Bill Thomas, and together the two men weighed and analyzed the perils and difficulties of reporting business and financial news. Their joint conclusions were later summarized by Thomas in an address to a group of businessmen:

"Until the Sixties, the press tended to rely almost solely on sources within the so-called establishment institutions. A crime story quoted police spokesmen; an economics story rested on business and industry and chamber of commerce sources; stories of racial problems came from the mouths of government spokesmen and sociology professors.

"One heard little from blacks, the poor, the dissident, the

accused criminal, and others who spoke without institutional blessing.

"In the 1960s there occurred a series of events that hurried things along: the black riots, the student uproar, the war protests—all focused attention on new areas of complexity; and newspapers began gradually to reflect far more diverse views than ever before.

"Really, all that has happened is this: where establishment voices alone were heard, others have gained access. To some, this is anti-establishment. To us, it is not only fair but the only way to bring about sensible, informed decisions.

"Here's where the quarrels start. When a government spokesman says one thing, and the story points out that he said quite another a few months earlier—and that a spokesman for an opposing viewpoint says still another—are we calling him a liar, or are we making the story more meaningful? Then, if we dig up and present facts that tend to support one view or another, are we taking sides?

"All this requires making judgments. Some calls are close, some are wrong.

"We worry about an increasing reliance on nameless sources making serious charges. We worry about what may seem to be a rush, under the impulse of competition, to join in attacks upon the latest institutional or governmental target.

"If the nation's leading papers, now so few and powerful, are perceived to be consistently unfair and lacking in credibility, the handwriting is on the wall—in the form of court decisions and laws proposed in recent years: they will lose their freedom to control what they publish. That would be bad for us. And imperfect as we are, that would be bad for you, too."

One key to the successful collaboration between Chandler and Thomas could be found in mutual belief in and emphasis

on the editing process. This is how Thomas later described
the experience to an interviewer:

"I began looking for new ways to deploy writers, working
either as a team or at least with supplementary help from other
writers. I also began looking for editors different from those
we'd had in the past—editors who could not only make assignments but structure the editing process, taking on responsibility for story ideas, experimenting with new areas of presentation and development of the news.

"In this connection, it's a helluva lot easier to find good
writers than good editors. One reason for this: good writers
do not necessarily make good editors, but good writers *require*
good editors. And as a good writer gets better, an editor has
to improve just to keep pace."

One editor who demonstrated rapid improvement is Bronx-
born George Cotliar, the managing editor. Wise beyond his
years but also eager and impatient, he walks with long loping
steps as if he were embarking on pole-vault practice.

He studied journalism at California State University and,
outside classes, landed a job as editor of a small chain of small
weeklies. Later he was hired as a reporter at the *Times* and
during the next twenty-one years moved upward through
eighteen different jobs, acquitting himself with distinction at
each one, and ultimately reaching the post of managing editor.

Like his immediate superior, Bill Thomas, fast-moving
George Cotliar is an effective boss not only because he has
sharp news instincts but because he is capable of swift, sure
decisions and knows the meaning of executive responsibility.

Recently he told an interviewer: "Bill and I both take great
care to stay out of hiring staff, and we both try to keep our
hands off assignments. There are exceptions, of course, but in
most instances the function of hiring staff belongs to the

department editors. The sports editor, the metro editor, the business editor, the foreign editor, the arts editor—each one has to hire those people he feels comfortable with.

"Similarly, assignments belong to the editors. Quite often reporters try to get me to intercede on their behalf. I won't do that, because it would destroy the editors who run the departments.

"Another thing: every afternoon at three o'clock we have a news conference in my office, where each editor has the opportunity to tell me what stories he thinks are for page one, and we proceed to lay out the page. I've known managing editors who created an atmosphere of, in effect: 'You can come to the news conference, but keep your mouth shut.' So the first thing I did, when I became managing editor, was to tell the department heads: 'I want you to contribute. I welcome your views.'

"I'm very comfortable letting people relate their feelings, and arguing about stories—as long as they realize that at some point I'm going to make the decision. You see, if I were to say, 'Dammit, I'm the boss, and I don't want you to argue with me,' then those times when the subordinate had a valid point, he wouldn't argue. He would just sit there silently, and that would defeat the entire purpose of the news conference."

Cotliar's assistant managing editor in charge of political coverage, political polls and a wide range of special projects is John Foley. Gray-haired and kindly, projecting the soothing air of a clergyman, he had, in fact, set out early in life to become a priest. He was raised in a strict Catholic family, first in Philadelphia, later in the South, and has vivid recollections of a distinct anti-newspaper prejudice in the family. "My father simply didn't trust the press. He'd say, 'They all lie.' One of his complaints was that the papers would often put out an extra—a big bold banner to sucker you in—and beneath it there was maybe a one-paragraph story, just one paragraph, telling you practically nothing. He said this was cheating, and I think he was right.

"I went into a monastery in Louisiana for four years in my teens, but when World War II broke out, I began to feel like a draft dodger. I went into the Navy, and by the time I came out, I hesitated about making an immediate return to the seminary. I applied for a job on the *New Orleans States* and they weren't hiring any reporters but they had an opening on the copy desk. I said to myself: 'What's a copy desk?' But I acted as if I knew, and the first day I wrote two headlines. I felt very pleased with myself, but later learned they had almost fired me."

With his bosses—Chandler, Thomas and Cotliar—John Foley pays attention consistently to the shortcomings of the press in general, and to making improvements at the *Times*. One measure of their collective achievement was noted by the *Columbia Journalism Review* in the summer of 1980, in a stern commentary on press coverage of the Reagan-Carter Presidential campaign. Setting forth the proposition that the press has a clear responsibility to provide "a leadership role to write about what's important," the *Review* observed that during a presidential campaign "it's up to the press to insist that democracy not degenerate into demagoguery or bullshit —that it not be just another advertising campaign." The *Review* monitored, among other media, the reporting of seven major newspapers including the *New York Times* and the *Washington Post*.

Reported the *Review:*

The papers that seemed most consistently to provide this sort of leadership were the *Los Angeles Times* and—predictably, per-haps, given its special mandate—the *Wall Street Journal*.

Beginning the political season with a December 5, 1979 editorial declaring the economy to be the most important issue—and inflation the chief threat to the industrialized world—the *Los Angeles Times* followed up with thoughtful, well-planned coverage coordinated by assistant managing editor John Foley. First came stories analyzing each candidate's background, then question-and-answer interviews and major stories about each candidate as viewed from the campaign trail. Most of these stories were featured on page one early in the campaign.

Not surprisingly, this approach yielded early dividends in illuminating issues. In a January Q&A exchange with George Bush, reporter Robert Scheer led off with hard-hitting questions about the economy which eventually revealed Bush's inability to clarify inconsistencies or to supply details about his basic economic proposals. Scheer's interview received a good deal of attention and was reprinted in other papers, including the *Washington Post,* precisely because it filled a gap in exploring the issues.

Harrison Gray Otis, who rose to lieutenant colonel during the Civil War, bought the editor's job and one-fourth ownership of the *Times* in 1882 with $5,000 loan.

Son-in-law Harry Chandler left editorial bombast to the colonel while he quietly schemed to build a bigger paper and a bigger city.

Once housed in a tiny print shop, the *Times* built this new
headquarters of granite and brick in 1887.

Chandler regularly arm-
twisted wealthy businessmen
to finance civic development.
They good-naturedly
complained that it cost $1,000
to have lunch with Harry
Chandler.

Unlike his fiery grandfather or empire-building father,
Norman Chandler earned a reputation as a cautious but
determined publisher.

Otis Chandler, fourth publisher (1960–1980), blazed the trail
for the modern *Los Angeles Times*.

The *Times* city room in 1922 when Ralph Trueblood,
seated at desk on left, held the editor's job.

Central Los Angeles in 1888. The *Times* building is the
turreted edifice in center of the photo.

The *Times* city room (1983) runs the length of a city block. It is located on same site as earlier building.

Central Los Angeles, 1983.

In 1910, during an era of bitter labor tension, the sturdy *Times* headquarters (which Harrison Gray Otis called the Fortress) was blown to kingdom come.

Marian (daughter of Harrison Gray Otis) and Harry Chandler survived the bombing, and went on to work and live together harmoniously for more than half a century.

Dorothy ("Buff") Chandler (seen here with husband Norman and son
Otis in 1961) gained enduring fame as the creative force behind the
Los Angeles Music Center. Her virtuoso performance as a fundraiser
earned her a reputation as one with whom it cost $25,000—or more—
to lunch.

(L. to R.) With sons Norman (now a *Times* production supervisor),
Michael (now a professional racing driver) and Harry (now a Times
Mirror cable TV executive), Otis shares his enthusiasm for speed.
This picture was taken at Watkins Glen, N.Y., in 1978.

Associate editor Jean Sharley Taylor.

Managing editor George Cotliar.

Media critic David Shaw.

Arts editor Charles Champlin.

Sports columnist Jim Murray.

Foreign correspondent Don Schanche.

Foreign correspondent William Tuohy.

Book review editor Art Seidenbaum.

Columnist Jack Smith.

Reporter Robert Scheer.

Business reporter S. J. Diamond.

Washington bureau chief Jack Nelson.

Cartoonist Paul Conrad.

"HAVEN'T WE MET BEFORE? DO YOU COME HERE OFTEN? CAN I BUY
YOU A DRINK? HOW ABOUT A SEAT ON THE U.S. SUPREME COURT?"

recorder with him. Nelson said, sure, it was in his car. He walked outside slowly, to conceal his eagerness, then broke into a run.

That night he interviewed Baldwin for five hours, Baldwin talking freely, Nelson demanding proof every step of the way, Baldwin documenting how he had been recruited to Nixon's reelection headquarters, detailing his relationships to White House aides Howard Hunt and Gordon Liddy. It was an important story, the first to connect the Watergate break-in directly to Nixon's reelection headquarters.

Baldwin spilled: "I had been using a walkie-talkie and acting as a lookout for James W. McCord [security director for both Nixon's Reelection Committee and the Republican National Committee] and his men, who were engaged in a bugging operation. For three weeks I had monitored conversations on a tapped phone in the Democratic offices. My mission had been to record all conversation. McCord appeared to be especially interested in any information on Senator George McGovern and the Democratic party chairman, Lawrence O'Brien, and anything having to do with political strategy. . . .

"I never questioned McCord's orders. I felt he was acting under orders and with full authority. After all, his boss was John Mitchell, the committee director and former Attorney General of the United States. If that was not enough to impress me with McCord's authority and official standing, we were surrounded by former White House aides McCord said were 'on loan' to the committee."

Baldwin went on to tell the details of his hiring, his mandate and the events of the night when he and his fellow operatives were caught in the Democratic National Committee's offices in the Watergate Hotel.

No sooner had Alfred Baldwin talked to the *Times* than other developments broke, aimed at blocking publication of the story. U.S. District Judge John Sirica issued an order barring principals from making statements on the case, and in the wake of his order federal lawyers working on the case warned Baldwin's lawyers that the government—which had agreed not to prosecute him, in exchange for his testimony— might consider its agreement broken if he spoke out. At the same time, Baldwin's attorneys urged the *Times* not to publish Baldwin's first-person story, or any story based on the interview; they claimed publication would compromise Baldwin's defense, and they threatened to sue the *Times* for damages if it did not halt publication.

Years later Bill Thomas recalled: "I was still new in the editor's job and more than a little bit nervous. I asked Bob Lobdell, our chief counsel, to take a look at it. There was never a question in my mind that we were going to run the story. But I was concerned about jeopardizing the *Times*. I asked Lobdell just how much exposure we had, just how vulnerable we were, threatened on one hand by a federal judge and federal prosecutors, and on the other by Baldwin's attorneys.

"Lobdell said, "It's a major exposure, but you've probably got to run the story, don't you?' And I said, 'Of course we do.' And we did.

"When the story appeared, all the promises were kept: the lawyers on both sides sent us their formal notices of action. This meant, in effect, the Baldwin lawyers were going to sue us for harming their client's defense, and the government was going to sue us for, in effect, screwing up the effort to prosecute the Watergate burglars.

"In a further twist, the attorney for White House aide Howard Hunt [one of the men caught inside Democratic headquarters that night] asked for the *Times'* tapes and notes of the Baldwin interview. He said he needed the information to prepare his cross-examination of Baldwin, and he had turned to the *Times* because Baldwin had destroyed his own copies of the tapes."

Although it was Baldwin, the government's witness, whose impeachment was sought, government prosecutors stipulated in a brief that they did not oppose the defense request.

Judge Sirica agreed, and subpoenas were served on the *Times'* reporters, Jack Nelson and Ron Ostrow, and on John Lawrence, who was then Washington bureau chief. The subpoenas directed the three men to appear in court and bring all materials relating to the Baldwin interview.

The *Times* refused to surrender the Baldwin tapes; and Nelson and Ostrow filed affidavits explaining that Baldwin had agreed to be interviewed only on the condition that everything he said would be confidential unless he approved it for publication.

Judge Sirica decided the *Times* was in contempt of the subpoenas he had issued, and he ordered bureau chief John Lawrence jailed for refusing to surrender the tapes, which were in his possession. Lawrence spent two and a half hours in a basement detention cell in the federal courthouse. He was released when the U.S. Court of Appeals intervened, to enable the *Times* to appeal to the Supreme Court. At that point Alfred Baldwin asked the *Times* to turn the tapes over to Sirica, and at the same time released Nelson and Ostrow from their pledge of confidentiality. Only then did the *Times* give the tapes to the judge.

Later Thomas remembered it was "a tense, anxious experience for all of us. Of course Otis Chandler was right in the middle of it, but he was a lot calmer than I. Not much rattles him."

Bill Thomas ran into another sticky patch when he pursued a hunch about a story closer to home—the Los Angeles Police Department (LAPD). "The image of the individual LAPD officer is one of brisk efficiency and incorruptibility," said Thomas to an interviewer. "He even looks good, in either his crisp uniform or smartly tailored civvies. But in actual fact just how good is he? Just how good is the LAPD?

"So far as I could learn, nobody had ever measured a police department anywhere, in sort of a report-card way, like, how good are they at dealing with homicide, rape, robbery, assault? How good are they at interviewing witnesses or even identifying all possible witnesses? How good are they at acquiring evidence useful and necessary for prosecution and conviction? Do they come into court prepared to testify? Overall, how effective is the LAPD at investigating violent and 'high-fear' crimes and following them through to convictions?

"Very few benchmarks exist for judging excellence. Statistics are deceptive because of a myriad of variables. The public generally thinks that a corrupt department is a bad department and that a clean department is a good one. But the fact is that a department may be corrupt in the sense that officers accept payoffs from vice merchants but still may be extremely effective when it comes to protecting citizens against violent crimes and making arrests that stand the test of the legal system."

The *Times* put together a team of eleven reporters to work on the story, and over a period of three months they conducted more than three hundred interviews throughout the Los Angeles area and across the nation.

The reporters found, among other things, that convictions were a sore spot for the Los Angeles Police Department. In homicide convictions, for example, it appeared that the County Sheriff's Department and even the Long Beach Police Department achieved a higher percentage than the LAPD.

Thomas continued: "When we go after a very large story, like our evaluation of the police department, we worry about something else of major importance. How do you get people to read it all? A book is obviously the best place to present all that material. But how do you deal with it in a daily news-paper?

"There were various ideas of how to package all those words. I called in nine ranking staffers—the managing editor, assistant managing editors, metro editor, assistant metro editor, and so forth. I gave everyone a chance to express an opinion. Then we took a vote. My nine colleagues voted unanimously in favor of running the story as a series. Mine was the only vote in favor of packaging it into one issue of the newspaper. It would be a huge, monumental reading task, but it seemed to me the best way to be fair, to present all the pluses and minuses about the LAPD in the same single issue of the paper. My solitary vote carried against the other nine. It was arbitrary, I suppose, but there are times when the editor has to be arbitrary.

"It turned out to be a helluva good balanced story, but predictably it pleased nobody. The LAPD's enemies claimed we didn't go far enough in our criticism, and the LAPD's supporters said we had done too much nit-picking."

Another storm burst around Bill Thomas when he grew curious about a recurring theme in the pages of the *Times*. He described the experience later to an interviewer: "I kept reading these one-paragraph, two-paragraph stories, sometimes separated by weeks, telling about crimes in well-to-do neigh-borhoods—incidents where the criminal was captured and it turned out to be somebody who had never before been in that neighborhood.

"It looked like a pattern of crime unknown in this century, but prevalent in Ancient Greece, Ancient Rome, in London during the Middle Ages, in Paris during the plague years, eras when there was an underclass removed from the rest of society, so that anybody with means traveled with guards; the only way of life for the underclass was to prey on the so-called overclass.

"I began to wonder if we were developing a permanent underclass of that nature in this country—people so totally submerged in desperation and hopelessness that their way of life consisted of preying on others.

"I sat down with the metro editor and several other staffers and we talked about it. I said, 'It's going to be a very troublesome story. We don't want a story that smacks in any way of racism or Blacks on Whites or anything as superficial as that. If my premise is correct, we need to put the story in a context so that readers can see and understand how people can reach a stage of becoming, in effect, a permanent underclass.' "

Times reporters began checking crime statistics, then followed up with detailed investigative studies of high-crime incidence in metropolitan centers across the nation. In Chicago they found a typical pattern: a family on welfare for three generations, overwhelmed by the struggle to pay their bills, locked in the nation's economic and social basement.

Bill Thomas said later: "The family was not unusual. There are millions of others like them."

Times reporters next zeroed in on the Watts section of Los Angeles. Working in a temporary office in an abandoned, boarded-up store, they spent four weeks talking with scores of persons, much of the time questioning those who steal from the middle and upper classes. The reporters learned of repetitive cases where marauders kick down doors to homes and rob and rape occupants; drive along streets and rob and shoot people at random; follow expensive cars and rob the drivers when they reach home; cruise residential streets and rob people taking out the trash or carrying in the groceries; deliberately bump cars and rob the drivers when they get out identification; roll up to telephone booths and rob people talking inside.

Times reporters quoted the deputy district attorney who prosecutes hard-core marauders caught in the prime West

Los Angeles County target area: "I've got fifty cases—burglars and robbers—and ninety-seven percent are from the ghetto. What scares me is the mentality. They have no remorse. One of them told me, 'They got it. I need it. I'm going to take it.' "

Bill Thomas later told an interviewer: "It was a very tough story to deal with. I'd look at the copy and agonize over it, wondering if there was some way to soften the impact. At night I'd toss around, telling myself: 'Geez, you're going to be called a bigot and racist and all kinds of foul things.'

"But I also know there is a certain kind of tension that comes with the territory. An editor might feel it would be great to forget about the problems and simply do his job. But after a while he realizes the problems are his job. And what the hell, when you get down to the bottom of a situation like this one, the answers are the same. You do your best to be fair, but there is no way to soften the impact. Does this mean we are not supposed to tell the story?

"Predictably there was a lot of negative reaction, a barrage of letters and phone calls telling us that we had exacerbated an already difficult situation, telling us the story was too harsh, telling us we had made it appear as if every black who's walking in a respectable suburban neighborhood is a potential threat.

"To make our position clear to all readers, it looked as if we needed an editorial summing up our views. I sat down with Tony Day, the chief of our editorial pages, and outlined the problem to him." Several days later the *Times* carried the following editorial:

The poor have no cushion against life's rude realities. They get sick, lose their jobs, go on welfare. It's that or starve. Babies come too soon and too frequently. These children can learn, but often don't. So no one wants to hire them when they grow up. Good intentions are killed by the poverty. Why bother when survival is nickels and dimes scraped out of the food budget to pay the rent increase?

If some hope and stability are not injected into the ghettoes and barrios, every city with any sizable underclass will be rendered uninhabitable.

The subject is especially sensitive because it is so interwoven with race. National studies show that blacks are more than three times as likely to be poor than whites, with Latinos about midway between. . . .

The old liberal answers haven't worked. Innovative—even radical—steps must be tried. Perhaps one such program would be a kibbutz-like environment that concentrates on educating the children and shelters them from the bad influences that surround them. For it is the young generation that may be the only hope for change. . . . The country must act soon, for it may take several generations to break the cycle of circumstances that creates the underclass.

This editorial brought applause to Otis Chandler and his staff from a wide audience of readers. But applause was only a sometime reaction.

Controversy and confrontation traveled with Otis Chandler even when he escaped from the immediate scene of publishing. He had many friends in high places, and he was fascinated particularly by the vitality and momentum of President Lyndon Baines Johnson. The President, in turn, did not conceal his admiration for Chandler. Johnson was nervous and suspicious about the press in general, but he enjoyed the company of the youthful publisher and regarded him as someone quite different from run-of-the-mill reporters.

Across the years there were many telephone conversations between the two men, invitations to the White House and to the LBJ Ranch in Texas. On one visit to the ranch Johnson took the wheel of his Lincoln Continental and, with Chandler beside him, toured the ranch at speeds exceeding ninety miles an hour. Chandler was himself fearless about high-speed driving—provided that the driver in question was both skilled and attentive. But it was Johnson's habit to keep a paper cup of beer on the dashboard and sip it as he drove. When Johnson noticed Chandler eyeing the instrument panel, the President casually perched his Stetson over the speedometer.

Soon after the 1968 election, when he left the White House and returned to Texas to spend his remaining years on the LBJ Ranch, Johnson indicated that he might be interested in selling various family-owned properties, including television station KTBC in Austin.

"I went to visit with him," Chandler recalled later, "to begin negotiations to buy KTBC. Quite remote from me—really a million miles away from my consciousness—there was another happening: a *Times* reporter in Texas was at work on an investigative story involving LBJ.

"From corporate colleagues I heard that LBJ was seething. I suppose he regarded newspaper stories as weapons, not as public business. Then one day he telephoned me and he was really upset. He said, 'How can we be negotiating friendly for the sale of KTBC when you're doing this to me? Otis, I want you to call off your reporter.'

"I said, 'I'm sorry, Mr. President, but we can't do that.' He was terribly unhappy with me, and he kept me in suspense for a while, but eventually he sold us the TV station anyway."

Another kind of pressure came from Richard Nixon. Defeated in his bid for the governorship in 1962, Nixon blamed his loss not on himself but on the *Times*. Six years later, when he won election to the Presidency, his rancor continued. He raged often, to those around him, that the *Times* deliberately stabbed him in the back again and again, a remark reflecting his bitterness that the paper held stubbornly to an independent course, giving balanced and equal play to Democrats and Republicans, declining numerous opportunities to pay unduly prominent attention to self-serving puffery from the White House.

Myopia about news coverage is an affliction suffered by all occupants of the Presidency; Nixon's affliction ran deeper, where the *Times* was involved, because the paper had once been his champion. His wrath was relayed to Otis Chandler via many routes. Presidential assistant H. R. (Bob) Haldeman, for one, sent letters complaining about the play given to Presidential news stories in the *Times*. Complaints from the White House increased when the *Times* shifted sharply in its position on Vietnam. The paper earlier had given editorial support to Dwight Eisenhower's Southeast Asian "domino theory," to John F. Kennedy's troop-building program in Vietnam, to Lyndon Johnson's escalation of the war effort.

Said Otis Chandler: "Then we began to realize that all three policies were bankrupt. I think we came to the conclusion, perhaps earlier than many Americans, that our government's policies were wrong. In June 1970, we called for a complete U.S. pull-out from Vietnam. To the White House this was one more sign of our complete political independence, and they found this terribly irritating."

White House tension peaked when Times Mirror's *Newsday* launched an investigative inquiry into the Florida real estate investments of and relationship between Nixon and his close friend Bebe Rebozo. Reports reached Los Angeles of a White House memo summing up high-level Administration reaction: *"Let's get Chandler."* Shortly thereafter these actions followed. First, the Internal Revenue Service began auditing his tax returns. Second, the Justice Department made a reconnoitering search for possible antitrust violations on the part of merger-minded Times Mirror. Third, the Securities and Exchange Commission embarked in hot pursuit of Otis Chandler when he became involved in the GeoTek case.

The GeoTek episode was a nightmare in the California dream of Otis Chandler's life. At the center of GeoTek stood Jack Burke, a strong, easy-laughing Irishman who had been a teammate on the Stanford University track squad. Chandler and Burke were chums on and off campus; they remained good pals long after college, visiting with each other's family and taking hunting trips together.

After Stanford, Jack Burke became a stockbroker in San Francisco, and he kept his buddy Chandler posted on investment opportunities. One time Burke urged Chandler to buy shares of stock in Apache Corp. The price of the shares dropped, but Burke expressed confidence it would turn around and he offered to buy the stock at Chandler's purchase cost at any time. Burke eventually did so, paying $72,800, roughly $4,000 more than Chandler would have gotten on the open market. Beyond his charming manner, Burke's action demonstrated that he was clearly an honorable man.

When Burke later asked Chandler to introduce him to people in Los Angeles who might be interested in putting money into oil-drilling funds—which offer special "shelter" advantages to those in high tax brackets—there was not much reason for Chandler to hesitate. But the publisher was cautious by nature, and quietly asked his own bankers, lawyers and accountants to run a check. "They all came back with the word that everything was 'wonderful, wonderful,' which simply confirmed my own feelings. There was just no reason not to trust Jack. I'd known him for more than twenty years, and in all that time no one had said to me: 'I'm suspicious of him.' We had so many mutual friends, and everybody loved him and trusted him."

By 1972, however, a wave of stories appeared in the press—

stories fully reported in the *Los Angeles Times*—dealing with an investigation of GeoTek by the Securities and Exchange Commission. The stories—published over a period of months —claimed that Otis Chandler was one target of the federal government's action.

One day in 1973, lawyers for the SEC marched into federal court in San Francisco and filed a civil suit complaining that GeoTek had violated federal securities laws and misled investors. The complaint charged Jack Burke with misappropriating millions of dollars for his own use. The action also charged Chandler with failure to disclose that he had received money and stock from Burke after introducing Burke to prospective investors.

Chandler replied that the SEC's charges against him were groundless. He had been a director of GeoTek, and more than a year earlier, he explained, "when I and my fellow directors first discovered possible improprieties in the management of the Burke companies, we immediately requested Burke's resignation and we installed a new chief executive. We hired independent accountants and we began a massive effort to evaluate and protect the interests of many public investors. At the same time we commenced litigation against Jack Burke." Chandler acknowledged that he had received promotional shares and "finder's fees" after introducing Burke to investors, but Chandler said: "I did not ask for the promotional shares and fees. I did not negotiate for them. I did not know on what basis they were calculated. And they were all returned for distribution to investors."

Chandler's defense did not stop there. His lawyers, including Robert S. Warren of Gibson Dunn & Crutcher, protested to the federal court that the SEC had inflicted "maximum and unnecessary personal injury" on Chandler by repeatedly publicizing groundless charges. "Whether by accident or design," Warren told the court, the SEC had delayed normal exchanges of testimony and documents, and instead subjected Chandler to "wave after wave of detrimental publicity." Warren also charged that the SEC had put off producing records and personnel for interrogation in Chandler's efforts to clear himself.

Chandler pointed out that his conduct contrasted sharply with SEC's: "My fellow directors and I caused GeoTek to cooperate fully with the SEC in its investigation. Every request for information was honored. Free access was given to all the company's records." Chandler also noted that he had supplied the SEC with "all requested information relating to my personal affairs, including private financial data. My right to privacy was voluntarily sacrificed in favor of disclosure to the government." He said he expected "similar candor and fair treatment from the SEC," but that instead the agency had not responded to normal requests for information "and it has been necessary to obtain assistance from the court to obtain this needed information." Summed up Chandler: "I have done nothing wrong. I want the facts out, and I desire to present my case rather than suffer a seemingly endless stream of charges" at the hands of the SEC.

A federal grand jury in 1973 indicted Jack Burke on charges of fraud in the GeoTek case. The indictment claimed that Burke had diverted investor funds and converted them to his own personal use, concealing these conversions from investors and prospective investors. The indictment outlined a complex scheme whereby corporations were organized with Jack Burke's brother, Robert, as the nominal president, and these entities then were used to siphon investor funds to Jack Burke—resulting in the investors being called upon to put out additional money to complete the development of gas and oil wells.

At Jack Burke's trial, Otis Chandler testified that he was "shocked and terribly upset" by revelations about the fraudulent activity. Chandler said he first learned of it when Burke telephoned him in 1972. "He told me he had something terrible to say," and Burke then detailed what he had done.

"I asked why and how he could have withheld this information from me," Chandler said. "He said he didn't think anyone would find out. He said he should have told me before and said, 'I'm sorry, sorry and sorry.'"

In 1975 Jack Burke was sentenced to prison, and the SEC dropped all charges against Otis Chandler.

In retrospect, Chandler attributed Jack Burke's downfall more to carelessness than to any other weakness, and the publisher speculated privately that he might have overlooked one distant early warning to the risk of doing business with Burke.

Prior to embarking on a trip, he would routinely make a complete list of the items needed on the trip. Once, preparing for a hunting expedition to Outer Mongolia with Jack Burke, Chandler reminded his friend that it was essential to plan carefully and keep a checklist of supplies. When they arrived at their destination, however, Chandler was astonished and dismayed to find that Burke had forgotten to bring rifle ammunition.

When the GeoTek bubble burst, Chandler's memory raced back to that incident. He remarked to a colleague: "I should have known—anyone who'd forget to bring ammunition on a hunting trip would someday get me into trouble, one way or the other."

The GeoTek episode contained a lesson in humanity for Chandler. Years later he remarked: "It hurt terribly, but it was an important experience for me to get whacked on the ass by the media.

"Never before had there been anything but positive stories about me in the press. Never before had I fully sympathized with people who came to me, as publisher, to complain about how they'd been treated by the *Times* and other media. I simply didn't know how it felt, until I had this humbling experience."

Chandler refused to wink at editorial responsibility on the part of the *Times* in the GeoTek case: his newspaper led the press parade in reporting the story fully. Later he told an interviewer: "My parents suggested we were overcovering it, we were telling much more than necessary, we could have given it less space. But I disagreed. The story had to be told in its entirety."

Chandler also took a fresh look at a problem confronting many publishing executives. In an era when the integrity and credibility of the press was a hot issue among newspapermen and society at large, he grew increasingly concerned with a corollary question: was it proper for an editor or publisher to be a member of the board of directors of an outside corporation?

Many publishers claimed that service on outside boards never colored their newspapers' coverage, nor did they pass on to their publications any inside information obtained as directors. Others argued, however, that membership on an outside board automatically put an editor or publisher in a suspect and embarrassing position. The risk was not so much that news coverage would be consciously compromised. It was rather that it raised the appearance of potential impropriety and thus it lessened public belief in the credibility of newspapers.

Chandler had immediate reason to be concerned, for he served on the board of numerous outside corporations. He canvassed his top editorial executives for their opinions, and they confirmed his own views: "The complete and demonstrable, unassailable independence of a newspaper is its greatest asset. This total independence applies to all those connected with it. And the independence ought to be not only factual but ought also to be above the shadow of possible public suspicion."

So saying, he removed himself from all outside boards.

Not even friends or (in some instances) family escaped Chandler's determination to practice responsible journalism. Many were shocked, for example, when *Times* art critic Henry Seldis wrote a series of stories casting a less than flattering light on the Los Angeles County Museum of Art and its management. The series produced shock because Chandler's sister Camilla and Times Mirror board chairman Franklin Murphy were both high-ranking trustees of the institution.

Museum director Kenneth Donahue, a personal friend of Chandler's, objected heatedly to the series and argued that one deplorable result would be to heighten the already monumental task of raising funds for the museum.

Chandler rechecked with knowledgeable sources inside and outside the staff of the *Times*. After satisfying himself that the Seldis series had been accurate, he wrote to Donahue:

"I can appreciate your problems, Ken, and the difficulties in raising money for the Museum. But I think you have to realize that you are a quasi-public servant and that you have to expect, periodically, a public airing of the activities of the Museum. It is the public's business and neither you, nor any member of the board of trustees, should attempt to delude or hide anything from the public. If I have any criticism in this whole matter it is of the *Times,* to the effect that we have not paid sufficient attention to the business affairs of this major facility. I assure you that we will continue to look at the Museum from all aspects and on a more frequent basis."

Chandler's deep-rooted sense of responsibility went further. If he was haunted by the awareness that his great-grandfather and grandfather had misused the power of the press, he did not say so; but his actions made clear that he championed editorial integrity.

He rejected arguments from Times Mirror's own board of directors and shareholders whenever they urged him to lend editorial support to the parent company's far-flung corporate interests; and inasmuch as Chandler family trusts owned some 30 percent of Times Mirror stock, his posture meant that he was prepared to pay the price, literally, of upholding journalistic integrity.

He told an interviewer recently: "For example, we hold substantial timberland to provide us with a continuing supply of newsprint for newspaper publishing. This is not a simple matter of cutting down trees and processing the wood into paper. Tree-cutting is done selectively and scientifically; the land is constantly reseeded so that every tree is replaced by a new tree.

"But there are arguments, differences of opinion, between extreme environmentalists on one side, and those who would cut certain acreage on the other. There are occasions when the *Times* and I will take a position in support of the extreme environmentalists, contra to those who would cut certain acreage. You could argue that this amounts to inflicting financial self-punishment. But actually it comes down to weighing each issue on its merit, making a choice on the basis of what's right."

Quick to understand and quick to support Chandler in matters of editorial independence across the years have been his highest-ranking corporate colleagues, board chairman Franklin Murphy and corporation president Robert Erburu.

Tall and heavyset, with large probing dark eyes, Erburu is keenly aware of the importance of editorial integrity. Small wonder. He majored in journalism at the University of Southern California, where he was appointed editor of the *Daily Trojan*. "But when I graduated at twenty-one, I didn't know precisely what I wanted to do in journalism," he told an

interviewer. "I went to see one of my professors, who happened to work nights as an editor at the *Times*. I asked him
for career suggestions and he said: 'Go to law school. Just for
a year. It will teach you the kind of disciplined thinking that
would be very useful to any reporter.'

"Harvard Law School hit me like a ton of bricks. Once I
got involved in it, I just wasn't going to stop at the end of
one year. When I graduated in 1955, I was hired by the Los
Angeles firm of Gibson Dunn & Crutcher, where I did a little
bit of everything—securities work, acquisitions, and so forth.

"Somewhat later an important client, Times Mirror, began
planning a diversification program, and asked about borrowing a lawyer to lend a hand more or less full-time. I was given
an office in the *Times* building, where I worked five days a
week. About six months later I joined the company and was
named general counsel. Each passing year has made my career
decision look good.

"As distinct from conglomerates involved in all sorts of
unrelated businesses, our emphasis, especially in recent years,
has been placed on growing as a media communications company with significant acquisitions in broadcasting and newspapers and cable. We have approximately three dozen companies under the umbrella of Times Mirror, and if there is
one thing I'm very clear about, it's that I would never, never
want to get involved in their editorial decisions. Those decisions are strictly and exclusively the responsibility of the
editors."

For the *Times,* the daily challenge of weighing the issues
and making choices is confronted by Anthony Day, associate
editor in charge of the editorial pages. He has journalism in
his genes. His father, Price Day, had been a reporter at the
Baltimore Sun, where in time he won a Pulitzer Prize and
eventually rose to become editor-in-chief.

Tony went to Harvard and then, through family and friends, was hired as a junior reporter on the *Philadelphia Bulletin*. Recently he told an interviewer: "I was absolutely terrified that I wouldn't do well. I got to know the city well, covering police, working all night, taking the full range of general assignment duty and discovering gradually that everyone has a story to tell."

In time the *Bulletin* assigned him to Washington and eventually named him bureau chief. In 1969 the *Times,* which was casting around for a chief editorial writer, offered him the job. "I began reading the *Times,* picking up copies in Washington, and I could see the paper was straining hard to become more comprehensive, more sophisticated. I knew very little about Otis Chandler, but it was clear that he was trying to pull the paper out of its past."

Day flew to Los Angeles to learn more about the prospective job. During a visit with Nick Williams, the veteran editor referred deadpan to a previous era when editorials were rewritten, at a high level, to conform to a strict Republican party line.

"Does it scare you?" inquired Nick.

Day, growing tense, gulped hard and asked whether the practice was still going on.

"No," said Nick.

"All right," said Day with a sigh. "Then it doesn't scare me."

He moved into the post with skill and professionalism, gradually imposing his own style and methods on the editorial writers. His mornings are characterized by tough, searching questions at the daily meeting of the editorial board, and he is invariably ready.

He begins his preparation some ninety minutes before the ten-thirty board session. It is his practice to visit shortly after nine o'clock most mornings with his deputy, Alvin Shuster.

"Alvin and I talk for perhaps fifteen minutes about what we

think the editorial writers should be doing that day and on the following days. At nine-twenty we sit down with our editorial writers in a conference room. We have a round table because it lends more of a collegial atmosphere. We ask each person, going around the table one by one, to express ideas on what we should be doing.

"Conversation darts about in a kind of zigzag fashion that would be bewildering to outsiders, because we tend to talk very often in code. We joke a lot and tell stories. But out of it there comes a list of the editorials we have in mind, and the writers who will be assigned.

"Then at ten-thirty we confer with the publisher, editor, managing editor and other top news executives. We exchange a lot of information. We check constantly, by the way, to make sure that we are factually correct in everything that appears on the editorial page. We certainly don't want to publish an editorial until we're sure of ourselves.

"Now, quite a few wheels are spinning at once. While some members of the staff are writing editorials—and more about that in a moment—others are at work on the Op-Ed page and the Sunday Opinion section. Op-Ed and Opinion require much more attention than meets the casual eye: we discovered some time ago that while we receive three hundred to four hundred unsolicited manuscripts every week over the transom, most of them aren't very good, so we try to solicit more pieces.

"We have a meeting every Monday to talk about the Opinion section, and we find that what works best—nearly all the time—are pieces written especially for us, at our specific request.

"For the Op-Ed page we buy a great many more syndicated columns than we can use. We spend a lot of money and time on them, not out of a desire to be extravagant but because we want to have some choices. We are literally flooded with material, and just reading all of it is a huge, time-consuming chore.

"We make a practice of keeping our options open, picking and choosing the material with great care, not running any item automatically or routinely.

"Art Buchwald, for example, was once a fixture on the Op-Ed page. He wanted to be run there, every day in the same spot, with his picture. I refused, simply because I don't want a daily commitment to any columnist. Eventually the paper found a regular place for him in the View section, and that was just fine with me.

"Our staff spends an incredible amount of time reading— our diet consists of all the principal newspapers and some ninety or one hundred magazines from all over the world.

"When I go home at night I try to turn it off by reading fiction or history. One of the great problems of daily journalism is that it's *daily* journalism, and you have to keep trying to stretch, to get away from routine, confined thinking.

"We try to be critical of what we do. In our editorials I'm concerned about being fair, being right, being helpful if we can. Occasionally we're startled at how little we know. When the hostages were seized in Iran, for example, we realized suddenly that we didn't know nearly enough about Iran.

"There are three great pitfalls for newspaper editorial writers: dullness, irrelevancy, pomposity. The hardest to avoid is pomposity, because the page is basically serious. The other day a letter arrived from a fellow who was furious at us. He wrote: 'I'm sick and tired of your Christ-like, everlastingly fair editorials.'

"We hear a great deal from our readers—an average of twelve hundred letters a week. We can't publish them all, of course, because there just isn't space, but we've increased the space three times, and each time the volume of letters has gone up. We publish letters on any issue, pro and con, in roughly the proportion in which they are sent in. I like the diversity of voice that comes across in letters. I like to hear the sound of a person talking. So we interfere with the letters' style least of all the things we publish on the editorial pages."

Occasionally readers hurl brickbats at the *Times*, claiming that the far-flung corporate holdings of the parent company, Times Mirror, preclude an honest approach to the news. A sharply different view emerges from a Ph.D. thesis written by journalism professor Jack R. Hart, who spent more than two years researching the *Times*. (His doctoral thesis was later published as a book, *The Information Empire*, in 1981 by University Press of America.) Hart found that Otis Chandler had shaped an enterprise where corporate affairs took a back seat to responsible journalism.

Chandler himself is quick to admit the existing potential for conflict of interest within a conglomerate operating newspapers. Recently he told an interviewer: "There are a great many issues of private enterprise rights versus the public interest, issues where our profits may be directly affected or threatened. You might expect the *Times* to react automatically, taking the side of greater profitability for the parent company. But it just isn't so. The *Times* invariably takes a position on behalf of the public interest.

"For example, one of our subsidiaries, Times Mirror Press, has as its largest customer Pacific Telephone and Telegraph— TMP prints all of their telephone directories. You might imagine the *Times* would either give editorial support to the telephone company or at least not antagonize it when a telephone rate is sought from the State Public Utilities Commission. But when our editorial board arrives at the conclusion, as it has, that a rate increase is not justified, our editorials come straight out and say so. More than once I've heard protests from our own Times Mirror executives to the effect: 'Hey, do you realize how much money we take in from the phone company? Do you understand we could be canceled out in a flash?' "

The editorial independence of the *Times*, however, is not self-evident to long-distance observers. Some critics cling to the suspicion that somewhere in the background there must be a devilishly clever self-serving policy—hidden from public view, yet still functioning.

A free-lance article in the *Columbia Journalism Review*, January/February 1981, stated: "The *Los Angeles Times* has worked hard in the last two decades, and with considerable success, to rid itself of its image as a parochial, pro-business instrument in the hands of the Chandler family. But memories of earlier days, and particularly of how the Chandlers used the paper to help bring water to their vast California holdings, die hard."

The *Review* article pointed to a controversial construction project designed to expand the state's water system, and noted that one of the large landowners that would benefit from the project was Times Mirror Company, which owned 50 percent of Tejon Ranch. The article implied that this ownership influenced the *Times'* news coverage and editorial opinions of water issues in California.

Tony Day tapped out a swift protest to the editors of the *Review:* "To state the obvious, our news judgment is strictly our own, and we arrive at our editorial positions utterly without regard to the views of the Tejon Ranch Co., into which we have never inquired. If the *Times* were the kind of newspaper your article intimates it is, none of us would be here."

14

Otis Chandler knows the dark history of the *Los Angeles Times*, the shadowy stories of corruption surrounding his grandfather and great-grandfather. And the dark history and the tales of corruption have made their mark on Otis Chandler: a psychohistorian probing his professional attitudes might conclude that here is a publisher reacting sharply to the sins and excesses of his ancestors. But it is not in Otis Chandler's nature to dwell on the past or to appear to carry a burden of shame for actions committed long before his time. He has a practical turn of mind, and he is concerned with the press of his own era. He is keenly aware that newspapers suffer at least one common failing: they examine and criticize practically every institution in society—but only rarely do they probe other newspapers.

Long before 1981, when the Pulitzer Prize was awarded to the *Washington Post* for a story later found to be a hoax, Otis Chandler reflected often on the weaknesses of journalism. Intrigued by an apparent unwillingness of the press to examine and criticize its own performance, he observed to William Thomas: "Somehow journalists are above reproach. We refuse to admit we make mistakes unless we are sued for libel, and then the admission appears in small print back in the truss ads. And we make no attempt to explain to readers how we function, no effort to shed light on our limitations, restrictions, ambitions, traditions, decision-making processes. I'm referring to us at the *Times,* but an 'above reproach' posture applies to the entire media—newspapers, magazines, radio, television."

Fascinated by this blind spot in the press and convinced that it was one reason why the press had lost a measure of credibility with the public, Chandler encouraged Bill Thomas to begin major coverage of the media. A longtime critic of the press, Thomas was delighted with the suggestion. To choose a reporter for media coverage, he searched the staff roster with elaborate care, and in 1974 finally settled on David Shaw, a slight, intense reporter, somewhat combative by nature, with an impressive ability to talk and write at flank speed.

Summoned to the editor's office, Shaw listened carefully as Thomas outlined a plan to provide regular coverage of the media. Shaw was characteristically skeptical; he accepted few statements at face value. He felt that a proposal, even from a top editor, was not above questioning, analyzing, resisting, modifying or rejecting. His capacity for independence and argument had earned him the reputation, among some editorial colleagues, of being outrageously abrasive. But Bill Thomas discerned in Shaw an extraordinary talent for tough reporting, clear thinking and good writing.

Shaw had learned early in life to be independent. He learned largely because he found himself on his own at an early age. The Ohio-born son of a photo engraver, Shaw stood apart in a family where "my parents were terribly unhappy with each other." His father suffered two heart attacks "after which he could no longer work, and we had to survive on his army pension. It was strictly poverty row."

To earn money, Shaw worked at a long list of jobs outside of classes in high school. Eventually he consolidated the heavy load into a forty-hour-a-week reporting routine, first at the *Huntington Park Daily Signal,* later at the *Long Beach Inde-*

pendent Press Telegram, and he structured his working hours to attend classes at UCLA, "but it took me five years instead of four to graduate."

By the age of twenty-five, when he was hired at the *Times,* Shaw had done "more than my share of covering police beats, fires, earthquakes and city council meetings. I had grown project-oriented and found satisfaction only in doing long, comprehensive pieces of reportage.

"Once I began to earn a good enough salary I began spending a great deal on food, travel and entertainment. My feeling is always: if I were to have a heart attack tomorrow, I could say, 'Hey, I had a pretty good life, I enjoyed it all the way.' "

Shaw applied the same intensity and energy to his reportage at the *Times.* "By nature I am obsessively disciplined and well organized. I spend an extraordinary amount of time on research, and then I write quickly. I don't waste time fumbling around looking for things."

From his first arrival in the *Times* newsroom Shaw did not need prodding; he generated a steady flow of story ideas on his own. Occasionally, however, Bill Thomas sent word that he had a notion for Shaw to explore. One day, in the early Seventies, Shaw was summoned to the editor's office. Thomas said: "It seems to me that the ACLU has stopped being a defender of free speech and turned into just another left-wing pressure group. Check it out."

Shaw went to New York, Washington, Chicago, Philadelphia, San Francisco and other cities, taking a month to interview dozens of sources. "What I found, of course, was that the ACLU had *not* really changed. In the context of the era—the Nixon Administration was in power, and the most frequent abuses of civil liberties were against people on the left—the most publicized cases gave the impression that the ACLU had turned into just another left-wing pressure group. But in fact they were also defending people on the right, just as before. This was absolutely the opposite of what Bill Thomas had sent me after, but my story ran on page one without a word being changed, and afterward Bill stopped me in the corridor and complimented me on it—and he doesn't hand out compliments lightly."

Later, Shaw told an interviewer, "when Bill offered me the job of media critic, I assumed he must have liked the fact that I was not intimidated by his views. But I declined. I wanted to remain free to range from subject to subject, writing on teen-age drug use, black militancy, the paramilitary right, urban sprawl, gambling, court reform, the sexual revolution, violent crime, football, poverty, or corruption. I liked to invest anywhere from three weeks to three months on a project, traveling widely, spending whatever money was necessary and writing four thousand to six thousand words—all virtually unheard-of freedoms on most newspapers."

Bill Thomas, however, was persistent and persuasive. He emphasized Shaw's unique talent and the singular importance of the assignment: no other newspaper had given a sharp investigative reporter a full-time hunting license to pursue big game in the media jungle.

Shaw promised to think things over. "One element that factored favorably into my thinking," he admitted afterward, "was my past dealings with Otis Chandler and Bill Thomas. Otis amazed me many times with his candor, his willingness to say things that other top corporate executives would duck away from. Once, for example, I did a piece on the future of newspapers and in the story I discussed their growing irrelevancy. I asked Otis how many of our readers would really miss us if we folded tomorrow, and he said, 'Probably less than half.' I was astonished that he made that statement and that he allowed me to quote him in print.

"Bill Thomas has a different characteristic that intrigues

me: he does not like a predictable story. No matter how well done a story may be, if it has no surprising conclusions, he is not going to be impressed with it. He can't stand knee-jerk reporting." Shaw remained cautious. He returned to Thomas' office the next day with a series of questions: "Will I be able to pick my own stories? I would want to be absolutely free to reject any story idea, from you or anyone else, if it bores me. Will I have complete freedom to criticize the *Times* and individuals on the paper by name, including you?"

Thomas gave Shaw all the right answers, and Shaw accepted the assignment. Then Thomas said, with a mischievous grin: "I hope you have a lot of friends outside the newspaper business. By the time you're through with this job, you may not have many left inside it."

Shaw's stories represented a new kind of journalism—a hard revealing look at the press itself, including the *Los Angeles Times*. One yarn explored the mystery of how and why newspapers miss important stories, and it gave an inside account (embarrassing to some *Times* editors) of how the paper itself failed to cover "promptly or adequately" a major story in its own backyard.

The central figure was David Begelman, a flamboyant Hollywood agent-turned-producer. He had taken charge of film production at Columbia Pictures when the studio was more than $220 million in debt. He had been widely credited with putting the studio back on its financial feet with a number of successful films, including *Funny Lady, Shampoo* and *The Deep*.

But on October 3, 1977, Columbia Pictures issued a press release announcing that the audit committee of its board of directors had "commenced an inquiry into certain unauthorized financial transactions between David Begelman and the company."

Wrote Shaw: "Why? What were his 'unauthorized financial transactions'? How much money was involved? How had Begelman been caught? Why had he done whatever he had done?

"Begelman was, it would seem, an ideal story for the press —and especially for a newspaper like the *Los Angeles Times*. Here was a tale of power, scandal and intrigue in the most glamorous business in the world, right in Hollywood."

But the *Times* "carried only a one-paragraph story on page eight of the business section, and the following day carried another short item, essentially restating the original story."

More than two months later Columbia reinstated Begelman as president and announced routinely that he had returned, "with interest," $61,008 in corporate funds obtained by "improper means." The *Times* again published a one-paragraph story. The rest of the press had been similarly indifferent.

But this time, Shaw noted:

The *Wall Street Journal* published a twenty-three-paragraph story, pointing out that Begelman had "obtained much of the money by forging checks . . . using the names of Cliff Robertson, the actor, and Martin Ritt, the film director. . . . " Five days later, the *Washington Post* published an even longer and more provocative story on the Begelman affair.

But not until five days after that did the *Los Angeles Times* run anything of consequence on Begelman—an edited-down version of the *Post* story, about one-third the length of the original.

In ensuing weeks and months, the *Times* began to show somewhat more interest in the Begelman story. But at no time did the *Times* produce a single story as revelatory as the original *Journal* and *Post* stories. It was not until July 22, 1979—19 months after the story first broke—that the *Times* finally published a lengthy, on-the-record interview with Begelman.

Why was the *Times* so passive, tardy and inadequate in its coverage of the Begelman affair?

"It was bad judgment," says *Times* managing editor George Cotliar. "A lot of us didn't even see the original story . . . [and]

once we blew it . . . the hardest thing for anyone to do is admit making a mistake. Subconsciously, we tried to wish it away. The editors made a terrible mistake. We screwed up on Begelman, and we continually compounded our error."

Shaw pursued the compounding of errors and uncovered a number of "structural deficiencies" at the *Times.* In essence, reporters and editors working in the entertainment or "soft" news departments routinely referred to the financial or "hard" news departments any story that seemed to have a hard-news angle. "Or, more often, they just assumed someone in those departments would logically handle the story. But reporters and editors in news and financial departments made just the opposite assumption: if it was an entertainment story—a change in studio personnel, a controversy in a network news operation or a rumor of rock-music payola—it was a story for the entertainment department to handle. Period.

"The result: In the absence of strong, head-to-head competition from another large metropolitan daily paper, it was easy for some stories to fall between the cracks in the editorial hierarchy."

David Shaw's relentless pursuit of the "missed" news story uncovered numerous errors of omission and commission, occasioned by the pressures of time and competition and by individual and institutional idiosyncrasies and shortcomings.

The *New York Times,* for example, found it inconceivable that the city of New York faced a financial crisis. In a column of "news analysis" dated April 11, 1975, the paper stated: "Can New York City default on its debt and go bankrupt? The answer is no, and it can be given without qualification, according to city and private financial experts. . . ."

But five weeks later, the paper was forced to concede in another "news analysis":

"New York could quite soon become a city with no available

cash, with poor credit, needing to borrow money from a financial market that is resisting. . . . In short, if the money is not
found soon, it could become a city in default."

Analyzing the *New York Times'* shortsightedness, Shaw
wrote: "One reason newspapers sometimes miss stories in their
early developmental stages is that they—and their editors and
publishers—are themselves part of the stories. The *New York
Times* is part of New York—in some ways, part of the very
New York establishment whose leaders (former Gov. Nelson
Rockefeller and former Mayor John Lindsay among them)
helped foster the conditions that made the fiscal crisis
inevitable."

"It was not so much a matter of the newspaper consciously
trying to protect its friends by suppressing bad news; it was
more a matter of the men running the newspaper and the men
running the city often sharing the same perceptions—and the
same misperceptions: They just didn't see the story early
enough. Sometimes, proximity, mutuality and personal relationships can combine with journalistic skepticism to distort
one's judgment."

Otis Chandler found particular pleasure in a series written
by David Shaw detecting "signs of life" in the long-ailing *Los
Angeles Herald-Examiner*. Once a crown jewel in the Hearst
Corporation's newspaper chain, with the largest circulation of
any afternoon paper in the country, the *Herald-Examiner* had
fallen on hard times in the Sixties and suffered a long-
running strike. For the next decade there were recurring rumors that the paper would close its doors. But late in the
Seventies the Hearst Corporation appointed an aggressive publisher, Francis Dale, and a brilliant editor, James Bellows, to
restore the paper to its former prominence.

Chandler took careful note when David Shaw, in a searching
appraisal, examined the efforts of Dale and Bellows to improve

the paper. Shaw reported that it "looks better and reads better, advertising is up and the long circulation decline may finally be abating."

Some press cynics suggested that it required little courage or generosity to praise the competition, since the *Examiner* was the journalistic equivalent of a mouse afflicted with malnutrition, in contrast to the elephantine, robustly healthy *Times*. But the cynics overlooked a key fact: Hearst Corporation itself was a major media empire, owner of such money-making properties as *Cosmopolitan* and *Good Housekeeping* magazines, and if it chose to spend larger sums on the *Herald-Examiner* to make it a more competitive paper, the Hearst organization had the resources to do so.

In another kind of hard, uncompromising look at the press, Shaw explored the question of whether newspapers can be trusted to handle competently complex scientific or medical stories. With characteristically thorough pursuit, he reviewed numerous newspapers in their efforts to deal with technical news. Among Shaw's findings:

"Three Rand Corporation researchers studied more than one thousand alcoholics who had taken part in treatment programs. The scientists concluded that *some* former alcoholics could safely resume drinking. But the researchers also expressed clear qualifications: their finding collided with the prevailing emphasis on complete and permanent abstinence; and they had not yet been able to determine which treated alcoholics could take up drinking without suffering a relapse. The researchers stressed: 'We are by no means advocating that alcoholics should attempt moderate drinking. Alcoholics who have repeatedly failed to moderate their drinking, or who have irreversible physical complications due to alcohol, should not drink at all.' "

But these qualifications were ignored by many newspapers.

Shaw found press headlines all across the country: "Alcoholism Study Opposes Abstention"; "Alcoholics 'Can' Drink Again"; "Study Says Alcoholics Can Drink Normally"; "Should Alcoholics Keep Drinking? Controversial Report Says Yes."

Shaw found even more inflammatory comment on editorial pages; one said Rand had "gambled with lives" in releasing its report. Shaw summarized:

Rand officials saw this widespread misrepresentation of their study as confirmation of a belief long held by many in the scientific community that newspapers just cannot be trusted with complex scientific or medical stories. Many scientists believe that newspapers, in trying to simplify such stories for their readership, often inadvertently oversimplify, sensationalize and distort information that has been carefully gathered, compiled and released.

The Rand study, for example, was 30 months in preparation, involved a bibliography of more than 300 sources, resulted in a formal 216-page report—and was withheld from public release for a full year while its methodology and findings were minutely cross-checked.

Then, in one morning, its conclusions—all couched in the most tentative and circumspect terms—were subjected to widespread distortion and ridicule.

This, Shaw found, was not an isolated phenomenon; scientists are shocked regularly by newspaper reports on birth-control pills, cancer cures, "life on Mars," earthquake predictions, breast X-rays, vitamin C as a "cure" for the common cold, megavitamins as a treatment for schizophrenia, new "breakthroughs" in genetics, links between marijuana use and various physical and mental disorders.

Shaw also pointed to one large reason why many newspapers fail to deal accurately with such stories: except for the largest papers, few employ experienced science writers, and as a result these stories are often covered by general assignment reporters who know little, if anything, about the subject and write the story quickly between assignments on a bank robbery, a city council meeting and a little old lady with an eight-foot tomato plant in her backyard.

Probing another weakness of the press, David Shaw turned a beacon on a highly controversial activity of some journalists: masquerading or deceiving in order to obtain a story. He cited specific examples:

—A reporter for the *Wall Street Journal* worked three weeks on an assembly line in a large factory to investigate charges that the company routinely violated fair labor practices.

—A reporter for the *Los Angeles Times* posed as a graduate student in psychology while working in a state mental hospital to expose conditions there.

—A reporter for the *Detroit News* posed as a Michigan congressman to prove how lax security was at a treaty-signing ceremony on the White House lawn.

Shaw asked: Were these unethical activities? Were these journalists compromising their professional integrity—and, ultimately and cumulatively, their professions' credibility? Do the special rights granted to the press under the First Amendment also impose upon the press special responsibilities that preclude deception and misrepresentation?

Or, asked Shaw, is the public benefit to be derived from the disclosure of certain conditions sometimes so great—and the obstacles to such disclosure sometimes so difficult—that reporters are justified in pretending to be what they are not? In short, does the worthwhile end sometimes justify the deceptive means?

Shaw found and reported in the *Times* widespread disagreement among reporters and editors over just when, and if, they could indulge in such activities. Some insisted that the press ought to be just as open, frank and straightforward as other people. But some journalists insisted there were special situations where masquerade was the only way to get a story.

For example, the *Chicago Sun-Times* assigned a team of reporters to operate the Mirage Bar for four months in 1977, without revealing their identity. The object: to expose graft and corruption in the city.

The team found that city inspectors agreed to overlook health and safety violations at the bar in exchange for money. Jukebox and pinball operators offered kickbacks. Accountants offered counsel on the fine art of tax fraud, and contractors served as bagmen for payoffs to public officials.

The *Sun-Times* stories were deplored by *Washington Post* executive editor Benjamin Bradlee, who said: "When cops pose as newspapermen, we get goddam sore. Quite properly so. So how can we pose as something we're not?"

Joseph Shoquist, managing editor of the *Milwaukee Journal,* disagreed with Bradlee. Shoquist said the widespread corruption uncovered by the *Sun-Times* "was a worthy subject that needed a dramatic presentation to capture the public's attention."

Further, James Hoge, editor-in-chief of the *Sun-Times,* noted: "We couldn't have gotten that information and presented it as effectively any other way. We had reported for a number of years on bribery in Chicago, with no effect." But Hoge called it a special kind of journalism to be used "only with extreme caution and selectively and only when certain standards are applied"; for example, the story should be of significant public benefit, and past experience, common sense and hard work should first demonstrate that there is no other way to get the story.

Shaw queried numerous editors and found that most seemed to agree, in principle, with the standards invoked by the *Sun-Times'* editor-in-chief. But Shaw pointed to a key problem:

practically every editor appeared to have his own definition for "significant" and "no other way."

Shaw constructed a hypothetical situation and posed it to more than two dozen editors across the nation: "Someone tells one of your reporters that there is a report by three doctors that a prospective gubernatorial candidate has a very serious drinking problem. That report is on a doctor's desk in the hospital, and all your reporter has to do is put on a doctor's white coat, walk into the office and copy it or photograph it. Would you let him do that?"

Nearly all editors agreed that such impersonation would be improper and unnecessary (if the candidate's drinking problem was serious, there would be other ways to learn about it) and that they would not let their reporters copy the medical material.

But the same editors were asked another hypothetical question: "Suppose the medical reports are from three psychiatrists who agree unanimously that the President of the United States is mentally unstable. Then do you tell your reporter to get the reports?"

This time nearly all agreed with *Los Angeles Times* editor William Thomas, who said: "You have to be very careful about doing that kind of thing in most circumstances. But in this particular situation, absolutely; you do it. You tell your reporter to do anything he has to do to get those reports—even if they're locked in a safe and he has to dynamite the safe. Christ, you're talking about an unstable President with his finger on the button." But, Thomas added, any journalist who actually broke the law to get a story would have to pay the penalty, "and the editor should make the call."

Hardly any subject involving the media proved too sensitive for David Shaw. To examine conflicts of interest among journalists themselves, he interviewed more than one hundred reporters, editors, civic leaders and politicians around the country, and he carefully included *Los Angeles Times* personnel, past and present.

He raised such questions as: Should reporters (or editors) help their government (as indicated by disclosures in recent years that many American journalists had worked for the CIA abroad)? Should they participate in civic affairs? Join the PTA? United Way? Should they march in demonstrations? Make political contributions? Participate in political campaigns? Should they leave their jobs to work for the government, then return to journalism? Should journalists even make friends with prominent politicians and civic figures? How about journalists' love affairs? Their investments? The civic and political activities of their wives and husbands? Do reporters and editors have essentially the same civil rights and civic obligations as other citizens? Or are they somehow "special"—subject to a different, more restrictive set of rules than their friends and neighbors?

Shaw wrote of his findings: "Bill Moyers [former press secretary to President Lyndon Johnson and later a television newsman] likens the journalist's role to that of a judge—'people in our society who have to try to be impartial'—and that, he says, means 'self-imposed moderation in the exercise of their legal rights.'

" 'Different professions simply have different standards of behavior,' says A. M. Rosenthal, executive editor of the *New York Times*, 'and you don't do anything that reduces your value in that profession. I can have a drink in my office, but a school principal probably shouldn't. Well, a journalist pretty much has to give up any kind of activity beyond voting. That's the price we pay for being newspaper people.' "

Shaw raised the question of whether editors and publishers

—who have policymaking responsibilities—should be even more circumspect in all matters than reporters; and then he wrote:

Many critics say *The New York Times* was unfair to students in its coverage of the 1968 riots at Columbia University, because *Times* publisher Arthur Ochs (Punch) Sulzberger is on the Columbia board of trustees.

Similarly, some critics say, the *Times* paid too much attention to the GeoTek story because of Chandler's involvement, but most say the paper would have been far more aggressive in its pursuit of the story had he not been involved. Editors at both papers respond to those charges with strong denials and with reams of clippings they say prove their integrity. But appearances can be damaging.

Shaw noted that in the early years of the *Los Angeles Times,* the owners were accused of self-serving boosterism and acquisitions.

Their purchases of land, combined with their editorial support of various water-bound issues to serve that land, opened them to repeated charges of conflict of interest—and worse. They were accused of "political manipulation" and of perpetrating "one of the costliest, crookedest, most unscrupulous deals ever."

Even today, the Chandler family's assorted landholdings occasionally open the *Times* to charges of conflict of interest—most recently (in December, 1977) when it was suggested that holdings by the Times Mirror Company and the publisher's aunt had influenced the *Times* to editorialize strongly against enforcement of a 1902 law limiting to 160 acres the size of farms irrigated by government water projects.

Much the same charges have been levied against the *New York Times* for its editorial campaign in support of a costly 4.2-mile interstate highway project for the lower west side of Manhattan.

"How much of their support is based on what Westway could mean to the value of the paper's real estate holdings in the city?" asks New York journalist Ken Auletta.

The *New York Times,* like the *Los Angeles Times* in the case of the 160-acre limit editorials, vehemently denies any connection whatever between corporate or familial economic interests and editorial positions. The people who decide on and write the editorials are not even aware of the financial holdings, they say. But skeptics, remembering what has sometimes happened in the past, are hard to convince.

David Shaw took full advantage of his freedom to criticize the *Times* and, by name, its publisher, editors and reporters. If some staffers were distressed by it, the publisher was not.

Otis Chandler explained: "Most of our department heads cannot understand why we publish Shaw when his stories criticize our own writers and editors. Many people, inside and outside the *Times,* were baffled by our willingness to quote Mayor Sam Yorty when he blasted us, for instance. There is one big answer to all these puzzles. We have an overriding responsibility to publish the news."

What did media specialist David Shaw find wanting about those journalists who functioned as critics? He called attention to serious shortcomings in the best-seller lists of books and he gave large doses of heartburn to writers who specialized in reviews of restaurants. With precision and sweeping force he reminded one group after another that the critical function is itself a most precarious one and never above criticism.

He pointed to flaws in the best-seller lists with a reminder of a time when:

Esquire magazine published the second of three excerpts from Truman Capote's long-awaited new novel, *Answered Prayers.* The excerpts confirmed for the book-buying public what had been rumored for months in the publishing industry—that *Answered*

Prayers was a gossipy *roman à clef* about the jet-set celebrities Capote had been cavorting with in the ten years since his last book, *In Cold Blood,* had catapulted him into celebrityhood.

Capote's reputation—both as a brilliant literary stylist and as a provocative social gadfly—seemed to guarantee instant bestsellerdom for *Answered Prayers,* and sure enough, inquiries and orders for the book flooded a number of bookstores as soon as the second *Esquire* excerpt was published. Demand for the book was so great, in fact, that at least two bookstores—one in Ohio and one in Washington—reported *Answered Prayers* to their respective local newspapers on that week's best-seller list.

There was, however, one small flaw in those bookstore reports: neither of the stores—nor any other store in the United States, for that matter—had sold one single copy of *Answered Prayers* (because the book had not yet been published).

So why did two stores report an unwritten, unpublished, unavailable book as a best-seller?

Because the compilation of newspaper and magazine best-seller lists is often so haphazard, so slipshod, so imprecise and—at times —so dishonest that, as one bookseller says, "If George Gallup conducted his political polls the same way, he'd have Harold Stassen, Mary Tyler Moore, Al Capone and Rin Tin Tin as America's favorite candidates for President. . . . "

Best-seller lists published in *Time* magazine, the *New York Times,* the *Los Angeles Times* and other newspapers are compiled from weekly telephone calls to selected bookstores and book departments of large department stores, and are based on sales in a given week, rather than on cumulative sales.

When a newspaper or magazine calls a bookstore, the store manager or clerk may just glance around to see which stacks have diminished the most in the last week. Or he may try to recall what books have been selling well. Or he may just read off the conveniently posted list of best-sellers published in the previous week's newspaper.

Publishing industry sources say these are the most common methods resorted to by bookstores for reporting best-sellers. Booksellers themselves admit this is so: "We just don't have the time to keep track of everything we sell, in order, on a weekly basis," one says.

Sometimes, if a store has ordered a large supply of a book that hasn't sold well—or one that sold well, then tailed off suddenly— a bookstore may try to spur sales by telling the newspaper it is actually a best-seller.

"Being on the best-seller list is the best free publicity in the world for a book," says Irving Wallace, the author of almost a dozen best-sellers.

Knowing that, authors and publishers do everything they can to make the best-seller list.

Booksellers say some less-celebrated authors will try to make the best-seller list by learning specifically which stores regularly report to the lists and then buying—or having their friends buy—a number of copies in each of these stores.

"Most stores just don't sell all that many copies of any one book," says Lou Virgiel, president of the Southern California Booksellers Assn. "Best-seller lists may be pretty reliable for the top two or three spots, but the next 10 titles are pretty inter-changeable; none of them sells more than a few copies each."

Remedying the inaccuracy of the best-seller lists would seem to be a relatively simple task: If the bookstores reported actual sales volume for each book, rather than just rankings, then the news-papers and magazines could add the totals, average them out and produce a reasonably reliable list.

But the booksellers refuse to supply their actual sales figures because (1) They don't want their competitors to know, (2) Most of them sell so few copies of each book that they think the figures would embarrass them, and (3) Recording and compiling each sale is an expensive and time-consuming process. . . .

Many people in publishing regard the *Publishers Weekly* list as the most reliable because it is reproduced quickly and is based on reports from individual stores, chains and other newspaper lists, which—cumulatively—represent more than 600 stores.

But since every newspaper that compiles its own list from local

she was, by nature, overly sensitive. In her view, however, the impact of Shaw's stories went beyond the minor irritations associated with an overly sensitive nature.

Taylor expressed her feelings to an interviewer: "When Bill Thomas first told me that we were going to have a regular media critic I knew immediately it was going to be a very difficult assignment for David, and for us. He would be, in effect, working for the editor and the managing editor. He was bound to keep his own lines fairly well protected. And this meant the people who were most expendable were the people in the soft news departments.

"He attacked the books' best-seller list at a time when we were vulnerable. We were late starting a book review, and when we did, Digby Diehl came to me and said. 'We've got to do our own best-seller list.' So we devised an imperfect thing. We asked the Marketing Research department to set up the demographics, and we assigned two persons to make a certain number of calls to a certain number of bookstores.

"To me this was honorable and honest. Maybe it should have been a lot better, but we were still in the toddler stage. Then along came David with a story telling how corrupt this whole system was.

"Sometime later we were talking and David asked, 'Do you ever go for a breaking news story?'

"I said, 'Yeah, David, that's what I was trying to do with the best-seller list. I was trying to get it going. And you came along and blasted it before I had a chance to get it going.'

"Another time David quoted someone, in paraphrase: 'Charles Champlin has never met a film he didn't like.' When that appeared in the paper, I was mad. I called Bill Thomas and I said, 'Why are we doing things like this?'

"Now Chuck may be a little too easy on some movies. But it seemed to me that there were ways of doing this in which he was not diminished.

"And what I said to Bill was: 'Chuck thinks it's coming from you.' Bill said, 'It isn't coming from me. I have great respect for Chuck Champlin. This is the media writer doing a story. I don't edit David's stories. He has to do what he sees. That's his job.' "

Otis Chandler listened patiently to the anguish over David Shaw's stories. He felt heat every time Shaw appeared in print. If the story found fault with the *Times,* Chandler's staff objected; if the story found fault with other newspapers, Chandler heard complaints from his fellow publishers.

But along with Bill Thomas, Otis Chandler stubbornly continued to protect Shaw's independence. Chandler did not necessarily agree with all of Shaw's conclusions, but the publisher knew that there was simply no other way a media writer could survive, maintain credibility and, most important, uphold the integrity of the newspaper itself.

15

Another chronic source of irritation—to presidents, governors and lesser mortals—is Pulitzer Prize–winning cartoonist Paul Conrad, a lanky, loose-jointed character with a high forehead, a formidable lantern jaw, large thick-lensed spectacles, a high-pitched voice, and a rush of laughter regarded as "ear-shattering" by more than one colleague.

Alternately savage, compassionate, brutal and ironic, possessed of a fanatic heart, Conrad employs pen and ink to puncture lies, hokum and corruption. He knows well the opportunities and limitations of his craft: in satirizing events and event makers, the cartoon refines material until only the ridiculous essence remains. Circumstances impossible in the real world are staged upon the cartoonist's proscenium: the politician comes face to face with his broken promises, hypocrisy assumes a human face, fingers are pointed, blame is fixed, responsibility attached to recognizable figures. No one believes that all editorial cartoonists are Daumiers working at top speed; daily deadlines can result in dreary clichés, fatigued metaphors, limp labels. But editors recognize that cartoons are getting better year after year and that, of all features, the editorial cartoon is a journalistic institution that at its best manages in a few square inches to encapsulate crises, expose hollow promises, puncture swollen egos, pierce pretensions.

Paul Conrad goes about his job as if he were deck watch officer on the Ship of State. Few public officials escape his scorn; the higher the office, the more tempting the target. Following Watergate, when the New York state bar association suspended Richard Nixon's license to practice law, Conrad sketched a saloon, identified as "New York Bar," with Nixon, having been tossed outside on the sidewalk, clenching a fist and hurling defiance at the bouncers: "I've been thrown out of better places than this."

When then-President Jimmy Carter announced a program to make it easier to fire inept federal employees, Conrad drew a bewildered Carter holding a notice: "Jimmy—you're fired."

Conrad has been an outspoken rebel ever since childhood. He grew up in Cedar Rapids, Iowa, the son of a railroad man whose hobby was painting watercolors. Railroad rate-structures were printed in large quantities on 8½ x 11 pages, the backs blank, and the rates were changed almost daily; the elder Conrad regularly carried home reams of scrap paper. Paul began drawing and quickly demonstrated unusual skill with pen and ink.

At the same time he rejected his father's political attitudes. He told an interviewer years later: "Every Sunday afternoon at three o'clock, whatever was going on around the house stopped. Shouting ceased. The dinner roast was turned to simmer. My dear sainted father tuned in the Atwater Kent, seated himself nearby, and we all listened for the next thirty minutes to the ranting and raving of a crazy priest, Father Charles Coughlin. I have great reverence for priests—we happen to be a devout Catholic family—but this guy didn't seem particularly Christian to me. In fact, he sounded like a goddam fascist.

"My father required silence in the house while Coughlin

talked, and this just drove me up the wall. I was only a teen-
ager, but it was awfully clear the priest was a phony rabble-
rouser. I felt like a witness at the royal ceremony where the
emperor displays his fine suit, and I kept wanting to shout,
'The emperor has no clothes at all.' I had to obey my father's
rule of silence, but ever since then I've been rebelling against
his politics, rejecting Father Coughlin, and in a sort of daily
reenactment I tell people that the emperor is not wearing
clothes."

After a World War II hitch in the Army Corps of Engineers, Conrad majored in art at the University of Iowa. Later
he landed a job at *The Denver Post* and soon *Time* magazine
tagged him as "probably the nation's hottest new cartooning
property."

When Otis Chandler inquired about the possibility of luring him to the *Times,* one high-ranking editor cautioned:
"He'll give you headaches," and pointed out that Conrad was
a creature of freewheeling independence and rip-roaring controversy, with an unlimited capacity for infuriating readers.

"Let's get him anyway," said Chandler.

Conrad joined the *Times* and he lived up fully to his advance reputation. Day after day sacks of angry mail arrived at
the paper. Some readers cancelled their subscriptions. Others
accused him, in effect, of feeding on bile and bat's milk.

He chipped away at Establishment nerves, *any* Establishment, and many of his victims were friends of the Chandlers.
At moments Conrad found himself besieged not only by angry
laymen but by outraged theologians. When the Vatican issued
a ruling barring women from the priesthood, Conrad sketched
the pope holding on his lap an infant pope with an identical
face. The caption: "Vatican prohibits ordination of women
as priests because Christ's representatives must have a 'natural resemblance' to him.—News item."

"Dear Paul," wrote Timothy Cardinal Manning, Archbishop of Los Angeles, "much as I admire your talent and its use for the causes of justice, I must, in conscience, write to protest your cartoon. The caricature of Our Holy Father and of his teaching was offensive, and a scandal. I hope that you will have an opportunity to undo the affront to him and to every loyal Catholic. We number two million."

Conrad penned a swift reply: "As one of the two million 'loyal' Catholics in the Archdiocese of Los Angeles, I was more than a little stung by your response to my cartoon. If you or anyone else found it offensive, I do apologize. However, I cannot agree that my drawing and its caption were either a 'scandal' or an 'affront' to the Holy Father.

"Just as your vocation carries with it a duty to 'hold and teach the Catholic faith,' mine obliges me to speak clearly for justice, in so far as my conscience allows me to understand it. In the formation of that conscience, I have always drawn on the teachings and tradition of the Church, but I find 'The Ordination of Women to the Priesthood' most troubling. I am certainly no theologian, but I do recall a principle of moral theology that goes something like this: to be good, a thing must be good in all its parts; to be defective, it need only be defective in one.

"It seems to me that the Vatican document is defective on two important counts. First, by denying women the opportunity to serve Christ in the fullest possible sense, it seriously weakens that complete sense of justice that should characterize relations among the People of God. Second, by relying on Aquinas' principle of 'natural resemblance,' the Vatican employs a source whose understanding of human biology was limited by the science of his time. It seems to me that the resemblance which should concern us is that which exists between souls. After all, God judges us not by our bodies, but by our souls, which were *all* created in His image and likeness. Why should the Church be any different?"

Conrad recently described his working process to an interviewer: "The subconscious mind keeps functioning twenty-four hours a day, and it always finds something. When I decide what current event I'm most interested in, I draw a rough draft, a cartoon concept. I take the rough around the office and show it to people. Does it make sense? Is it important that this statement be made? Collecting reactions, I look not simply for a 'yes' or 'no' but I watch the corner of the eyes. Some people say 'yes' but mean 'no' and vice versa.

"If the consensus is favorable then I show it to my editor— my editor being not a censor but a judge of the sense of the material itself. From there to the drawing board to do the finished work, which generally takes about an hour and a half.

"I do not think in terms of the *Los Angeles Times* syndicate, even though it provides a rewarding source of income. The syndicate can either starve or, I hope, get fat on what I do, but the syndicate is sort of beside the point of the creative experience. The *Times* itself is always uppermost in my mind. I need it more than I need the syndicate because this is where the nurturing goes on, this is where I talk to people and get their reactions, this is where I come into focus, this is where I zero in on what's current, what's hot, what needs to be said and the right way to say it.

"I try not to think in terms of *Times* editorial policy, or how Otis Chandler or any high-ranking editor feels about a particular issue. I just try to put on paper the way I feel about current events, and I try to put it in perspective for the guy who doesn't have all the background that I've picked up.

"Luckily for me, the editors never suggest anything to me. They know the quickest way to turn me off is to say, 'Why don't you think about this?' or 'Why don't you try that?' They might have the right idea, but they know it's better to let me grope or just go my own way. For some reason I just turn off to suggestions from others.

"The ideas come along like cars on a freight train, traveling along peaks and valleys. Some days you can see a whole series of them, other days you have to search hard to see anything.

"Someone once asked me what I'm trying to achieve. Buckminster Fuller has pointed out that our own time fails to provide us with an instruction booklet. But I have faith that society *can* change. I believe society *will* learn *how* to act upon the fact that man's humanity, his dignity, must be preserved at all costs.

"There is a quote from Woodrow Wilson which I believe should be tacked to every cartoonist's drawing board, pasted to every reporter's typewriter, and hung on every editor's wall, and might be read daily by mayors and TV commentators and chiefs of police and presidents and vice presidents:

" 'What happens to the least of men everywhere, happens to all men everywhere.' "

Conrad's busy conscience brings waves of angry mail, day after day, much of it directed to the attention of Otis Chandler. Although Chandler routinely refers such protests to staff deputies, he makes a special effort to acknowledge personally complaints from friends. "An editorial cartoonist makes his point with a single graphic statement," Chandler wrote to one angry acquaintance. "The limitations of his medium do not permit the kind of balancing that the written word permits—he cannot, for example, depict a man doing something reprehensible and at the same time indicate that the man has redeeming qualities, or even that his record as a whole is good. It's an inflexible art.

"That creates no problems if the cartoonist concerns himself with minor matters or if he seeks chiefly to depict the happier aspects of life. But Conrad is a social critic, commenting chiefly on the turmoil of these times and those who play a decisive role in it. His cartoons, admittedly, are often angry, often bitter, almost always derisive. Being harsh in nature, they stimulate harsh reactions, approval or disapproval. No one, not even his admirers, has ever written me to say, 'he's such a sweet guy.' "

Conrad's cartoons also add to the workload of the *Times'* legal staff; more than once, harsh reactions have taken the form of libel suits. "I'm lucky," Conrad says. "I work for a newspaper that can afford to defend the stuff I do. I wonder just how many stories never get written and how many cartoons never get printed because publishers are afraid of lawsuits. It takes a lot of money to put up a defense, and they can harass you to death in the courts."

16

THE formidable task of defending Paul Conrad and other *Times* staffers falls to chief counsel Robert Lobdell. A courtly, soft-spoken, Stanford-trained lawyer, he gives the impression of suffering in silence, especially on any occasion when a reader with a bizarre turn of mind takes offense at an item published in the paper and rushes into court with a nuisance demand for damages.

Assisted by a team of crack deputies including witty, resourceful William Niese, Lobdell confronts legal problems day after day. Some items:

When Bantam Books hosted a cocktail party at the Beverly Hills Hotel in honor of famed writer of westerns Louis L'Amour, *Times* reporter Dave Smith devoted a good portion of his piece to the antics of a character on the scene known colloquially as Freddy the Freeloader. Smith described him as "a professional party crasher," and went on, "His short-portly gray suit looks a little slept in and the pants have about three parties to go before the waistband fails completely, but within those pants reposes a truly happy man. He works his way down the canapé table like a Dempster Dumpster. . . ."

Freddy the Freeloader claimed he had been libeled and asked for damages. But the suit collapsed like a party balloon when Freddy was required to answer detailed questions as to his life-style.

When President Gerald Ford visited San Francisco on a speaking engagement in 1975, a spectator named Sarah Jane Moore drew a revolver and fired shots at him. The gun was deflected and the shots sent astray by the quick reaction of a husky ex-Marine, Oliver Sipple.

Reporters for the *Times* and other publications promptly went about gathering information on the ex-Marine and his heroic action. Sipple proved to be a well-known activist on behalf of gay rights; and some of this already-public material crept into stories on the ex-Marine who had now saved a President's life.

Sipple, however, filed a lawsuit claiming his privacy had been invaded. Attorneys for the *Times* countered that he had catapulted himself into widespread attention by his heroic action; there was a bona fide public interest in his personality and background. Further, his gay-rights activities were widely known prior to his public act of heroism. A trial court ruled against Sipple.

The Sipple case underlined—not only for *Times* lawyers Lobdell and Niese, but for their peers at other publications, and for journalists across the nation—a task of extraordinary delicacy: the continuing challenge of trying to balance freedom of the press with the rights of the individual. That balancing act, often central to the controversy over lawsuits for libel and invasion of privacy, was once described by former U.S. Supreme Court Justice Abe Fortas in this way:

"The courts may not and must not permit either public or private action that censors or inhibits the press. But part of this responsibility is to preserve the values and procedures which assure the ordinary citizen that the press is not above the reach of the law—that is, special prerogatives, granted because of its special and vital functions, are reasonably equated with its needs in the performance of these functions.

"For this court totally to immunize the press—whether forthrightly or by subtle indirection—in areas far beyond the needs of news, comment on public persons and events, discussion of public issues and the like would be no service to freedom of the press, but an invitation to public hostility to that freedom."

Another equally delicate balancing act confronts the courts on most libel and invasion of privacy cases—that of truth vs. falsehood. This is what U.S. Supreme Court Justice Byron White once said about that balancing act:

"Neither lies nor false communications serve the ends of the First Amendment, and no one suggests their desirability or further proliferation.

"But to insure the ascertainment and publication of the truth about public affairs, it is essential that the First Amendment protect some erroneous publications as well as true ones."

In court decisions dealing with a person's right to privacy, and the public's right to know, the only constant element is change. *Times* attorney Lobdell recently told an interviewer: "The courts hold, at one end, that each of us has a zone of privacy, a right to be left alone, an area of living that need not be scrutinized by others. But the courts have not drawn a clear line as to what's private and what's public. Every court decision may be applied *ad hoc* to the facts of each case, and the decision may well hinge on other questions. To what extent is the person who claims privacy already in the public eye? To what extent has the person asked to be public through an effort to become a celebrity, a famous performer, a public official, a public spokesman, a participant in public causes? Has the person who claims privacy attempted to mold or cater to public opinion, or to win public approval?"

Libel suits spilled into many areas, with ripple effects on the *Times* and other publications. When television entertainer Carol Burnett sued the gossip tabloid *National Enquirer,* seeking damages of $1.5 million, and subsequently a Superior Court jury in Los Angeles awarded Burnett a $1.6 million judgment, many libel lawyers gasped in horror.

Burnett's suit arose from a 1976 article dealing with an encounter between the actress and Henry Kissinger in a Washington restaurant. According to the article, a "boisterous" Miss Burnett engaged in a "loud argument" with the former Secretary of State and then "traipsed around the place offering everyone a bite of her dessert."

In her suit Burnett charged that the *National Enquirer* article implied she was drunk and had behaved in an "undignified manner." She denied that she was "boisterous," had argued with Kissinger or had offered everyone bites of her dessert.

A major issue in the trial was whether the *National Enquirer* had shown "reckless disregard" for the facts in printing the Burnett item.

To many publishers and editors and their legal staffs the significance of the Burnett award loomed large. It seemed clear that libel suits had become costlier and harder to defend against. The alarm was genuine; the trend in court decisions made it easier for plaintiffs to pursue libel causes. Libel charges that were once promptly dismissed were now being granted jury hearings. The difference between prompt dismissal and lengthy trials added up to huge defense costs and occasionally resulted in spectacular judgments.

The alarm fed also on the belief that a large monetary award could serve as an invitation to popular and well-known people to "punish" publications like the *National Enquirer* for their general content or coverage of the plaintiffs rather than for specific falsehoods. Legal experts were also troubled by the large amount of damages, troubled because Burnett's lawyers proved no medical expenses, loss of reputation or loss of occupational income. Had she won $10,000 in general damages alone, libel lawyers said afterward, there would have been no impact on other media. But an award of $1.6 million "became a clear signal," as one said, "that you can make a lot of money if you can get to a jury, even if you haven't suffered damages." Subsequently trimmed to $800,000, and much later—after months of expensive negotiations—reduced to $150,000, the sum was still deemed "unwarranted and excessive" by most libel lawyers.

"All this has a chilling effect," said *Times* general counsel Robert Lobdell, "which means an increasing danger of self-censorship on the part of the press, a reluctance to deal with or even a deliberate avoidance of stories where there is a risk of prolonged litigation. The result: the public interest is not served."

Even more alarming to Lobdell and other media lawyers has been a pronounced trend toward closing the courts to press coverage, especially in cases involving criminal defendants. The Sixth Amendment guarantees the right of an accused to a trial by an "impartial jury." Press coverage has been attacked for allegedly undermining the impartiality of present and prospective jurors.

The problem became acute in 1966 when the U.S. Supreme Court decided that the conviction of wife murderer Sam Sheppard should be reversed because the trial judge, among other things, failed to protect against the harmful effects of highly prejudicial press behavior. Subsequently, trial judges grew increasingly alert to the effects of potentially prejudicial publicity and employed several methods to curb its effects.

Some courts applied "gag" orders directly on the press, ordering reporters not to print information already obtained in open court or elsewhere. But gag orders proved unwieldy and largely unworkable. Gradually the courts turned toward closing off some of the most volatile sources of potentially prejudicial information: the pretrial hearing, and occasionally other parts of the judicial process including the trial itself.

Although Bob Lobdell and numerous other media lawyers argued that courtroom closures violate both the "public trial" guarantee of the Sixth Amendment and First Amendment guarantee of freedom of the press, the U.S. Supreme Court gave its blessing to courtroom closure. In one landmark decision, *Gannett* v. *DePasquale,* the high court ruled in 1979 that the Sixth Amendment guarantee was solely for the benefit of the accused and could not be raised by the press or the public; and it also ruled that if the First Amendment required an openness at all, its requirements were overcome wherever there was a "reasonable likelihood" of prejudice to the defendant.

"It was a terrible decision," said Bob Lobdell. The following year the high court rendered another judgment (*Richmond Newspapers* v. *Virginia*), not directly overruling the Gannett decision but to some extent limiting the broad sweep of closing off trials to the press. "The fact remains," said Lobdell, "we continue to get pretrial closures. Time after time, a judge somewhere decides to bar the press from a pretrial hearing. It is bad judicial policy and bad public policy. It ignores our own history, which holds that our courts should be open.

"Much of the work of the criminal justice system takes place in pretrial hearings: plea bargaining, confessions, the indication of whether evidence was lawfully obtained and can be used in the main trial, the questioning of jurors and other motions heard in advance of the trial.

"All too often we find that a judge may simply have a

predilection for a closed courtroom or a feeling that the Sixth Amendment rights of the defendant are better served by keeping the public and press out of the hearing."

In one case Otis Chandler himself was the protagonist. He made a decision to ban from the pages of the *Times* all advertising for pornographic films. "It was not something sudden or impulsive," said Chandler. "Over a period of years I'd received protests about porno films. People demanded to know by what right a family newspaper carried ads for porno films.

"Some were movies from major studios with major stars. The advertising was not offensive but the film itself was. Others were strictly X-rated films, very explicit stuff. I tried to excuse it away, pointing out that national magazines carried much more daring or offensive material than could be found in the *Los Angeles Times,* but the protests didn't stop. People said the national magazines were simply not the *Los Angeles Times,* which happens to be *inside* the home every morning and is seen by children.

"I kept hoping the issue would go away, but it lingered on. Parents kept objecting. Pornography began exploding all over the landscape. Films and even television got more and more explicit. Finally I asked our advertising department to review the situation and let me know what it would cost to simply ban all porno advertising. The figure that came back to me was several million dollars a year. I said, 'Okay, let's get rid of it.'

"I told the staff, 'Yes, porno activity exists in our society. We will cover it from a news standpoint. But I don't like the idea of making money by advertising the stuff. We are big enough and strong enough to survive without the $3 million. We are a home-delivered newspaper, a family newspaper, we have a certain set of standards.'

"What happened was, we were sued by the theater owners. They even looked into the question of whether we conspired with major movie studios to put the porno houses out of business. But we won everything hands down, including the right to reject advertising. And we also won an extraordinary amount of goodwill. For years afterward I heard from people, by mail and in person, who assured me that one of the best things I ever did was to take out those damn porno ads."

The publisher's office, Chandler knew, served as a constant magnet for mind-boggling problems and time-consuming conflicts. But he also knew that he must not lose sight of priorities; he must keep in mind always the ongoing goal of pushing the *Times* forward.

Part Six

WORKING AT THE *TIMES*

17

O N a typical day Otis Chandler arrives at Times Mirror
Square before nine o'clock in the morning. (His transportation to the office, however, is *never* typical. He rotates
vehicles often, one day driving a Honda motorcycle, another
day a Rolls-Royce Silver Cloud, a third day a Porsche Turbo,
another day a Toyota truck.) By the time he arrives at his
large, airy, glass-walled office, his mind is filled with thoughts
of the *Times:* not only recurring anxieties about the safety
of *Times*men around the world, but all the challenges of managing the affairs of an international newspaper.

He pushes himself hard on every front. He delegates many
tasks with ease and skill—he has a knack of inspiring his deputies to push hard—but not everything is susceptible to delegation. He is in motion constantly as the boss of a company,
Times Mirror, with revenues close to $3 billion annually.
He is also confronted directly week after week with crucial
decisions on, for example, opportunities to buy other newspapers and major properties.

He makes lists of everything he plans to do, day by day,
both in hobbies and business. He arrives at the office every
morning with lists of the tasks to be done—letters or memos
to be written, people to see or call.

Entering his walnut-paneled office on a typical day, he settles into a polished chrome-and-leather chair, designed by Mies van der Rohe, and pulls it closer to a Stow Davis walnut desk where a stack of messages await his attention. Some are from personalities in the news, ranging from Presidential candidates to high-level businessmen to civic leaders, expressing a wish to confer with him. There are speaking invitations from universities and press clubs and chambers of commerce. There are personal messages: calls from his five children wanting to talk with their dad; a call from one friend to plan a big-game hunting trip; a call from another to plan a motorbike journey into the desert; invitations from other friends to lunch or dinner.

The volume and variety of messages are part of the regular daily routine. Possessing wealth, power and a cluster of colorful pursuits outside the arena of publishing, Chandler has long been a celebrity's celebrity, a bona fide newsmaker. Each new achievement—a fast race, a triumphant hunting expedition, a rare car added to his collection, a major newspaper or television acquisition, another journalism prize won by the *Los Angeles Times*—amounts to a newspeg, a reason to interview Chandler; and requests flood in from newspapers, magazines, radio and TV seeking to learn more.

The object of attention wherever he goes, he finds many social situations oppressive. Privacy eludes him because he is readily recognized, "even in surprising places. I've been on my surfboard out on the ocean when suddenly a stranger will paddle over and say: 'Hey, Otis'—all surfers are on a first-name basis—'why doesn't the *Times* give more coverage to surfing?' "

He does not, however, allow the loss of privacy to interfere with his outside activities. He regards his athletic pursuits and hobbies as necessary balance, for like many another top executive who finds himself caught up all too often in a web of business affairs that reach through evenings and weekends, Chandler knows how debilitating it can be to become over-worked, exhausted, irritable and snappish. He perceives, quite sensibly, that a person's efficiency and creativity climb impres-sively with regular periods of relaxation. He encourages his staff to take time away from work, and he himself continues to seek a change of pace in numerous ways, understanding that outside interests would bring a sense of renewal and refreshment.

To his closest acquaintances he is known not as Otis but as "Oats" because he gives more than routine attention to nutrition, health and body-building exercises. He works out regularly in a well-appointed gymnasium located at a sub-terranean level of the *Times,* pumping iron (he routinely presses 250 pounds) and performing other heavy weight-lifting exercises.

His multiple and diverse activities require a careful allo-cation of time—more careful than a casual observer might guess, for he has on his agenda a full involvement with his immediate family. Divorced in 1981 from his energetic, out-going wife Missy, he married Bettina Whitaker, a slender beauty from Pasadena who prior to marriage had been a mar-keting and sales executive. He maintains close rapport with his five children—Carolyn and Cathleen, both students; Mi-chael, a professional race car driver; Harry, a television pro-grammer who works for Times Mirror's TV cable division; and Norman, who has been a management trainee and is now a production supervisor at the *Times.* He talks with them regularly by telephone and sees them often, as well as his four grandchildren, of whom the oldest is Otis Yeager Chandler, age six. He also keeps in immediate touch with Buff, his widowed mother (his father, Norman, died in

1973 at the age of 74); and with his sister Camilla and her husband F. Daniel Frost, managing partner of Gibson Dunn & Crutcher, the largest law firm in the West.

The close family connection reveals occasional surprises in the usually gentle nature of Otis Chandler. Inclined to be a self-critical perfectionist, he deems it natural enough to apply the same rigid standards to members of his family, and at times they are jolted by his great expectations. Says Chandler: "Very often at the end of a day I'll analyze what I've done and, in effect, I'll be very rough in my judgment. I can be objective about myself. But when I turn objective toward others, they find it hard to deal with. For example, my kids have always known I loved them, but they've also known I could be tough and demanding in terms of accomplishments. They had to go out and find jobs, clerk in drugstores, find housepainting chores, do something to earn money. There were some protests, but I just wasn't about to have any spoiled rich kids in the family."

Norman, the eldest, is tall, handsome and possessed of a candor that makes instant friendships wherever he goes. He told an interviewer that he had once allowed himself to imagine that the dynastic torch might someday be passed *automatically* from father to son in one grand sweeping gesture.

But Otis made it clear to the youth: There was no chance the publisher's job would be handed over to him arbitrarily. For the *Times* was no longer the exclusive private preserve of a family. Times Mirror had become a publicly traded giant in the hotly competitive media world, and there was at least one fundamental prerequisite to its survival: the company's board of directors must determine every key appointment strictly on the basis of merit, without regard to family name.

Norman understood clearly. "Nothing is guaranteed to me," he remarked to an interviewer as he made his way from one assignment to another in the training program. He found special challenges built into it. "Every time I go into a new department, I'm under the gun because I'm the boss's son. There's a certain amount of tension in the air. I make an effort to diffuse it, going out to lunch with my colleagues, joking with them, getting to know their interests so I can rap with them. At the same time I have to do a first-class job. Then, just about when I've learned to do the job, learned everybody's name and made friends, just about the stage where much of the pressure has been diffused, it's time to move into another department and start all over again—advertising, circulation, pressroom and so forth. There is one great part of it, however, that outweighs all the negatives of pressure: everybody seems to like me, everybody seems to want me to succeed."

18

WHEN Norman's management-training odyssey began, in 1980, the moment arrived for Otis Chandler to change roles. He was ready, after a twenty-year hitch as publisher, to become chairman of the board and editor-in-chief of all Times Mirror activities, a move that freed him to spend more time on the new technology of the communications world. At the same time his predecessor in the role of board chairman, Franklin Murphy, would become chairman of the executive committee.

Chandler applied to himself the same rule he had put into place for others many years earlier: every executive must groom two assistants as possible successors. Thus he was surrounded by men of uncommon ability and talent in the parent Times Mirror—board chairman Franklin Murphy, corporation president Robert Erburu, vice-presidents Dow Carpenter, Charles Redmond, Phillip Williams, Peter Fernald, Charles Schneider, John Flick—and all had special qualities essential to leadership of the company.

On the *Times* itself he developed an additional reservoir of topflight executives: general manager Robert Nelson, editor William Thomas, advertising director Vance Stickell, controller Don Maxwell, general counsel Robert Lobdell, personnel chief Robert Flannes, and many others.

Ever the long-range planner, Chandler—in his late forties—began casting seriously for a successor, endeavoring to narrow the field of many possible candidates down to a single choice.

"I didn't want to continue as publisher until death or retirement," he told an interviewer recently. "I could see myself getting burned out in the publisher's job. It was time to look ahead to moving into a different corporate chair. It was time to choose the person who could do the best possible job as publisher."

The action centered on W. (for Wyatt) Thomas Johnson, a hard-driving, plain-talking executive in his mid-thirties. Chandler's first impression was that the man might have a freak memory, a trick vault of the mind, a midnight valise for all the cerebral potpourri that fades silently away from most men.

That first impression was gained in 1973 at a large reception in Texas, when Times Mirror bought television station KTBC-TV from a company owned by former President Lyndon Johnson. At the reception, Otis Chandler was introduced to the business leaders of Austin, including KTBC's advertisers.

Chandler later recalled: "President Johnson wasn't feeling well, but Lady Bird and I stood in a receiving line for about two hours. In back of us was Tom Johnson. He was executive vice-president of LBJ's various businesses, although I'd never heard of him, and at first I didn't pay much attention. But then I noticed something special. As each couple approached us in the receiving line, he whispered to Lady Bird: 'This is Mr. and Mrs. So-and-So, Betty and Bill. They spent $45,000 with the station last year.' Or 'This is Mr. and Mrs. So-and-So, Eunice and George. They have cut down their budget at the station.' He went on this way, identifying more than a thousand people and their various relationships to KTBC, enabling Lady Bird to greet each person by first name.

"It was a remarkable performance, remembering all those names, and all the amounts spent at KTBC. Another time Tom took me over to the offices of KTBC and introduced me to every person, from janitors and clerks up to senior management, scores of people, all with first names. It was just astounding. I began asking questions about him."

What Chandler gradually discovered was a man of extraordinary intelligence and decisiveness, with impressive connections in Washington and other power centers around the world. What Johnson possessed, beyond uncommon gifts of the mind, was a powerful need to succeed.

He had grown up in Macon, Georgia, where his father sold watermelons and firewood from the back of a pickup truck. The father suffered ill health; Tom's mother was often the family's breadwinner.

Tom told an interviewer recently: "She clerked six days a week in a small grocery store. She instilled in me at a very early age the belief that I could do anything I wanted with my life. Even so, at this same tender age, I felt sort of socially unacceptable because my parents were not among the more affluent people in town.

"At the same time, watching my mother struggle, I felt a responsibility to help earn money. My ninth-grade English teacher told me the Macon newspapers were looking for a stringer to report high school sports scores, and the pay was three dollars a game, which sounded like a tremendous amount of money. I was fourteen, and the job became important for much more than money. Seeing my by-line on those little stories gradually gave me a sense of identification, and I suddenly realized I loved the newspaper business."

Quick and serious, energetic and thorough—qualities that would help to carry him a long way—Tom apprenticed himself to a tough and demanding sports editor who helped the boy develop as a reporter and writer. It was precisely the kind of encouragement Tom needed. His exceptional enthusiasm caught the attention of Peyton Anderson, the owner and publisher of the *Macon Telegraph and News,* and when Tom finished high school, the publisher gave him a scholarship to study journalism at the University of Georgia, plus a full-time reporting job to provide extra money.

Tom soon developed an ambition to pattern himself after the publisher. Perceiving this, and reasoning that a publisher should be fluent in numbers as well as words, Peyton Anderson urged him to seek a master's degree in business administration and backed up the advice by financing Tom's way through Harvard Business School.

Harvard seemed a foreign land to a hungry, ambitious youngster from the backwoods of Georgia. Tom pressed hard to do well not only at studies but at winning friends. With an MBA in hand, he won a year's fellowship as an intern in the White House; he was chosen from among three thousand applicants to be an assistant to Presidential press secretary Bill Moyers.

Moyers later recalled: "When I first saw Tom he was lean as a hungry rabbit. Fortunately he had something more: staying power, subtlety in its best sense, and a passionate ability to couple hard work with good judgment. As I came to know him, I felt much like a coach who discovers a rookie who is a real triple threat."

At the end of the year's fellowship, President Lyndon Johnson wrote to Macon publisher Peyton Anderson: "Tom feels a strong moral commitment to return to Macon because of everything you have done for him. His conscience won't let him just walk away from that commitment. I also believe that he has a great opportunity here to make a significant contribution. I have told Tom that I would like for him to

stay on if he could do so without breaching your confidence
and faith in him. If you feel you can spare Tom Johnson, his
country and his President need him." Anderson bowed to the
President's request.

Tom stayed on at the White House for three years, becoming special assistant, occasional whipping boy and Presidential
confidant. When LBJ returned to Texas in 1968, he persuaded Tom to accompany him to assist with a number of
projects, including work on the Presidential memoirs and on
plans for the Presidential library. Two years later Tom was
named executive vice-president of LBJ's various businesses,
including television station KTBC in Austin, radio stations,
photo-processing plants, and cable TV, as well as ranching,
banking and other companies.

After careful observation and inquiry, Chandler hired Tom
Johnson in 1973 as editor of the *Dallas Times Herald,* a property Times Mirror had only recently acquired, and gave him
a mandate to inject fresh life into the paper. Johnson set in
motion a series of major changes designed to transform the
afternoon *Times Herald*—a lackluster second choice among
Dallas readers—into a hard competitor and spirited alternative to the *Morning News.*

Within eighteen months he was named publisher. He recruited a new editor and together they hired a lively staff and
added considerable emphasis to consumer reporting. The
paper also launched extensive coverage of the arts and stepped
up its political coverage. Morale, circulation and profits
climbed. "I could see," Otis Chandler remarked recently,
"we had a talent that we could use almost anywhere in the
company."

The best place to use him, Chandler decided, was in the
top managerial position of the *Los Angeles Times:* to appoint
him the paper's president, with the possibility of becoming

publisher. It was a shrewd move that offered a solution to the quest for a successor.

Tom Johnson moved into the presidency of the *Times* with winning determination. He smiled easily but he was intensely serious. He spoke calmly but there were outbursts of passionate emphasis: he made dramatic use of his hands, illustrating points with long, lean fingers, now jabbing and slicing the air, now clasping the tips and pumping up and down as if engaged in vigorous prayer.

In March 1980, when Tom Johnson was named publisher, Otis Chandler set forth the immediate challenges at a ceremonial dinner. With a light touch he outlined the paradoxical nature of the task:

"Tom, since I am leaving you with a business that is financially at its all-time peak of success, that has the loyalty of all its employees, the appreciation of its owners—the shareholders —the goodwill of its customers and the admiration of its competitors, the position you are inheriting should be a rather pleasant one, rather easy, just coast along, no pressures at all. You have plenty of leisure time to enjoy long vacations with your family.

"But before you start planning a long vacation, there is some unfinished business—a few goals for the future. Among them: Always continue to improve the product, and profits, at the same time. . . . Continue to review the general editorial direction of the paper in light of the social changes in this decade and the decades ahead. . . . Though perfection is impossible, always push toward it. . . . Encourage your editors. Give them the resources, but do not ever hesitate to question them on stories or changes in the paper. . . .

"A publisher must guard against inside and outside forces that try to subvert him. He must not give in to the demands of advertisers, or even, heaven forbid, our own advertising sales staff who occasionally make requests which could adversely affect the integrity of the paper. I mean, like putting the opening of a new department store on the front page of the paper."

Otis Chandler paused to let the laughter ring out loud and clear. Then he turned serious:

"My mandate to you, Tom Johnson, is to accept your new position not only as a sacred trust, but also as a unique opportunity to serve this enterprise, this community and our nation by publishing the *finest* newspaper you possibly can."

19

PUSH, drive and determination are evident all across the *Times*. During his twenty-year hitch as publisher, Otis Chandler had put into place a topflight newsgathering organization, and the results of its work are visible in the paper day after day.

Not always apparent to readers, but known intimately to Chandler and to his successor, Tom Johnson, is the extraordinary amount of behind-the-scenes energy and intelligence that goes into the task of reporting important stories to the readers. In November 1979, for example, only a few months before Chandler passed the publisher's torch to Johnson, both men knew that Washington bureau chief Jack Nelson, among others, was scrambling desperately in Washington, seeking to make sense of a chaotic diplomatic situation thousands of miles away in Tehran, where the United States embassy had been seized.

They knew that Nelson and key members of his Washington staff were seeking to get an idea of what, if any, retaliatory action the United States government might be planning. There was no question about Nelson's expertise. Slight of build, with a rosy complexion, heavy-lidded blue-green eyes, a reassuringly soft Southern accent, and a mind like a steel trap, he had been named to the coveted post of Washington bureau chief not only as a result of his craftsmanlike reportage for the *Times,* including his work on the Watergate break-in, but because he was, in effect, a well-connected insider in a company town.

Shortly after the embassy seizure in Tehran, Nelson went to the grand ballroom of the Mayflower Hotel in Washington, to attend a luncheon where a number of members of Congress were scheduled to be among the guests. It was a more or less routine affair, an event which ordinarily would not command a place high on his list of priorities. But the circumstances were no longer ordinary; the startling news from abroad had suddenly turned the luncheon into an occasion of journalistic opportunity. It was a place where he could connect in rapid succession with a handful of key lawmakers, marching them off one by one to a quiet spot in a corner of the ballroom or out to a corridor, quizzing each one on weekend briefings conducted by the President's staff aides for certain members of Congress.

Not that Nelson lacked sources at the White House. He had been around Washington a long time, with excellent sources inside the Oval Office and on Capitol Hill. His head swam with history and he knew the lunacy of politics. But the Iranian experience that weekend was something else, as if politics once and for all had become unhinged. There was no discernible sequence or thread, so far as he knew, only the chaotic thrust of a mob lunging at the gates of the American embassy in Tehran.

When he first heard of the attack, Nelson began calling the White House, where his sources included President Jimmy Carter. He knew the President well, a relationship dating back to an era when Nelson, then based in Atlanta, had covered the Georgia state legislature, among whose members was an ambitious, grinning, upwardly mobile Jimmy Carter.

But Nelson's efforts were thwarted. His usually accessible contacts in the White House had refused to take his calls; a curtain of silence had descended. He speculated on activity behind the scenes: the President was undoubtedly monitoring the Tehran crisis on a minute-to-minute basis. The President's rapport with Capitol Hill was not a hallmark in effective liaison, but it was a good bet that he had begun to share some information. It was always thus in a time of crisis: a handful of lawmakers had to be kept informed.

Now at the Congressional luncheon in the Mayflower Hotel, Nelson intended to learn just what substantive information the President and his staff had shared with lawmakers. Nelson glanced around the red-carpeted ballroom. His gaze fastened on an influential senator. Nelson knew him well, and after a careful greeting he led the senator out to a corridor. They swapped stories for a few minutes, laughing together, and gradually Nelson zeroed in for specific information on the bizarre turn of events in Tehran. The senator obliged. He did not know how much the White House was holding back, but he was willing to pass along some of the fragments he had picked up.

To Jack Nelson it was a familiar kind of challenge, sparking an electrical charge of excitement: the beginning of a major story. He had come a long way from the tiny town of Talladega, Alabama, where during the Depression his father had operated a fruit store.

When the Nelson family moved to Biloxi, Mississippi, Jack answered an ad for a general assignment reporter at the *Biloxi Daily Herald*. As a street-wise eighteen-year-old who could talk credibly, he had no problem persuading the publisher to take a chance on him. Almost at once Jack began writing stories about gambling payoffs and slot-machine concessions, and he soon grew accustomed to death threats from local hoodlums.

Several years later he landed a job on the *Atlanta Constitution*, where his sleuthing and investigative reporting turned up widespread corruption in Georgia, including plenty of governmental protection for gambling, prostitution, voting frauds, lottery rings. One time he tracked down a piece of massive road-working machinery that the Georgia Bureau of Investigation claimed it could not find. The *Atlanta Constitution* promptly published a map showing where the machinery could be found.

Another time Nelson picked up a tip about a major scandal at Milledgeville Central State Hospital. He was rebuffed at first; the doctors would not talk. But Nelson refused to quit, and by sheer persistence documented a portrait in horror. Afterward he wrote a series of articles charging the hospital administration with using experimental drugs on mental patients without the knowledge or permission of relatives. The hospital also had on its staff doctors who used alcohol and drugs while on duty, and nurses were allowed to perform major surgery when doctors were absent. As a result of his stories the hospital underwent a major shakeup, and Nelson won a Pulitzer Prize.

Hired by the *Los Angeles Times* in 1965, he opened a news bureau in Atlanta and ranged across the South, covering politics and the ongoing civil-rights struggle. His reporting grew sharper year after year. Transferred to the Washington bureau of the *Times* in 1970, he demonstrated outstanding ability, and in 1974 he was promoted to head up the office of twenty-seven reporters and desk editors.

A bureau chief sets the tone of news coverage for his staff. He hires and fires and handles a maze of administrative details. He walks a thin line between the role of ambassador for his newspaper (particularly if, as in the case of the *Los Angeles Times,* it is rarely seen by news sources in Washington) and the hard ongoing responsibility of reporting the news.

Nelson's newsgathering competitors gave him high marks at his complex job. *Time* magazine in 1980 characterized his bureau as "one of the two or three best" in Washington.

Among the numerous and diverse tasks confronting a bureau chief, there was no doubt about Nelson's top priority: he perceived himself first and last as a reporter.

Now, within hours of the seizure of the U.S. embassy in Tehran, as the Iranian riots gathered momentum, Jack Nelson patrolled the aisles of the Congressional luncheon in Washington. He had a long way to go before a story could be pulled together. Not until much later would he learn details about the Administration's top-secret planning to mount a rescue mission. Right now he was taking only small steps. As he began, he wondered how—amid what obstacles—the reporting adventure proceeded in Tehran itself.

20

DON Schanche carried his luggage, including portable type-writer, into the lobby of Tehran's Intercontinental Hotel. It had been a long hot flight, overcrowded and noisy, and he needed sleep.

He slept fitfully, however, knowing there were serious problems ahead. This time he expected the worst. He remembered how unsuspectingly he had arrived on his first assignment to Tehran one year earlier, how peaceful and undisturbed the city had seemed as he strolled toward the campus of Tehran University. There was no hint of trouble, no wild dream of seizure of the U.S. embassy, as he approached the campus. His purpose in visiting the university was "to get the feel of the place before making the usual round of embassies, government offices and political contacts."

That was Schanche's style. He had been a military affairs specialist for *Life* magazine and later managing editor of *The Saturday Evening Post* before signing on as a foreign correspondent for the *Los Angeles Times*. He knew his way around the Middle East, and, in turn, he was known and respected by the diplomatic community.

Cerebral and energetic, Schanche had a reputation for wit and resourcefulness. He was recognized as a reporter who did his homework, preparing himself conscientiously for each assignment. He had known before his arrival, on that first assignment to Tehran one year earlier, that there was unrest in the Iranian mood; he knew that students at the university, located less than a mile from the hotel, were winding up a week of nonviolent demonstration honoring "national solidarity."

As he approached the campus on that year-earlier visit, two young men flanked him and simultaneously delivered sharply driven fists to his shoulders. Then the young men laughed and one said: "Get out of here. It is very dangerous for foreigners."

Schanche retreated a short distance. "But abruptly I cursed my own timidity, reversed course and walked purposefully toward the university's main gate. Suddenly, however, a crowd of panicked students and onlookers surged out, racing to escape the pop-pop-pop of automatic-weapons fire. I glanced around and discovered black smoke billowing from a flaming Pepsi-Cola truck. [Pepsi became a favorite target of the Islamic revolutionaries because the owner of the bottling company in Iran was a Bahai, a religious sect considered heretical by Shia Muslims.] Within minutes the panicked crowd was pounding up Los Angeles boulevard, a broad thoroughfare that stretches between the university and the Intercontinental Hotel, leaving behind the Shah's angered troops and some fifty victims (ten dead, forty wounded)."

Half an hour later, as Schanche sat in the hotel coffee shop making notes on the unexpected violence, rioters gathered outside. They set two fire trucks aflame and barricaded the road with a municipal bus, to which they also put the torch. They shattered the ground-floor picture windows of the hotel with bricks. Moments later they stormed into the coffee shop, hurling tables, chairs and heavy glass ashtrays through the elegant shop windows of the adjacent hotel arcade.

Schanche recalled: "I made a hasty retreat to my fourth-floor room, covering the remainder of the riot from my window overlooking the street. Hotel employees turned high-pressure fire hoses on the demonstrators and washed them out. Curiously, the Shah's troops, after firing into the crowds at the university, did not intervene until the riot had spent itself in broken glass and bonfires."

Violence in the streets became a daily occurrence for the next three months, and for the forty U.S. correspondents who regularly covered the revolution it was a frustrating and dangerous story to report. *Los Angeles Times* correspondent Joe Alex Morris, Jr., standing at a second-floor office window to observe the fighting in the streets, was shot to death in February 1979.

Schanche recalled: "Trusted by neither the rioters nor the army, there was no safe place for us to be, whether inside our hotel or out on the streets. We were often sandwiched between their lines, running from gunfire on the one side and dodging trucks and rubber-tire bonfires on the other. Yet as the violence escalated it was essential to keep eyeballing it and literally attempt to count the victims, because the rioters grossly exaggerated the numbers of dead and wounded, and the government and military routinely denied there had been any clashes at all."

At least a dozen correspondents were injured, some by gunfire. Two *Newsweek* reporters, Loren Jenkins and Barry Came, endured a two-hour beating at the hands of the Shah's police. Don Schanche suffered a painful but lucky break. He had been standing between rioters and army troops on the main thoroughfare in front of Tehran university, watching as students hurled stones and paving bricks.

An officer fired his pistol into the air, and suddenly his troops knelt and leveled their German G-3 automatic rifles at the mob. Expecting them to raise their guns and fire only warning shots, Schanche moved toward the demonstrators, prepared to walk away from the scene with them. But the troops kept their guns aimed at knee and waist level and, from a distance of twenty-five yards, opened fire.

Schanche ran toward a nearby corner to escape the line of fire. "My right foot slipped into a sidewalk pothole and simultaneously I was pushed from behind by another panicked runner and sent sprawling. It was a providential spill, because as I scrambled to my feet I saw several Iranians crumbled beside me, apparently hit by bullets from a fusillade. Around the corner I tried to duck into the door of an idle ambulance to escape the green, slippery antiriot foam spray of a giant water cannon that had rounded the bend with me. As I reached into the open door a fellow correspondent, Mike Burns of the *Baltimore Sun,* who had already arrived at the sanctuary, slammed it, crushing four fingers of my right hand. It was several hours and three bloody street demonstrations later that I began to suspect that my right foot, which I thought might have been sprained, was broken. An Iranian, who identified himself as the Shah's personal physician, set the break and applied a cast that evening."

Four days later *Los Angeles Times* correspondent William Tuohy noticed that Schanche's toes, where they protruded from the cast, had turned a suspicious blue-black in color. Tuohy led Schanche promptly to Maherabad Airport (newly reopened for the triumphant return to Tehran of the Ayatollah Ruhollah Khomeini) and put him on a Pan American flight to Germany. Schanche went immediately to an American orthopedist at the U.S. Army hospital in Heidelberg.

"The cast is as tight as a rubber glove and there's no circulation in your foot," the doctor said. "If you had worn it another day or two, I would be taking off the foot, not just the cast."

"But the Shah's personal orthopedist put it on."

The doctor nodded. "Ever notice the Shah limps?"

When Schanche's injuries were healed he returned to Tehran, an assignment he shared alternately with *Times* correspondents William Tuohy, Doyle McManus and Kenneth Freed. It had become a love-hate experience. "It's a deeply fascinating country, but it turned into such a thoroughly disagreeable place during and after the uprising against the Shah that most of us secretly welcomed the decision of the revolutionary authorities to kick the Western press out in mid-1979."

But the doors to Iran abruptly opened again in November 1979, when Iranian mobs seized the U.S. embassy and took hostages. Schanche's previously unusable long-term multiple-reentry visa, issued almost a year before by "the Imperial Embassy of Iran," was suddenly deemed acceptable by revolutionary immigration officials.

Now he had flown into Tehran once more. Tossing fitfully in his sleep, trying to anticipate the depth of problems ahead, he geared himself to expect the worst. For several days, however, he found little hostility directed by Iranians against American reporters. But late one night there came a loud pounding on the door of his room at the Intercontinental Hotel. "It was past midnight. I was at my desk writing while Stuart Auerbach of the *Washington Post* sat in a lounge chair making notes.

"I opened the door, with the husky Auerbach behind me, to find the Iranian night manager of the hotel standing almost apologetically apart from five thuggish-looking men.

" 'These men are from the Komiteh [revolutionary committee] that controls the hotel and they want to search your room,' the night manager explained.

"As politely as I could, I told him that my room was the premises of the *Los Angeles Times,* and that unless the gentlemen had a warrant or some official document from their government authorizing a search, they would have to walk over me and Auerbach to get in.

"The frightened night manager interpreted my remarks to the Komiteh thugs, who appeared flabbergasted. But after a hasty conference in Persian they turned and left. A few minutes later the night manager telephoned to apologize. 'They thought you had a woman from the American Broadcasting Company in your room,' he explained.

"In revolutionary Iran, the mere presence of an unaccompanied woman in the hotel room of a man is prima facie evidence of skulduggery, not to mention adultery, and cause for flogging or worse as an act of corruption against Islam. I thanked him, bade him goodnight and finished writing my story for the *Times*."

By the time the Tehran crisis ended, with the release of the U.S. embassy staff in November 1980, Don Schanche had been assigned to another post: Rome bureau chief. It was not, on the surface, a perilous assignment, although some reporters could have argued the point later when a would-be assassin fired shots at the pope.

But Schanche shrugged off the risks for, as he told a friend at the *Times,* when one considered it in perspective, there were considerable hazards merely driving the freeways of Los Angeles.

The *Times'* foreign staff had grown at an impressive pace. Much of its growth occurred, oddly enough, in an era when foreign reporting by most newspapers underwent a steady decline. During the Sixties and Seventies one publication after another gave up its overseas staff under the pressure of mounting costs; among the best were those of the *New York Herald Tribune, Chicago Daily News, Washington Star, Boston Globe, Chicago Sun-Times,* and *Philadelphia Bulletin,* plus the entire foreign staffs of three major chains—Knight, Copley and Scripps Howard.

By the early 1980s the *Los Angeles Times* and the *New*

York Times, with the *Washington Post* in third place, led all other American newspapers in the volume of foreign news published. A few other major papers—notably the *Wall Street Journal,* the *Christian Science Monitor,* and the *Baltimore Sun*—kept staff reporters abroad, but not on a global scale.

Otis Chandler knew that the steady decline in quantity and quality of foreign reporting was traceable mainly to the substantial expense of maintaining staff correspondents overseas, expense that soared even higher when reporters were called upon to travel vast distances in pursuit of stories. It was Chandler's longstanding practice to give close scrutiny and analysis to budget data, questioning every major item and poring over summaries prepared by his financial staff. He heard echoes of his father's grim warnings against reckless expense, and the echoes reverberated every time another newspaper, or its foreign staff, went out of business. But Otis had made up his mind: international news reporting of the highest order was essential to the *Times,* and he refused to order cutbacks in the foreign news budget.

Reporting of the highest order also involved amassing a sizable quota of odd experiences, and occasionally the aggressive approach to newsgathering was intermingled with sharp flashes of humor. In New Delhi, Tyler Marshall was given medical advice on how to avoid an epidemic of conjunctivitis raging through the nation: stay out of crowded places.

"In India?" Tyler asked.

Danger and dark humor were inseparable. "Guatemala is a spooky place," Dial Torgerson, Mexico City bureau chief, memoed to foreign editor Robert Gibson after a first visit to the Central American country. Because a CBS reporter had been stopped at the airport the month before, Torgerson was curious to see if he would have trouble entering.

"They didn't look my name up in the book when I came in, but they did look my name up in the book when I went out," Dial reported. "Guatemala is the kind of place I'd rather not get into than not get out of."

One place Dial did not get out of was Honduras, close to the Nicaraguan border. In the summer of 1983, to check out reports of fighting between the two countries, Torgerson and free-lance photographer Richard Cross traveled over a dirt road in a white Toyota Corolla. When their vehicle struck a land mine, both men died instantly.

A foreign correspondent, in the role of special observer abroad, is the eyes and ears equivalent of an ambassador. Although a correspondent is not required to be a diplomat, as an agent abroad any reporter has the clear-cut capacity to pile up grief and embarrassment for the home office.

One blushing example of reportorial embarrassment occurred in Uruguay in the 1960s when President Lyndon Johnson held a summit meeting with leaders of nations of the Western Hemisphere. For security reasons, the Uruguayans sealed off Punta del Este, the site of the summit meeting, and to get inside a correspondent had to be accredited.

Foreign editor Gibson recalled the incident: "We sent a reporter in early to scout living accommodations for the meeting. Let's call him John Doe. He informed us the hotels were all booked, but he said he could lease a house for a couple weeks, and this would enable us to put up a second correspondent—let's call him Rex Roe—who would also be covering the summit conference. We said fine.

"When Rex arrived on the scene, he discovered John had also furnished the house with two sensational-looking women. John had obtained accreditation for them, and they wore little badges indicating they represented the *Los Angeles Times*.

"Rex was terribly upset by this. He considered it improper, embarrassing and—if his wife ever heard about it—potentially disastrous to his marriage. Rex ordered the women out of the house, but John stood his ground.

"News of a mess travels fast. I heard about the incident, and discussed it with Nick Williams, who was then editor. John Doe had been on shaky ground for some time, and this was cause for dismissal. When we sack somebody, we don't use cable or telephone; we do it eyeball to eyeball.

"I hurried off to the summit conference and told John he was fired. He just couldn't understand why we were upset. I said, 'You can't have a couple of women representing themselves as *Los Angeles Times* correspondents, at a summit meeting of all places, when they are obviously not correspondents. It's terribly embarrassing to the *Times*. It simply doesn't reflect well on us.'

"John continued to protest. 'You're wrong,' he insisted. 'These women were absolutely beautiful. Their appearance brought great credit to the *Times!*' "

"You were lucky to get me back from Ulan Bator," Hong Kong correspondent Michael Parks memoed his editors in 1980, following a story assignment to Mongolia.

When the first train reservation was canceled, I didn't mind—I wanted to stay until the end of the week, and that canceled reservation gave me three more days. When the second train had no room for me, I began to get a bit, well, concerned, and when the train officials said there was no room on the next train either, the old travelers' tales I had read—the ones about being trapped for three years in Mongolia, subsisting on indescribable diets of mutton—began to go through my head.

Getting out was an adventure in the absurd. You can't buy a ticket without a reserved place, of which there are none, though with a ticket you can probably get on the train and find a seat.

Here's what it took to get me out on Monday, 5 July: the British ambassador and wife in person talking with Mongolian tourist officials on the train station platform, an official of the Mongolian foreign ministry getting the station manager to open up earlier and bring a cashier from home to sell the ticket, a Chinese embassy second secretary prowling the train (a Chinese train from Moscow with a Chinese crew) for a seat and a Soviet correspondent, an old friend from *Izvestia,* to buy the ticket with his hard currency credentials.

The Catch-22 that required all this help was, as mentioned, an inability to buy a ticket without a seat—but the train left half an hour before the cashier opened, the ticket had to be paid in Tugriks, the Mongolian currency, purchased at the bank, which of course was closed on Sunday and not nearby anyway. So while the Chinese and I searched the train, the British ambassador remonstrated with the tourist authorities, the foreign ministry fellow got the station manager to get the cashier to sell the ticket to the Russian correspondent who brought it to me, a seat having been found. Whew!

All this was incidental to the major problem of reporting—an almost complete inability to make any plans. Requested interviews would be scheduled and then canceled, even forgotten. Mongolians never want to say no, so it is always yes, which may or may not be real. (Even confirmed train reservations mean nothing, I discovered.) Said a Soviet specialist, "They are like children who just learned to tie their shoes—sometimes they stay tied and sometimes they don't but you never know."

The people, however, leave a very positive impression—friendly, open, hospitable, gentle. After a couple of days, I was wondering how Genghis Khan mobilized them to conquer most of the known world and how they could terrorize anyone.

Tall and husky, with a fleshy face and casual slouch, foreign editor Bob Gibson possesses the voice of a rumbling basso and the empathy of a kindly master sergeant. "The most urgent thing I do is deploy a staff correspondent, one or more, in a fast-breaking situation. If there's a revolution in Iran, or a Lord Mountbatten is assassinated, or a war is erupting somewhere, we have to move very quickly. Even though we have nineteen overseas bureaus, there are times when we don't have enough staff available or propitiously located to cover a story. I will go in and bargain with the metro editor or the national editor to borrow one of their people to help us in an emergency.

"Now, you just can't put a parachutist into a foreign country and expect to get the kind of quality reporting that you are proud of, but you try to do your best anyway.

"I'm not by nature a person given to anxieties. I don't get easily upset. I'm actually rather low-keyed and steady. The nearest thing to anxiety I have is when a correspondent is having trouble getting to a hot spot. I worry because we're probably not going to have his reporting in hand. At the same time, if we do receive his copy, hardly anyone is going to appreciate what it took to get him there. Practically nobody, except the correspondent himself, fully appreciates how difficult it can be at times just to get from, say, East Africa to West Africa. Strangely enough, not all of our editors are sensitive to the logistical problems involved. They'll say: 'Gee, is it really that hard to get from Cairo to Riyadh?'"

The problems of the press are of particular interest to the *Times'* London correspondent William Tuohy. Tall, slim, elegantly dressed by conservative Italian tailors, he carries Gucci luggage and even a Gucci-made case for his portable Olivetti typewriter. He is not a dandy, however, but a practical man who learned early in his career that "a journalist is quickly sized up by the way he dresses himself, and dealt with accordingly."

The Chicago-born son of a judge, Tuohy majored in liberal arts at Northwestern University and later was hired by

Newsweek on a trial assignment, "swinging from one back-of-the-book section to another. Gradually I learned to tighten stories, as if with a wrench. I concentrated on compression, transitions, keeping a story in focus, telling a story through anecdote, detail and quotes rather than through simple indirect discourse."

Tuohy learned quickly and was elevated to permanent staff, a promotion that brought him into close contact with a colorful and tempestuous editor, John Denson. A veteran of *Time, Fortune, Collier's,* the *Miami Herald,* the *Los Angeles Herald-Examiner* and numerous other publications, Denson had gained a reputation as "the loosest foot in American journalism." His itinerant nature was spurred by impatience and a sizzling temper. He took a personal interest in stories dealing with the media, and during his tour of duty at *Newsweek* his frequent reversals made life especially difficult for the senior editor in charge of the Press section. Denson had a ferocious habit of grinding teeth, as if munching a snack, while he diagrammed changes in a story. Following one stormy session in his office, a newly hired researcher inquired of the Press section's senior editor: "What kind of nuts was Mr. Denson chewing on?" "Mine," replied the senior editor.

Bill Tuohy learned gradually to deal with erratic editors and even to overcome a deep-seated fear of flying. *Newsweek* assignments led him later to Vietnam, where "after spending a certain amount of time in helicopters, with enemy tracers coming toward me, I wondered whatever had made me so uneasy about flying in a big, safe, commercial airliner."

Like other newsmen in the mid-Sixties Tuohy heard frequently of rapid improvements occurring at the *Los Angeles Times.* Offered a post as Saigon bureau chief, he signed up.

In the midst of the Vietnam War Tuohy tried to live with a certain amount of style. Later he told an interviewer: "Out in the field, among troops, a colleague and I carried along cans of pâté and Beaujolais from the French supermarket. I also carried cognac in a pigskin pewter flask. The idea was to show a little panache—that the war, however ghastly, could not grind you down, at least not into rubble." To Tuohy it was a simple process of rationalizing the predicament. "Everytime I got into a dangerous situation, I'd remind myself: 'What the hell, I could be dying of heart disease behind a desk in Los Angeles.' "

What he reported from Vietnam, writing with uncommon grace and style, often reflected his own ambivalence about the war. "No. 1 Tu Duc Street was a tall, handsome, French-style villa at the quiet intersection of a pleasant, middle-class neighborhood in the northeast part of Saigon," he noted in one dispatch. "On Monday morning, No. 1 Tu Duc Street was blown to rubble by Vietnamese government sappers."

At the end of his Vietnam tour in 1968 he boarded a plane for the United States. Taking a last look at the country below he wrote: "The once-lovely green and brown rice fields bear the ugly pockmarks of war: The long trails of B-52 craters reach almost to Saigon's suburbs. Four years ago, the fields around Saigon were like velvet. The war has done its dirty work."

Next he was assigned to Beirut. "It was a period of intense Palestinian guerrilla activity, and overall a story even more crucial to the fortunes of the West than Vietnam. The Middle East had oil, politics, the Arab-Israeli conflict, the involvement of the superpowers—in a way, the story had everything, including the usual risks to limb and life."

Transferred in 1977 to peaceful London, Bill Tuohy discovered that it also offered special risks. He told an interviewer recently: "One—perhaps no different from other important cities—is getting too close to government officials, particularly those articulate personalities who can make out a very good cause for their point of view. The British are past masters at working their policy into persuasive briefings, so one has to be constantly alert for the special pleading involved. Another danger is going too soft, especially for a journalistic fireman who is always on call to cover trouble anywhere it breaks out. London can be beguiling, and I have to guard against not being able to tear myself away from it, especially when the breaking story is in some hot, dusty, uncomfortable place, where it's hard to work, difficult even to survive. It's the third-world countries that often make news these days, and their concept of a free press is rather different from ours; forceful, fair reporting can land you in jail.''

One London story that intrigued Bill Tuohy was the drama of Fleet Street itself, the home of Britain's national news-papers. In or near Fleet Street, within eyesight of the towering dome of St. Paul's, stand the massive stone offices of sixteen morning and Sunday-only papers. The area is laced with Dickensian pubs and candle-lit wine bars frequented by edi-tors, reporters and printers.

Long confronted by mounting losses, labor strikes, con-stantly rising costs and a general business recession, the British press often appeared to be faced with collapse. Taking a care-ful look at Fleet Street and making intensive inquiry among labor and management, Tuohy made detailed notes on the causes of the continuing chaos. His notes described "a depress-ing picture of near anarchy, with just about everyone sharing the blame; incompetent executives who couldn't manage; left-wing journalists with ideological axes to grind; and right-wing printers determined to squeeze every penny out of em-ployers while outrageously feather-bedding the work force. Among the printers there was little or no loyalty to the papers paying their salaries; instead, a sense that if a paper went under, 'too bad, Jack.' They would get their severance payments and catch on at a job printing shop. There was absolutely no realization among a paper's workers that the introduction of new technology, which they resisted, could in the long run insure a paper's future and thus save jobs rather than junking them.

"At the same time the British class system permeated labor relations. The senior executives came from the upper middle classes and, literally, did not know how to communicate with the shop stewards of the working class. Thus, they did not sense the early warning signals sent out by the work force. The working class considered the executives unfeeling, incompetent snobs. So it was a kind of upstairs-downstairs transferred to the newspaper industry, a them-and-us psychology, the chaps and the lads. Given these deep-seated class differences, and the anarchic power of the local union-chapels to abrogate any contract, one crisis after another became inevitable."

In early 1981, even as Bill Tuohy filled up notebooks on the deepening troubles of Fleet Street, the Telex machine in his office clattered with a message from Los Angeles, conveying word of Otis Chandler's interest in the possibility of a story on the problems of Britain's national press.

The message did not represent ESP but firsthand knowledge on Chandler's part. He had visited Tuohy in London only a month earlier, and had gathered up insights to the chaos of Fleet Street. At the same time Chandler had received a message from the Thomson organization, owners of the London daily and Sunday *Times,* inquiring whether he might be interested in buying the properties.

Chandler declined politely, but privately he was surprised by the naiveté of the inquiry. Not that he carried an ancestral baggage of prejudice against labor unions. Three of his company's metropolitan papers—*Newsday,* the *Denver Post,* the

Dallas Times-Herald—had contracts with unions. But Chandler had built a singularly consistent record of profitable acquisitions; he avoided like the plague all money-losing properties. There was nothing to tempt him to involve his company in Fleet Street's mind-boggling problems.

His lack of interest in owning a piece of Fleet Street did not, however, diminish the possibilities of a story on Britain's lively and colorful national press. Bill Tuohy, with notebooks propped up next to his typewriter, tapped out a report: "Fleet Street, taken literally as well as figuratively, suggests the great press lords: the elder and younger Lords Thomson and Rothermere, Lord Beaverbrook, Lord Astor, Lord Kensley and Lord Hartwell, who bought or created newspapers more often for power and prestige than for profit.

"But for publishing experts, Fleet Street has come to signify a quagmire for owners and investors, a perilous place characterized by near-anarchy, with management and labor locked in tooth-and-claw battles against each other and among themselves. Consequently, the once-profitable national press is in deep financial difficulty, with few papers making a reasonable profit and some seemingly headed for extinction.

"Fleet Street is beset with rising costs, falling advertising and stagnant circulation. It is also afflicted with what some observers call 'the Fleet Street disease'—the constant threat of wildcat strikes that frequently disrupt newspaper production. Louis Heren, deputy editor of London's *Times,* calls the situation that prevails in the composing and pressrooms organized industrial blackmail."

Tuohy noted that in one recent six-month period an estimated 75 million copies of the *Times* failed to reach readers because of wildcat strikes; the daily and Sunday *Times* together were staring at a deficit of $36 million, following on some $95 million lost during an eleven-month shutdown the previous year. Lord Rothermere's *Evening News,* the country's largest afternoon paper, had also announced it was going out of business, leaving London with only one evening newspaper. Tuohy continued: "Once there were harmonious relations on Fleet Street, and British printing unions were considered a model of efficient production. But as profits rolled in during the 1950s and 1960s, newspaper owners competed for labor, and shop-floor stewards concluded all sorts of private production deals, leading to entrenched practices over which senior management had no control—or even knowledge in some cases."

Among other ailments, Tuohy reported: "Local unions put elderly retired workers on the active payroll, or forge signatures to earn paychecks for men who did not work. Another dishonest practice is forcing production managers to grant up to half the shift as time off. The workers then walk across the street to work those hours at another paper.

"The British Sunday papers, which operate separately from the dailies, even when there is common ownership, have been troubled by the fact that since their pressrun occurs only once a week, on Saturday night, they have traditionally employed a large 'casual' work force. The problem with casual workers is that they do not care a hoot and there is nothing whatever the company can do about it.

"The chaotic labor situation on Fleet Street has caused costs to soar. The *Times* management recently calculated that the paper could be printed in Washington, D.C., flown to London, sold for fifteen pence (about thirty-five cents), and make a profit. Instead, the paper is printed on Fleet Street, sells for just under fifty cents and suffers a considerable loss.

"In the past, many union leaders and shop-floor workers assumed that if a newspaper were in financial jeopardy, a rich backer would step in—and in the past that has usually happened. But now, according to one newspaper owner, 'There just aren't any more fairy godmothers out there ready to rush in and take over a newspaper.' "

The supply of fairy godmothers had, in fact, disappeared all over the world. It was clear, as the ranks of newspapers thinned late in the twentieth century, that prudent management and harmonious labor relations had become a prerequisite to survival. It was also clear that the best of the press brought to its readers a total package of abundant and relevant information—news, features, entertainment, service information—not available on a regular daily basis from other sources.

21

O NE major contributor to the total package of information
at the *Los Angeles Times* is Robert Scheer. Trim, clean-
cut and soft-spoken, he wears Palm Beach suits, puffs non-
chalantly on expensive cigars and has the relaxed, civilized
air of a plantation owner traveling on a holiday among civilized companions.

But Scheer is, in fact, a complex and tough-minded reporter,
a self-styled "Berkeley radical" who works with an unusual
charter. Trained as a scholar and academic, he had a mandate
"to spend incredible amounts of time to understand just one
little facet of a complex subject."

When his curiosity leads to crucial questions about men
at the top of corporations and institutions—do they measure
up to their claims and pretensions? and if not, precisely where
and how do the claims and pretensions fall short in performance?—he pursues those questions as if he were preparing
to write a doctoral thesis, patiently and elaborately sifting
through mountains of data, building up solid documentation.

Occasionally (although he laments that it does not happen
often enough) one large research project flows into and illu-
minates another. For example, during the White House years
of Jimmy Carter, Scheer put together a profile of the President's special assistant for national security affairs, Zbigniew

Brzezinski. With surgical precision Scheer (who knew far more about Brzezinski than Brzezinski realized) punctured a myth that had ballooned around the man's public image.

Scheer wrote, in part: "A widespread misconception has it that Zbigniew Brzezinski, the 'Polish Kissinger,' is a passionate anti-communist whose politics derive from a distraught emigré condition.

"This image persists despite the fact that [he] spent only the first three years of his childhood in his native Poland.

"[His] determined struggle to his current position as the President's most trusted foreign policy adviser is marked by a passion centered far more on making it in American society than on liberating a foreign country he has barely seen."

Shortly after the story was published, Otis Chandler attended the annual dinner of the Gridiron Club in Washington, D.C. There he was accosted angrily by Zbigniew Brzezinski, who denounced Scheer's story as "outrageous."

Chandler said calmly, "Well, I'll go back and read it again." This second reading persuaded Chandler that the story was first-class and he instructed the public relations department of the *Times* to reproduce it for promotional mailing to a wide audience of editors, publishers and other opinion leaders across the nation.

The promotional mailing provoked a swift protest from Brzezinski's press assistant. He telephoned Scheer and demanded to know the basis for the story: "How could you write it without interviewing Brzezinski?"

Replied Scheer: "If he told you that I haven't interviewed him, you'd better check with him again. I spent an entire summer with him, up in Maine, interviewing him day after day for a book I was working on. When he was appointed national security adviser, I called and told him I was going to use the material I had gathered in the past, because I was doing a portrait of him for the *Times,* and I wanted to talk to him. He wouldn't give me any more time, and I went ahead with the story."

Brzezinski's press assistant confessed this was news to him. He promised to check back with his boss and then to discuss the situation further with Scheer. But Scheer never heard from him again.

Less challenged by writing personality profiles than by dealing with major issues, and armed with a keen instinct for irony, Scheer chooses often to explore sociological problems. If his carefully documented stories prove more instructive than sensational, the results are nevertheless disturbing and thought-provoking to readers. His approach appears to stem from his background. His parents were garment workers who met on a picket line; Scheer was raised in a one-bedroom walk-up in the Bronx. He told an interviewer: "My bleeding-heart liberalism made sense in terms of the experience and environment and politics of where I grew up. Roosevelt was a hero, and a left-wing attitude was not considered weird.

"My father had very strict views: when you worked, you became a man. So at age twelve I began working." He delivered milk in the morning, groceries in the afternoon, and sold soda pop at Yankee Stadium in the evening. Later, while he went to City College, he worked as a clerk at the post office, and it seemed to him that he was spending three or four hours a day on the subway, getting from home to classes to work, back and forth.

"I went to graduate school at Berkeley. The academic work was supposed to be in economics and Chinese studies, but I kept getting involved in nonacademic things, like collaborating on a book about the Cuban revolution."

He found no sense of excitement about academic life and he spent more and more time in San Francisco, listening to jazz and poetry readings. "I got a clerking job at Lawrence Ferlinghetti's City Lights bookstore in San Francisco, and since there weren't any customers until twelve o'clock or so, I'd go to the store early in the morning and read the papers and magazines coming in from all over the world. It was a marvelous education.

"The more I read about Vietnam, the more it seemed to me that there was a book to be done. Keep in mind this was the early Sixties. I borrowed enough money for round-trip air fare, and afterward wrote an article about CIA involvement in Vietnam. It was published in the *Realist,* and when it was reprinted in *Ramparts* it became that magazine's first big exposé. I also wrote a pamphlet on how the U.S. got involved in Vietnam. It was published by the Center for the Study of Democratic Institutions, and it became something of a blockbuster, with a lot of pass-around quality.

"I went on the staff of *Ramparts* and in a very short time became managing editor. It was a tremendously exciting time, with lots of important stories, but there were two things wrong.

"First, because I'd been identified as someone who had some knowledge about Vietnam, I was forced into more of an activist position than I wanted to occupy. Second, I was very proud of the *Ramparts* work, but it was a day-by-day battle to stay afloat."

Eventually Scheer grew weary of the suspense. He quit *Ramparts* and began free-lancing for magazines, including *Esquire, New York* and *Rolling Stone. Playboy* assigned him to a number of interviews, and one of those gained national attention when the interviewee, Presidential candidate Jimmy Carter, confessed that in his heart he lusted after women.

Said Scheer: "A friend at the *Los Angeles Times* called to ask if I was interested in a job. I said, 'Not particularly'—a lot of magazine assignments were being offered, and book contracts were dangling. I mean, I was busy and earning a good living.

"But people at the *Times,* especially Bill Thomas and Mark Murphy, who was metro editor at that time, kept after me. No matter what questions I raised, they had answers. I explained I'm not a newspaperman because I don't know how to deal with the pressure of a daily deadline. Sometimes I can do a story in three days but sometimes I need three months. I take an academic approach to a story, reading all the background literature before I do anything else. Most newspapermen simply don't have time to read much more than the clips of their paper. Thomas and Murphy said that was fine—they wanted me to work in-depth."

Scheer also explained that he needed a researcher who could go to the library and gather up extensive background, before he began interviews. "I kept explaining my habits and feelings and independence. I almost expected them to say, 'Now you've gone too far.' But instead they kept saying, 'That's fine, that's fine.'

"The more we talked, the more appealing it became. They said, in effect: we know some story projects won't work out, and we'd rather know it than have you fudge and put it in the paper. You might spend weeks on what you think is a good story, but maybe after all your investigating, you find the results disappointing. Then the responsible thing would be to say: Look, this story has turned out to be boring, so let's forget it.

"Their attitude was: your job is not just to fill up space. We have plenty of staff. No reporter at the *Times* should feel he's got to be pumping in words every day, just to fill up space."

Scheer had some second thoughts after he joined the staff, because "I've never been part of a large institution, except when I worked for the post office many years ago. Suddenly I was working for a big corporate giant. The first thing I saw in the lobby was a statue of Harrison Gray Otis, with a slogan about industrial freedom. Keep in mind my parents were union organizers. So on my very first day I began to feel uncomfortable. I thought, 'Hey, I'm going to split; this place isn't for me.' But Thomas and Murphy picked up on this immediately. They told me I didn't have to come into the office—I could do my writing at home or wherever I felt comfortable writing. They were just very good about everything.

"They were particularly understanding of, and encouraging about, my individual approach to stories.

"No matter what project I get involved with, my feeling is: I have to become a leading expert. One time I was talking with Bill Thomas and he asked if I had any interest in television. I said, sure. Then he began to tell me all the things he wanted to know about television that he'd never read anywhere, like how does the profit-making work, and how does that influence the news, and how do the business and creative ends of TV connect up.

"These were questions that fascinated me, and I had plenty of my own. Television, like many subjects, is incredibly complicated. Just to understand one little facet of the business, I had to spend weeks talking with people.

"For example, I was curious to learn how and why one network TV news personality had been hired. When after many attempts I finally reached the head of the network news department, he said flatly that she was hired on the basis of her sound news judgment and extensive journalistic experience.

"I said, 'You're insulting my intelligence to offer an answer like that. I've checked her out and she has absolutely no news experience, so it's silly to suggest otherwise.'

"He got very angry with me, and afterward he called Bill Thomas to complain that I'd been abrasive. To his everlasting credit, Bill told him: 'For the money we're paying Scheer, I should hope he'd be abrasive.'

"Now this was just one tiny point of a very complicated

story. A lot of time is spent getting to the stage where you can sit at your typewriter and feel confident that you know what you're talking about. My rule of thumb is: when I can provide better answers than the people I'm interviewing, then it's probably time to write the story.

"The amount of work that goes into one of my stories is way out of proportion to its lifetime as a piece in a daily newspaper. It drives me crazy. A piece in a magazine is out for a month, and a book—at least in theory—is out there forever. But with a story, well—the next day there's a new newspaper, and that realization can kill you.

"Every time I begin a new project, I have to start cultivating sources all over again, introducing myself to secretaries, being put on hold, waiting and wondering if the calls will ever be returned.

"What's even more time-consuming is this: I'm challenged more than most reporters because my copy is controversial. It sticks out. My stuff is read before it goes in the paper, not just at the desk level but by the metro editor, national editor, assistant managing editor, managing editor and the editor.

"All those challenges keep me on my toes. I'm writing for the average reader of the newspaper, and those editors are there to tell me what the reader is going to be able to get, what makes sense, what's arguable.

"Take a story on immigration. It was not a hot issue in my life; I had never really thought much about the subject. I got into it accidentally. A congressman I'd met on another story called one day and asked if I'd like to go eat some Puerto Rican food. He happened to be head of a Census committee. He was going to the Mexican border the next day and he invited me to go with him.

"I was shocked by the spectacle at the border, people trying to get into this country, a sort of crazy confusion, half comic, half tragic. I spent a couple of days there. When I got back to Los Angeles, I said I wanted to write about it, but no one was interested in the subject. Okay, I'm not about to spend weeks or months working on a story if the editors aren't interested in it.

"But I kept thinking about it anyway. I went through our clips on the subject, and it looked as if our stories had been done basically from the point of view of old-line immigration agents, who are very conservative characters.

"I heard the U.S. Commissioner of Immigration was coming to Los Angeles and, strictly on my own, I asked his people if I could meet him. He was a person of considerable insight. I began to see the possibility of a story that would be a sort of summing up of a changing situation. I'd found an emerging consensus among scholars and politicians, taking a different approach to immigration, seeing it less as a problem and more as a resource.

"I approached the editors once more, and when I got a go-ahead on the story, my researcher started pulling together a body of literature—everything available from the Center for Immigrant Rights, the Chicano studies department at UCLA, all the standard references in *The Readers Guide,* and so forth.

"In the process of gathering a mountain of material, we began picking up names of people who have specialized in the subject, professors and so forth, and this led to still other source material, some of it highly technical.

"Then I had to sit down and read all of it. This can be terribly boring, because it's not written for general interest—you really have to force yourself to wade through it, not to find anything that can be used in a story, but to reach the stage where you can ask intelligent questions.

"Okay, that's academic research, and it's a preparatory step that can take at least a month. Meantime, I was checking off the names of potential sources and starting to interview them.

"The journalistic legwork, doing interviews and discovering new questions and following up with more interviews, and going out on raids with agents of the Immigration and Naturalization Service, and following up with still more interviews—all this consumed still another month. Then there was another round of researching and interviewing. Altogether the story took about three months, most of it spent getting to the point where I could sit at the typewriter and feel confident that I knew what I was writing. The actual writing required the smallest amount of time.

"The most controversial story I've done was an idea offered by Mark Murphy. He said, 'We always see references to the Jewish community and we don't know anything about it. Why don't you take a look at it?'

"We talked about it for a couple of hours. New York has more Jews than Los Angeles, but the *New York Times* had never taken a look at the Jewish community in its own backyard. The 450,000 Jews of Los Angeles make up six percent of the county's population. By most accounts they have the highest per capita income, and per capita are the best-educated, most productive and socially active citizens to be found. But the Jewish community remains, according to some of its leading citizens, as insecure as it is prosperous and as socially isolated as it is officially accepted.

"My challenge was to explore the question: What is it like to be a Jew in Los Angeles today? I interviewed a vast cross-section and eventually—it took months—put together a three-part series. Before turning it in I passed the story around to some thirty reporters on the staff, many of them Jewish. I wanted to get their reactions. Not one of them found the story offensive."

To convey some of the complexities and contrasts of the Jewish community, Scheer quoted numerous Jews—ranging from poor to wealthy, from ill educated to scholarly, from obscure to powerful and influential. Scheer also sketched numerous personalities, attitudes and scenes to provide multiple insights.

Despite his care, caution and sensitive approach, the series provoked a torrent of objections from Jewish readers. Otis Chandler and Bill Thomas were jolted by complaints and protests. Said Thomas: "It was a proper subject for journalism. I read every word of the series in advance, and it was obviously compassionate, honest, illuminating, all of it done with goodwill. I could anticipate an emotional reaction, but factually there was nothing to take exception to."

Otis Chandler added: "The reaction spun far deeper than we had expected. For months afterward, wherever I went socially, I got the cold shoulder from very close friends. And I was deluged by mail. The bottom line was a belief in the Jewish community that this was a subject better not dealt with at all in the press, no matter how good and honorable our intentions."

Scheer was distressed by the uproar. "I told Otis that I was sorry about causing him so much grief, and he said very courageously: 'Look, it's okay, all the commotion means people are reading the paper, and reading it carefully.'

"But I know the heat was terrible. I told Bill Thomas: 'Maybe you didn't bargain for all this trouble when you hired me. I'm perfectly willing to leave. I'll go quietly.' But he was gutsy, just like Chandler, and he told me not to worry about it.

"I get a tremendous amount of feedback on most of my stories, and it's quite different from appearing in the national magazines. When I write something for *Playboy* or *Esquire*, I'll hear from a small circle of friends in New York, but magazines basically go to specialized audiences; they aim at a very narrow slice of the public.

"When my work appears in the *Los Angeles Times,* my New York friends may not see it unless I send the stuff off to them, but there is a marvelous feedback here, of course, and in a great many cities where the stories are reprinted. A newspaper takes a much broader cut of the public. A newspaper story is something to pass around. When I have a hot one going, people clip it and send it to their relatives, and you get letters for weeks and months afterward.

"For instance, I did an interview with the head of Standard Oil, in the midst of the gasoline shortage, and I couldn't believe the response. Wherever I went and introduced myself, people said something about it, like: 'You're the guy that did the Standard Oil story.'

"It gives me a good, strong feeling to get that kind of feedback. Even when feedback is negative, it's still good for my work. It keeps me awake, because I know that people are reading my stuff. I think what kills a lot of journalists is, they don't have a sense that people are reading them. And when feedback happens to be positive, it really spurs us toward achievement."

22

TRIM and athletic, she has plenty of power but seldom makes a show of it. Carrying the title of associate editor, Jean Sharley Taylor reigns over the huge dominion of "soft" news, a territory encompassing Books, Movies, Television, Society, Fashion, Travel, three separate Sunday magazines, direct responsibility for the work of 140 staff editors and writers, plus a larger number of free-lance contributors.

Problems large and small are tossed like tennis balls into her office, and, occasionally—in her view—there were problems bordering on the absurd. One involved a column by *Times* columnist Jack Smith, a whimsical piece on the drinking habits of birds. Wrote Smith:

"Whatever doubt I may have had about my observation that birds are heavy drinkers has been evaporated by letters from readers who have come to the same conclusion from their own empirical experience. I am also gratified by the letters of encouragement I have received as a result of my mentioning that when my wife and I go to England next month, I hope to see some British tits, which I am told are notorious drinkers.

" 'Should you find yourself in the vicinity of Wells Cathedral while in England,' writes Mary Thompson, 'treat yourself to a visit to the Cathedral Book Shop, where you will find a wonderful collection of fascinating books. An entire shelf is devoted to books about birds, including one very dignified volume simply called 'British Tits.' Have a wonderful trip.' "

Smith then quoted another reader, who wrote:

" 'The birdman, Jack Smith, has brazenly announced a trip to England that includes having a look at some British tits. How does the *Times* plan to cover this?' "

Smith continued:

"The *Times* plans to cover this as usual, by sending its best tit man."

In addition to protests from readers, Jean Sharley Taylor received a blistering memo from a staff writer employed by the *Times'* metropolitan department: "Jean: I'm too far behind in my own work to spend time bitching about other people's, but I can't let Jack Smith's column today go by without expressing outrage. I don't normally read him as his attempts at down home folksiness are not to my taste, but someone pointed out his tasteless comments about being a 'tit man' and I blinked in disbelief that a major American newspaper would indulge a columnist in what he must have thought was cleverness. As a woman, as a writer, and as a *Times* employee I feel thrice insulted. At his age I don't suppose his mentality is likely to change, but I hope that as his editor (at least the people out here in Metro say he is your responsibility) you will scrutinize his 'work' more carefully in the future. Such smutty jokes are better suited for the locker room or men's toilets than the *Los Angeles Times*. (signed) Lois Timnick."

To which Jean Taylor replied: "Lois: We are not, contrary to your surprising opinion, oblivious to our editing responsibilities.

"But the judgment calls on columnists are difficult because the columnist, like the cartoonist, must be permitted to shape a highly personalized image and Jack's image—a humorous shading—is of the middle-aged innocent, contemplating a fast-moving world and retreating back to a single, harmless vice—girl-watching. The device occasionally moves him right to the edge, at which point we make a decision. We made it— the copy editor, the news editor and I. If I had to do it again, I'd still run the column.

"I'm sorry you don't read Jack to get a totality of view. He has written more than 4,000 columns for the *Times* and most of them have much to do with manners and gentleness and human regard. His readership is amazing—especially among women. (signed) Jean."

Jack Smith, who received carbon copies of the exchange, sent along an additional comment: "Dear Ms. Timnick: The funny thing is, I'm actually more of a leg man."

Jean Taylor deals with protests at a briskly efficient pace, whenever possible, for she follows a breathless routine: her multiple departmental schedules often tend toward collision. Recently she told an interviewer: "I arrive at the office about nine-thirty, take messages and try to get ready for the ten o'clock meeting of the View section. There's no leeway here; if we're even ten minutes late in our deadlines, we can deter other sections of the paper waiting to get on the presses.

"While we're putting together a cover for the View section, I usually indicate things that I feel we should have inside. I leave that meeting in time to rush down the hall to the editorial board meeting, which begins at ten-thirty, and includes Otis Chandler, Bill Thomas, Tony Day, George Cotliar and so forth.

"By eleven-fifteen I get back to my office and there begins a procession of editors and writers. I have pretty much an open-door policy. Sometimes people argue out in the hall and they continue the argument as they stroll in. They forget I'm there and they sort of feel at home. Each section editor is operating on a different schedule, printing at a different time, with different type. This applies especially to the various Sunday sections which go to press on different days. So there are little island problems that need to be solved.

"Overall I try to create an atmosphere in which the editors do not feel that I'm looking over their shoulders. But I want also for them not to be ill at ease if I drop in with a suggestion.

"Some changes require only the lightest touch. Take Travel, where we have a really strong editor in Jerry Hulse. My involvement might be to tell him a particular piece on the cover is not quite right, and he knows instantly what I mean and how to fix it. Or if I happen to suggest a piece that combines travel with environmental concerns of pollution and energy, Jerry is right on top of it; he comes up with an idea for a regular column touching on the environmental element in terms of travel.

"The Real Estate section was something else. In the old days it was essentially an advertising supplement which featured openings of houses and these were connected, more or less, to nearby placement of ads. We have gradually moved away from this to build a fairly strong editorial section—a news approach to real estate—and we brought in environmental, architectural and financial writers from elsewhere on the staff. So it became a sort of horizontal approach to improving a section—borrowing people from different departments to apply their expertise.

"Some changes are terribly tough to make. It's most difficult to convince people, who have been doing something a certain way for many years, that you are not overly critical in suggesting change. One of our Sunday magazines, *TV Times,* was fairly typical of this. It employed loggers—individuals who sat there, like characters out of Charles Dickens, and laboriously copied by hand, hour after hour, day by day, the TV schedules for an entire week, covering some twenty-four separate TV channels in the area.

"Then we became aware of the availability of computerized TV logs. They didn't quite work for us because they were designed for cities with only a few channels. But we hired an expert who adapted the technology to our needs. One thing we were able to computerize, for example, was our own summary reviews of hundreds and hundreds of movies—the stars, the producer, the critic's rating—and when a movie is scheduled, either on national, local or cable TV, all we have to do is push a button and retrieve a capsule review.

"Take the next step. Instead of spending money to employ Dickensian loggers, we can use the money to employ additional TV critics, specialists who write about cable, pay TV, satellite transmission, TV's effect on our lives, and so forth.

"Now, these things just don't happen. All the decisions have to come from higher up. Obviously I wouldn't do anything unless Bill Thomas said okay. When I have his permission, my next job is to convince the people in my various sections that this or that change would be good for the paper. At the same time—and this is much harder than it appears—we cannot let the upgrading of the system deter us from our main goal, which is to be a newspaper and to be first in our particular areas with the news. It would be a terrible mistake to wallow in fancy machinery and dazzling techniques, and yet lose sight of our larger responsibilities.

"Some readers think we are uncaring about the community, especially because we cannot carry long lists of golden weddings, births and deaths, except for obits of major personalities. But if we cannot carry endless lists, then we have to put some humanism of another nature into the paper. This takes a lot of determination not readily apparent to the casual observer."

Determination helped to shape Jean Sharley Taylor. The daughter of British-born parents who struggled to make a living in Detroit, Jean was brought up in a household where tea was served every afternoon, regardless of financial setbacks.

"In high school, when I said I wanted to become a newspaper reporter, the teachers told me that girls couldn't be reporters. I decided one way to make a start was to slide over through an advertising department. The summer I finished high school, at seventeen, I got on a streetcar and rode to the J. L. Hudson Company, a huge department store. I stood in line a long time at the personnel office and eventually they hired me as a messenger for the advertising department.

"This job continued when I was at college. One day the ad manager asked me to write a poem for an ad. It was a corny poem, but gradually Hudson's let me write little items of retail advertising for their fashion ads.

"This went on for six years and after I finished Wayne State, Hudson's took me on as a regular member of the advertising staff—and all that time my parents were kind of wondering what I was doing. Girls, you see, did not become writers.

"One day I heard the *Detroit Free Press* was in the market for a fashion writer. The *Free Press* had never hired a woman reporter—I was the first—and even though I knew something about fashion, I was really green in terms of reporting, and I wrote some crummy copy. But gradually I improved and they sent me on New York trips to cover the fashion shows. This went on for three years until the paper shifted me over to write features. Immediately I decided I was a hotshot reporter. I just reveled and stayed with the *Free Press* for many years, until I was hired to be women's editor of the *Arizona Republic,* and then came an offer from the *Times* to work on the women's pages here.

"An editor has an awesome responsibility: to make substantive changes in the paper. For example, what was once a women's page, consisting of a few items about club meetings and narrow social events, has become the View section reflecting the very important needs of women in terms of their families, their social status, their self-respect and their esteem, and the changes in the woman's world in terms of jobs. The same section has gradually added an element of humanism with excellent regular columns on health, food, fitness, manners.

"Instead of offering a tiny window on the world of the wealthiest few, View has become a place to take a very wide, across-the-board look at people. Now the section even crusades for reform, in some stories, and if legislation is the result, that's fine."

Jean Sharley Taylor's top deputy, Charles Champlin, now carries the dual roles of arts editor and principal book critic of the *Times*. Courtly in demeanor, he possesses an arsenal of enviable attributes including swift understanding, a literate nature and an anecdotal turn of mind. A kind and generous state of mind frames his own window on the world; he is puzzled and grieved by others who might judge him in less kind and generous terms.

For many years he was the paper's principal film critic and arts editor. The two jobs led him to screenings four or five times a week and, in addition, gave him immediate responsibility for some three dozen colleagues who dealt collectively with film, theater, books, television, music, art, and dance.

Beyond his wide-ranging tasks at the newspaper, which more than fill a five-day week, Champlin has engaged in other pursuits: he conducts a regular program of on-camera interviews with film personalities for a cable television network; he has taught a class in film criticism at Loyola-Marymount University; and he turns an occasional half-day toward writing a book.

He manages to pack many varied activities into a day because he writes swiftly and, it seems, almost effortlessly. Recently he told an interviewer: "I know others, including colleagues on the staff, for whom writing is a terribly slow, agonizing process. Luckily I don't have that problem. I'm a compulsive writer, and it flows for me. I must give all credit to a lot of years with *Time* and *Life*, where the discipline of writing under deadline pressure was an absolutely terrific postgraduate education.

"My day usually begins at the typewriter, at home, between eight and nine in the morning. I find it very hard to write at the paper, because of all the administrative distractions. So I flail away at the typewriter until perhaps eleven, and then I belt downtown to the office. If it's a piece that I'm doing for the next day, I get in just under the wire with my copy. Three or four times a week it's a review, and for Friday it's a Critic-at-Large column, which may be anything from a piece on jazz to a book review or any other option that I seize on eagerly—eagerly because it gives me an opportunity to write about something other than movies. Then, after turning in my copy, I face up to the administrative chores."

To Champlin this means, among other challenges and opportunities, dealing with numerous job applications, some from within the staff, from persons in other departments who would like to participate in arts criticism. It also means, Champlin observes, traffic with "an awful lot of applications from all over the world. The *Times* has become a mecca for anybody who wants to write about the arts. And it means dealing with an amazing number of problems that arise in terms of trips that people want to take, to develop projects they're involved in: a cultural reporter to Washington for a story on federal funding of the arts, a music specialist to New Mexico for an unusual series to be done there, a TV reporter to New York on a TV story back there, and so forth.

"These are very ripe areas for attention. We struggled for several years, for example, trying to define just what we should do by way of covering television, not only reviews but news about cable and satellite transmission and the entrepreneurs, plus of course the visible TV personalities. We've been trying to balance reviews against news features, trying not to get so solemn that we lose the readers' interest. There are all kinds of balances to worry about.

"If you are a film critic and you work at the *Times,* you are conspicuous. You have a certain amount of power and responsibility. It sounds pretentious, but the *Times* gives you an influential voice and you become a kind of synapse, a junction point for producers and distributors. They want to show their films, and mostly as a favor you will go to see them. Or a local exhibitor may be debating whether to run a film, and he invites you over.

"So you spend an awful lot of afternoons schlepping out to see the latest Balkan masterpiece. For one reason or another— perhaps an executive decision not to release a film because it isn't commercial—some of these movies are never shown theatrically and are never reviewed, but a large amount of time has disappeared with them.

"And then the big commercial Hollywood studio screen-ings tend to be in the evening at eight-thirty. So the day begins early at the typewriter, and ends quite late as the lights come on after a film.

"It takes an awful lot of hours, and I'm inclined to think it's not so much a skill as just a habit of hard work. I came out of a small-town Depression background, and neither then nor at any time since have I found any effective substitute for hard work.

"For seventeen years I worked for another very potent or-ganization, *Time-Life,* and I was the beneficiary of all the power and prestige and popularity of the company. I'd have been a damned fool if I assumed that I was sought after because I possessed some innate gift of charm; I was nothing more than an entree point for others to make it onto the pages of *Time* and *Life*.

"This was an invaluable lesson to learn, not cynicism but skepticism. When I was hired by the *Times* in 1965 to be entertainment editor, I could see what it must be like to be a beautiful woman: the publicity departments of the major studios courted me nonstop. If you overwhelm easily, you're in real trouble.

"One day I was looking around for an idea for a column, and it struck me that the hardest of all the arts in Hollywood is survival. Longevity is the glittering prize, the gift to be treasured above all others. And I did an essay on people who'd survived. They may not have been any good in the first place, but if they survived they became folk heroes within the film industry. The piece cited the case of Jack Warner: nobody ever said that he was an easy guy to get along with, but he was always given a big hand at banquets because he'd been a survivor for fifty years in a tough town. That was all—just sort of a throwaway line.

"That night when I got home there was a bottle of brandy with a note from Jack Warner's top publicist saying: 'The Colonel thinks you're a flaming genius.' The nature of press agentry is very strange indeed.

"Dealing with press agents, unfortunately, increases one's vulnerability to criticism. We have our own in-house critics, such as David Shaw, who dismiss my film reviews as being too generous, too kindly, too gentle, especially when other film reviewers blast the very same movies.

"Given a choice, I would rather be fair than colorful. It's awfully easy to be scathing. You can destroy everything from

Michelangelo's *Pietà* to *Gone with the Wind* if that's the goal of the critic, but destruction is kind of a mug's game.

"Once I did an interview with a director named Joseph Losey. He did a film which drew unfavorable reviews from practically all the critics, including me. Afterward he sent me a note saying: 'Chuck, at least you tried to see it as a movie and not as a crime against civilization.' I rather cherished that, because I had tried to be fair.

"When there are complaints about my film reviews, I can get terribly annoyed. But if you try too hard to explain and clarify, you begin to sound like Captain Queeg rolling steel balls around in his hand. It's just not worthwhile. I'd rather walk away from it."

Champlin stayed with movie reviews for fourteen years before switching to a new endeavor. Following his appointment as principal book critic in 1980, he explained in a column: "Writing about books feels both like a beginning and a return to my own beginnings as a compulsive reader as well as a compulsive writer. I look forward to being a galley slave."

He continued, of course, in his influential behind-the-scenes role as arts editor, overseeing the work of numerous colleagues. And he collaborated closely with Book Review editor Art Seidenbaum.

Scrunched down at a desk heaped high with galleys, Seidenbaum is visible only as a gleaming bald head among stacks of pages. Not until he raises his round, unlined face and rubs his alert, sky-blue eyes does it become apparent that he is searching for something among the scattered sheets of paper: a lengthy reminder list detailing specific books to be assigned to specific reviewers.

The act of searching annoys him, for it consumes time, of which there is too little, and it further irritates him because he is inclined to be precise and well organized; he does not often lose assignment lists.

Art Seidenbaum speaks with a style to match his writing: the brittle observations conceal a sensitive and sentimental nature. He talks at length, if necessary, with authors and reviewers, but he prefers the clean, nonargumentative, time-saving method of sending written guidance to a widely scattered legion of book-reviewing contributors. He finds it necessary to budget his time carefully, for he also reviews books. And he makes a singular effort, in his "Endpapers" column in the Sunday Book Review section, to give some meaningful illumination to life behind the scenes in the book-reviewing process.

Following a large promotional bash hosted by Bantam Books, he wrote:

"The literary cocktail party is usually a kind of quiche-me-quick affair. Hundreds of people hurry through lines of small talk to make as many contacts and mend as many fences as time permits. Dozens of conversationalists look over shoulders to find the next person to pounce upon while finishing off the person face-to-face. A few photographers from places like *People* magazine stalk the wild celebrity.

"The big Bantam party at the Beverly Hills hotel had all the proper ingredients: Hot and cold running canapés. A spring line of executives to introduce a roster of big-time writers. . . . The trouble with sprawling Los Angeles is the contradictory impress of the book community. The Rodeo Room of the Beverly Hills hotel offers no place to hide. Anyone serving a sentence knows everyone else doing publishing time."

The son of an advertising man with whom he played Scrabble and other word games as "a constant source of amusement," Art Seidenbaum grew up in Yonkers, New York. After graduate school at Harvard he found a job at Time Inc., as a staff writer on *FYI,* the house organ. Recently he told an interviewer: *"FYI* provided young people with a hunting license to find a somewhat better job on one of the Time Inc. magazines. I was promoted, if that's the word, from editorship of *FYI* to messenger on *Life,* and later from messenger to reporter, which meant writing captions for picture stories.

"When an opening developed in the Los Angeles bureau, I asked for it. I found reporting, outside the confinement of New York, a very luxurious way to exercise one's own curiosity and to be a student forever.

"When *The Saturday Evening Post,* which was supposed to be enjoying a renaissance, invited me to run its West Coast bureau, I took the job, but the magazine was in terrible shape, and very soon thereafter, in 1962, I went to the *Times,* where Otis Chandler had only recently become publisher. Culture was at that point a national buzz word, and possibly because I had worked for a couple of distinguished magazines, the *Times* offered me a chance to write about culture.

"The emphasis on culture rapidly became more and more sociological and less and less artistic because the *Times* itself was growing so quickly under Otis. That is, instead of one art critic, there were soon two. Instead of one drama critic, there were soon two or three. Jazz had been one of my passions, but all of a sudden there was a jazz critic. Suddenly there was also a writer specializing on higher education and it wasn't necessary to cover the colleges the way I had been, in a kind of slapdash way.

"As the paper put more and more experts into place, there were fewer and fewer fields open to me, and my work became more of a commentary column than a subject-oriented column. It lived on the front page of Metro and in various other sections. It went on for sixteen years, appearing various places in the paper. I worked at home and came into the office once or twice a week to dump copy, read mail, mend fences.

"Those were deliriously pleasant years for me. Writing a regular column, however, tends to become more and more difficult. Readers get tired, which I think is understandable. Writers who have some ego about being fresh begin to wonder whether they haven't dredged the last new adverb or noun out of the well. Only two and a half years after taking on the specific assignment of writing about architecture—not a long time at all—I grew restless and began looking for something else to do."

Coincidentally, the *Times'* book editor, Digby Diehl, had begun clearing off his desk and emptying out his office in preparation for a move to the East Coast. A facile writer and skilled editor, Diehl had lent his voice to the chorus of book-lovers demanding a regular weekly package of book reviews. Prior to 1975 the *Times* published a page of Sunday reviews, but efforts ambitious enough to be classed as book sections were produced only at widely spaced intervals, ranging from monthly to quarterly.

When in 1975 the *Times'* advertising department found, however, that it could sell enough ads to support a regular weekly section, the Sunday Book Review was launched, pushed forward aggressively by Chandler and Bill Thomas, then developed carefully in collaboration between Digby Diehl and a small staff, all supervised closely by Jean Sharley Taylor. Diehl swiftly won recognition in book-publishing circles as a book editor of uncommon talent, and he was invited to join a New York publishing subsidiary of Times Mirror. (Later he became book review editor of the Los Angeles *Herald-Examiner*.)

Recently Art Seidenbaum recalled: "When I heard the *Times'* book editor's job was open and announced my wish to succeed Digby, I imagined my bosses would throw their arms around me and say, 'Wonderful, wonderful.' Instead, they interviewed very carefully. I was lucky to become book editor.

"Much of the reviewing process is a guessing game. A major frustration to me is my somewhat impossible desire to have the flow of books, more than forty-two thousand published each year, match the number of pages available to the Book Review section, where we can cover only about three thousand of them. Every time we guess, we guess wrong. The pendulum is always swinging from one end to the other and not stopping in the middle. We either have more reviews than we have room for, or a sudden richness of room and shortage of reviews, governed in part by the quality of the books—and that's something of which we have no control.

"One large problem arises when we deal with celebrity reviewers. For example, in 1979 a book came in written by Henry Kissinger, and it was obviously a very important book. My notion was to get Ronald Reagan—who had not yet announced his Presidential candidacy—to review it from the political right, and George McGovern, the liberal Democrat, to review it from the other side of the spectrum. That would give us two balancing views of one book and place Kissinger somewhere in the middle.

"Reagan declined, saying he was too busy, so we enlisted Senator Sam Hayakawa, whose political views are roughly similar to Reagan's. McGovern reviewed Kissinger the man, more than the book, while Hayakawa simply quoted from the book and said almost nothing as a human being about it.

"Both men were late with their copy, and Hayakawa's didn't qualify as a review. What to do? If we ran just McGovern, without Hayakawa, we would appear to be embracing McGovern's point of view. It was much too late to ask Hayakawa for a rewrite. So I sat down to write a brief precede that would be a cosmetic powder. But it didn't work. I wrote three or four precedes and, rather than covering the wart, they seemed to call attention to it. So we ran Hayakawa as he wrote it. The resulting mail was very angry and, I think, rightly so.

"Another time we received a review copy of *The Brethren,* a big controversial book about the United States Supreme Court. It was written by two *Washington Post* staffers, Woodward and Armstrong. Their paper had serialization rights, and thus had no difficulty doing an early review. The *Washington Post* owns *Newsweek,* and this meant there was no way the rest of the world could catch up to those two publications. Adding to all this, the book's publisher, Simon & Schuster, was so nervous about being true to its *Washington Post* sponsors that the book was sent out in some secrecy. They sent my copy to me at home, loose pages in a blue box.

"I invited Shirley Hufstedler, a member of the United States Court of Appeals, to write a review. But she was about to be appointed to a Cabinet job in Washington, so she quite sensibly turned us down. I then asked Dorothy Nelson, the distinguished dean of the University of Southern California law school, to do the book. She took it with her on a weekend trip, and afterward she said, in effect, it was delicious reading, but no one connected with the judicial system would likely review this book. It was great fun, but just too tender to deal with.

"At that point I enlisted an outstanding UCLA historian, and the review was written for us. But those kinds of delays really make our life difficult. We spent perhaps more time on that one book than on ten others.

"In addition to our five-hundred-odd reviewers we have six columnists who appear in rotation. One deals with original trade paperbacks, the slightly more expensive, larger-format paperbacks. Another week we have a reviewer dealing with what's called mass-market paperbacks. We also carry regularly a list of worthy reprint books. Another week there is a list of thrillers (crime, spy, detective). Still another week there is a list of Hollywood and theatrically oriented books, and another week there are children's books. Each of those six columnists has fifteen hundred to two thousand words in which to cover ten to twelve books.

"Sometimes I sit down and write a piece. And since I used to write pieces on the average of four times a week and now it's once a week, it's a delight. I wash a lot of our dirty laundry in that space, including conflicts of interests.

"We send each of our reviewers a form that says, essentially, 'You owe every book two things: understanding what the author was trying to do and some summation of what that attempt was and what the book is about. And then you should provide us with your own interpretation of how well that author succeeded or failed. That is, you should not praise the book simply because it was beautifully written, without talking about what the content is.'

"It is very difficult to find somebody who will admit to liking best-sellers, who will treat popular fiction for what it is and not for what the reviewer would like it to be. The tendency is for a reviewer to want to have a urinating contest as to who can create the most negative trajectory for this or that book. And, in effect, to star by despising that which is too easily attacked anyway. So I think there's righteous criticism that we tend to be stuffy sometimes.

"We make every effort to be completely ethical and honorable. We will not assign a book to be done at the reviewer's request. The reason: sometimes the reviewer, unknown to us, turns out to be the sweetheart, cousin or advertising director of the author.

"Two ugly incidents brought about this stricture. In one, a good writer requested a specific book but didn't tell us that he had already given the publisher a publicity blurb to use in the promotion of the book. Conversely, there was the case of an academic who asked to review a book written by one of his colleagues. We didn't know they were colleagues because the author writes pseudonymously."

Seidenbaum finds another area of distress in the refusals, by some reviewers, to deal with certain books—for reasons not reflecting well on the critics. He wrote about it in a recent column:

Now and then—unfortunately more recent nows than long-ago thens—reviewers turn books back to us, not wanting to announce critical judgments. They have that right, of course. Most of our reviewers work free-lance, for pleasure and peanuts.

Usually the reviewer says no because the work in question is unpleasing, because the reviewer cannot find enough kind words in conscience to make the piece.

Too often, however, the reviewer says no to keep the peace, because the reviewer doesn't want to be a barracuda in troubled literary waters. The refusal then becomes a reluctance to speak harsh, tough—or even true—to the public, a sort of restraint of critical trade, self-imposed. Grandma may have been correct: If you can't say something nice, then don't say anything at all.

The book family is too small, of course, for critical comfort. John doesn't want to knock a Doubleday author when he, himself, would like to be a Doubleday author. Jane is reluctant about panning a George Diskant client because she's a Diskant cousin herself. And Jean tries to be all love to all agents and publishers and editors. Such pussy-footings are fine for Pollyanna's world but they hardly advance the craft of criticism. I suggest public regret is a better expression than private refusal. Candor is served; readers are warned.

But the joyful experience Seidenbaum finds in books outweighs all other considerations. He says: "I read for pleasure. Even if I were not book editor, I'd try to read three or four books a week. Another nice thing about the job is that it's sort of like seeing theater on the road. If you take galleys before there are any reviews out, then your judgment of the book is pure. I have a good time with that."

Under the massive tent of the *Times,* Otis Chandler assembled a large and varied collection of star writers. Among them, the by-line "S. J. Diamond" gives no clue to gender. What nothing can mask is Susan Judith Diamond's talent. A former staffer at *The New Yorker,* her craft is classy writing, and she applies it to the Business section.

She says: "Even though I'm part of a big metropolitan newspaper, I still work like a magazine reporter. Where other people may deal with a story in a single day, most of the feature stories I do will take two, three or four weeks.

"In the early stages of a story I have a sense of time, because I go to the office, do interviews and research, observe other people, take lunches, listen to the telephones ringing. I'm aware of the hours clicking by because there are appointments to keep and things are happening all around me.

"But in the second half of a story, when I am ready to write it, I work at home. I have a rule that I can't get out of my bathrobe until I have done three pages, and I can't take a shower until I have done three more pages. What it means is, the day has no humps in it at all. I can work from early morning right through lunch or dinner, and often until midnight or one o'clock. It's a long day but it runs more smoothly and is less tiring than schlepping back and forth from home to the office.

"Afterward I spend at least as much time rewriting my early draft. By the time I have rewritten the story, no line is the way it was.

"I also work like a magazine writer by keeping at my fingertips a list of story ideas. I revise the list every couple of months and take it to the business editor. I say, 'All right, which one interests you the most? Which shall I do first?' I'll develop the stories one at a time. There is some attrition—some stories die off while they're waiting on the back burner. But I keep adding new suggestions to the list, so there is always a big backlog ahead of me.

"Not that everyone on a newspaper is accustomed to or willing to accept the rhythm of magazine writing. One of the first things an editor in my section told me was, 'Look, you can't worry so much how you say it, you have to remember that by three o'clock it will be at the bottom of a bird cage.'

"As a magazine writer, you don't think about that, because you are writing for a glossy-page publication that will be taken by a subscriber, who places it carefully on a coffee table or shelf. Later, in leisure, the subscriber can sit on the couch, put up his feet and read it thoroughly—in effect, reliably reading every word. This is quite different from the newspaper reader who—I am told—wants to go through the paper quickly.

"There is another expression among those editors who want me to turn out copy at greater speed. They say, 'Don't assume that anybody will read past the jump.' In effect, you had better get your story into the first five paragraphs because probably most of our readers will not stay with the story beyond that point.

"This attitude bothers me, of course, but not enough to make me change my ways. I suspect it would be better for my career if I were faster, if I could do things a bit more casually, but I'm not successful at that.

"Nobody is really interested in how long it takes me to do a story, so I always try to make it sound like I spend less time. I don't tell people I've stayed up late six nights in a row, working on a story, because not only is it not appreciated, it is disdained.

"They are, in fact, right in wanting me to be faster. I think it would be better if I could care less. And basically what am I here for? I'm here because I want to reach more people. Why does anybody write? To reach as many people as possible, with as many stories as possible. Do I, by spending twenty percent more time on something, get twenty percent more readers? Probably not. I mean, if I'm going to write for the layman, I should write more for the layman; I should not write for the people who are going to notice the sentence in the middle of the piece. It's a self-indulgence that I think one has to give up.

"Now, I'm not referring to an investigative-type story that may take months to develop, but just a feature that I think should be written well. Okay, am I shortchanging quality when I say this? I've been told that twenty percent less quality would still be quality material. I have enough faith in myself so that I think, yes, if I were writing only eighty percent as well, it would still be good writing, and I would be writing more stories. So, I'm not sure that I'm on the wrong side of the argument. So, it's a problem for me. I want there to be some great place in the sky for people who always want things to be the best, but I find there is not necessarily time for the best in life."

Susan grew up in Boston, studied for a Ph.D. in English and landed a job at *The New Yorker*. Following her hitch there she moved to Los Angeles, where she became a busy and much-sought-after free-lance correspondent for a number of magazines including *Time, Money, Fortune* and *People*.

"Although I was a general reporter," she told an interviewer recently, "I found that almost everything I covered—whether the subject dealt with medicine, science, a movie personality

—ultimately involved a story of marketing in some form, marketing in terms of assessing how and why an idea became popular, and how much of the public would buy how much of it.

"Another name for it is business. I found that more and more people who did not necessarily comprehend business did understand they were affected by it and wanted to read about it—and somebody had to write about it for them in layman terms. It appeared to me that traditionally, business pages were written for people who were also reading the *Wall Street Journal,* while I found I could write for a reader who might not see or understand the *Journal.*"

Diamond's special talent is shared by others on the staff. Jim Murray, the kingpin of sports columnists—and widely syndicated by the *Times*—writes for readers who might not see or understand or even care about spectator sports. Says Murray: "I write about people."

Tall and husky, with a ruddy complexion and a broad New England accent, Murray is as well known as—and vastly more entertaining than—most of the people he writes about. Fourteen times in seventeen years his colleagues in the National Association of Sportcasters and Sportswriters have honored him as the best in the business.

Otis Chandler, in 1960 during his first year as publisher, looked around for a breezy sports columnist to brighten up the pages of the *Times,* and his gaze fastened on Murray, then a writer on the staff of *Sports Illustrated.* Murray soon proved himself to be one of the quickest, funniest, most irrepressible sports columnists in America. His staples were similes and hyperbole, but he was equally adept at irony and satire. Some samples: "He fields a ground ball like a guy groping for a towel with soap in his eyes." On prizefighter Floyd Patterson: "Send him out for the Holy Grail and he comes home with an empty Coke bottle. Put him in charge of a ship in a storm and he runs it aground. He's that kind of guy who goes through life spilling soup on his boss's wife. He's not a fighter, he's a situation comedy."

Reporting from Moscow on the 1980 Olympics, Murray wrote of the Russians:

These are certainly the happiest cast of people I have ever seen in my life. You know they're happy because they don't have to show it. I mean, you know how they put on these plastic smiles in Hollywood and on Broadway and in Palm Springs and Palm Beach? Pretend they're having a good time?

Well, these people don't bother to put on any fronts. Of course, it may be that smiles are just another shortage in this glorious workers' paradise. There are, after all, certain things you have to give up to insure the Revolution. You have to watch these things. It starts with a smile, you know, then a laugh—and the next thing you know, they think the government is funny.

It may be that smiling requires a special permit or that you can only buy them in the stores marked for foreigners' use only. You have to queue up for everything else in this proletarian Eden. Maybe you get to smile only every other Thursday between the hours of two and four. In the morning. Maybe now that the dissidents and the refusedniks and the subversives who are apt to burst right out laughing have been removed from the city and put out of the way—much the way titled families used to lock the idiot sons in the attic when company called—the KGB's main function is to keep an eye on the smilers.

The real problem with Russia is you forget how to smile. I have made up a list of instructions to myself when I return home. "Pull down on the left corner of your mouth, pull up on right corner. Show off your teeth. Try to think of something pleasant."

Only trouble is, I'm afraid one of the government agents will find it and accuse me of trying to undermine a form of government where the people are so happy they can afford to frown all the time.

Some more samples of Murray:

Indianapolis is America's only sanctioned 33-man suicide pact. There are some accidents where all they need is a whisk broom and an ashtray.

If I were a horse today. I'd be tempted to throw a party—champagne, fillies, barn dancing, all kinds of horsing around. You see, George Edward Arcaro, the well-known bongo drummer and horseback rider, has decided to hang up his tack. To understand what this can mean to a horse, just imagine the feeling of the crew of the *Bounty* when they put Captain Bligh to sea in that lifeboat, or the Russians when they got word Stalin was running a temperature. There are two ways to win horse races—by guile or by terror. Eddie Arcaro chose the knout. His riding style, as far as the horse was concerned, was early Cossack, a combination of Attila the Hun and Jack the Ripper in goggles and silks. The horse was running not for his oats but for his life because he knew the quicker he got to the finish line, the quicker he could start to heal.

Football is, in many respects, the most American game of them all. It used to be played by scholars who, after a hard day in the chem lab, felt the need of a little violent exercise to get their sluggish blood going and the smell of the Bunsen burners off their fingers. Then, one day, it hired a coach. And football has never been the same since. You will never get it back from the coaches without a struggle. For football coaching is an obsessive profession. It is as fascinating as playing chess with real men. The only thing more exhilarating for a human being with a desire to play God is war.

There are 6 million people who attend horse races annually in the state of California and they are like no other breed, animal, vegetable or mineral, anywhere on earth. They are the largest congress of philanthropists in the western world. Thanks to the cut the state takes of their wagers, they donate to charity, build schools, finance county fairs, underwrite employment for boys handicapped by size, and restore wildlife. The next time you see an elk grazing on a state preserve, just remember that behind every elk stands a guy with frayed cuffs and holes in his shoes smoking a cigar stub he just rescued from an ash can by the $2 window.

Murray is also an attentive witness to the drama of aging. In one column he wrote:

I woke up Tuesday morning and went to look in the mirror. The guy in there was having a birthday. I won't tell you which one. Suffice it to say, he's much older than I.

I check on him every ten years or so. I can't seem to get rid of him. He keeps getting older while it's well known I'm growing younger. I'm somewhere between thirty and thirty-five. He's God-knows-what. He's got these pouches under his eyes. His skin is kind of blotchy. God knows, my skin is clear.

He's always getting heartburn while it's well known I can eat a taco, chili relleno and polish it off with a flagon of Dos Equis and not even belch. His hair is getting gray around the edges while mine is as black as Rudolph Valentino's. He's always trying to get me to go to bed early, but I fool him. I stay up clear through the eleven o'clock news some nights.

Until 1979 Jim Murray wrote five columns a week. Then one day in Miami, just before a football game, he ordered an egg salad sandwich.

This is about the whitest thing you can have on a white plate with a white napkin underneath it. Except this one looked as if it were growing red worms.

I decided it was time to find a doctor and I was chauffeured to a hospital where I sat for about two and one-half to three hours amidst a whole waiting room of people who had fallen off skate-boards. I was finally ushered into the presence of a doctor who said my vision was all right. I think he was the same guy who told the captain of the *Titanic* full speed ahead.

Eventually I learned I had a detached retina. Now a detached retina is something that happens to preliminary prizefighters—not guys who make their living hitting typewriters instead of floors.

Other operations followed, first in Miami, later in Los Angeles. For ten months Murray endured near blindness. Then delicate eye surgery gave him a reprieve; 72 percent of his vision was later restored in his right eye, with the left permanently blind.

His column disappeared for an interval, but eventually Murray addressed his readers again:

I feel I owe my friends an explanation as to where I've been all these weeks. Believe me, I would rather have been in a press box.

I lost an old friend the other day. He was blue-eyed, impish, he cried a lot with me, laughed a lot with me, saw a great many things with me. I don't know why he left me. Boredom, perhaps.

We read a lot of books together, we did a lot of crossword puzzles together, we saw films together. He had a pretty exciting life. He saw Babe Ruth hit a home run when we were both twelve years old. He saw Willie Mays steal second base, he saw Maury Wills steal his 104th base. He saw Rocky Marciano get up. I thought he led a pretty good life.

One night a long time ago he saw this pretty lady who laughed a lot, played the piano and he couldn't look away from her. Later, he looked on as I married this pretty lady. He saw her through thirty-four years. He loved to see her laugh, he loved to see her happy.

You see, the friend I lost was my eye. I don't know why he had to go. I thought we were pals. He recorded the happy moments, the miracle of children, the beauty of a Pacific sunset, snow-capped mountains, faces on Christmas morning. He allowed me to hit fly balls to young sons in uniforms two sizes too large, to see a pretty daughter march in halftime parades. He allowed me to see most of the major sports events of our time. I suppose

I should be grateful that he didn't drift away when I was twelve or fifteen or twenty-nine but stuck around over fifty years until we had a vault of memories.

Limited vision has hardly stopped him. Writing out of his Bel-Air home, he dictates his column by telephone to a machine in the Times Mirror building. His fundamental task remains the same. Says Murray: "The trick to writing a column is to avoid boredom. You have to keep people interested, but first you have to keep yourself interested. That isn't always easy. Boredom is the joker in the deck, the loose board at the top of the steps in the dark. There's a story in every man and woman. The challenge is to find it."

Another *Times* writer who finds stories everywhere is columnist Jack Smith. He is slim and sharp-featured as a bird, with a crest of silvery hair, and has a soft voice and hesitant manner.

Blessed with a shining imagination to illuminate the commonplace, Smith at his typewriter has debated philosophy and drama with a college-age son; explained—while up to his knees in running water—why his wife had always done the plumbing; visited a nudist colony. He shares every adventure with his readers.

There have been many memorable crises in the life of Jack Smith, but none more touching than his experience with the family's old Renault. The car, he wrote,

was sick and growing sicker day by day. When it started up it shook like a wet dog. It refused to climb our hill, except in low. It coughed itself out at every stop. The prudent thing to do was get rid of it. But it isn't easy to get rid of an old and ailing automobile. Nobody wants it, even for junk. Unlike a dog, it can't be put humanely to sleep.

Finally I drove it—over its protests—to Emile's. The French are eccentrics. They are impatient and moody, and treat cars as if they were women, not machines. They are prone to caress, not operate. The Renault was beyond caresses. I left it with Emile and took a bus to work. Later he phoned me at the office. "You have z' broken piston," he said. "It is no good. *Fini.* I am sorry."

Fortune saved me in the person of one of my son's college roommates. He was a man of some skill with engines, and he desperately needed a car. I gave him the Renault, pink slip and all. For the next ten months I kept track of it, in a casual way, as one keeps track of a relative who has moved away. Now and then I would hear of its exploits, or temporary illness. Once or twice I even saw it, though we made no attempt to renew our old relationship.

Then it was gone; and its end, I was sad to learn, was sordid. At the last it was lonely and unloved—in fact abandoned. I don't know what finally became of the old Renault. It was carried off. I don't believe in reincarnation, but sometimes, when a Datsun or Toyota passes us, I think I hear it humming "La Marseillaise."

Another time, Smith wrote:

Before going to serve the nation at an Air Force base in Wichita, our son Curt flew home on an eighteen-day furlough. He had complete his course in radio repair and maintenance with honors. I took pride in that. I admire anyone with a grasp of circuitry, wavelengths, frequencies and all that. It's all I can do to turn a radio on or off. I was glad to find that he took pride in his new expertise too. It so happened that the day he flew home the electric system in the dashboard of our car had gone ape. The turn signals didn't work or worked when you didn't want them to, or blinked left instead of right, or vice versa. The air conditioning went on and off at will; the radio too.

"What do you suppose it is?" I asked him on the way home from the airport.

"Hard to say," he said professionally. "I'll troubleshoot it for you in the morning. Probably a lose connection somewhere." I liked the verb "troubleshoot." It's the troubleshooters that keep things going in the technological world of ours.

As we rounded the corner by our house I pressed the button on the genie. The garage door opened and the light in the garage went on. It was new to him. We didn't have it when he joined up.

"How far away from the house will it work?" he asked.

"Just about that far," I said. "When you turn the corner."

"Well, I can amplify it for you, if you like, so you could open the door all the way from the airport. Of course, you would also open every other door in Los Angeles on the same frequency."

"That's a little more power than I care to have," I told him. "We'd have the FBI on our necks in 24 hours."

When we got in the house, the first thing that caught his eye was the new combination radio/phonograph/TV set, a monster of a machine with half a dozen dials.

"One thing I'm starved for," he said, "is good music. You don't hear much good music in Biloxi."

"It's much too late tonight," I said. "You can play it all day tomorrow."

We told him about our recent burglary. "It's the second one in a year," I said. "I've been thinking of buying a couple of big dogs. Those poodles wouldn't scare an Avon lady."

"Hmm," he said, "I'll rig up something electronic. A burglar alarm system. It shouldn't be too hard."

"I don't know," I said. "It sounds like something I'd accidentally electrocute myself with."

"No. I could make it foolproof."

We didn't call him for breakfast the next morning. We knew he would enjoy the luxury of sleeping in. I remembered what a lovely experience it was to doze through half the morning without a reveille. He had left a sheaf of large folded sheets on the table. They were charts of radio circuits.

"They look absolutely Greek to me," my wife said.

"I wouldn't fool with them," I told her, "they may be top secret."

We went to work without waking him up.

At mid-morning he phoned me at the office. "I hate to ask you this," he said. "Go right ahead," I told him. "That's what I'm for, what is it?"

"How do you turn the new phonograph on?"

Another time, Smith encountered the lost generation of flower children:

One Sunday morning in June, I drove down to Will Rogers Beach for a love-in. I had heard the hippies were gathering there. A reporter I knew, who had gone to a love-in at Elysian Park, told me a beautiful young girl he had never seen before had handed him a flower and said, "Love."

I drove down to the beach and parked on a cliff above the surf. I had dressed in tennis shoes, old blue jeans rolled halfway to the knee, and a Portuguese fisherman's shirt, and gone without shaving. I knew I could never look like a flower child again, but it wouldn't hurt to add a touch of protective coloration. I stood on the Palisade and looked down at the sea. It was a poor day, overcast and clammy. A dozen surfers loafed on their boards, waiting for a wave. No hippies out there. A youth with a red beard and long red hair, like an Irish Moses, walked up with a barefoot maid. Her hair was yellow; her cheeks were borscht and sour cream. A flower child? "You got a cigarette?" the young man asked. "Oh, uh, no," I stammered, "I don't smoke." They looked at each other understandingly. How square can a man get? They walked to a new dark green Chevrolet Impala, got in and drove off up the highway. I couldn't be sure whether I had experienced a true encounter or not.

During World War II Jack Smith joined the Marine Corps as a combat correspondent. Later he worked for half a dozen different newspapers—"I was really a grasshopper"—before landing at the *Times* as a general assignment reporter in 1953.

To earn extra money during off-hours, he began writing a twice-a-week column for the Op-Ed page. Gradually, it became a lightning rod for fan mail, and one day in 1970 Nick Williams and Bill Thomas inquired whether he could step up the frequency to five times a week.

Smith replied, "Sure, but not in addition to working in the city room. The column has to be a full-time job."

And a full-time job it became, a charming circle of glorious and universal trivia, Smith feeding goldfish, feuding with cats and blackbirds and deliverymen, Smith dancing along the sharp edge of the knife of frustration, without ever bleeding much.

Recently he told an interviewer: "My sense of responsibility makes me an achiever, although in limited ways. I don't have to impress anybody, except through the column. I don't have to be good in any other way, really, and that's great for me.

"Whatever problem I have is the lonely creative one of what I'm going to do, to conjure up the next column. I'll read the paper and cast about through the mail and look at my desk and shuffle through a stack of things that have been saved up, hoping some idea or topic can be found. Many times I've gone to the wastebasket and retrieved letters or clippings that were earlier discarded, and I find the gestation period has been going on all the time.

"No one really has that many things to write about, and in fact, when I began doing the column, I figured it would last just two or three months, maybe a few dozen columns, by which time I would use all the ideas and quit, and become a general assignment reporter again. I'd have said everything that had been saved up all my life, and I'd be at the bottom of the barrel. But I didn't quit. I've been scraping the bottom of the barrel ever since, and I've written more than four thousand columns.

"I began worrying about repetition, but discovered by continuing that life *is* repetitious. I am a different person each day, so nothing is ever quite the same; my attitudes change. I gave up worrying about not having anything to say, and decided to write a column about what was uppermost in my mind, day by day."

Jack Smith's observation—*life is repetitious but never quite the same*—applies equally to an entire newspaper and to the fascinating city surrounding it. They have grown together, newspaper and city, worked together, fought each other, nourished each other for a remarkable century.

From a dusty pueblo of twelve thousand inhabitants in 1882, Los Angeles has been transformed into a vast metropolitan complex covering nearly five thousand square miles— an area as large as Rhode Island—and containing a population of nine million. The ethnic mix of the 1880s has multiplied with large arrivals of Indochinese, Armenians, Cubans, Koreans, Samoans, Filipinos, South Americans, Japanese, Chinese, Serbs, Lithuanians, Croatians and many others.

Times reporter Richard Meyer recently described the new melting pot: "Within ten blocks on Figueroa street, Colonel Sanders sells California kosher burritos, T.B. Chew sells Famous Chinese Herbs and a woman everyone calls Sister sells barbecue beef and pork. The Orpheum theater, where Al Jolson played in blackface, offers Anglo movies with Spanish subtitles. Students in Glendale Unified School District speak forty-four languages, including Filipino Tagalog and Arabic."

Along with its rich ethnic mix of cultures the once raw desert has become a stunning tapestry containing more than seventy-five university and college campuses, a vast network of science, technology and skilled manufacturing (the aerospace industry alone employs more than 277,000 persons), bright pavilions for the arts including music, dance, drama and painting, a massive marketplace for merchandisers and shoppers, a tourist attraction for the rest of the world.

Entering its second century the *Los Angeles Times*—having begun as a four-page sheet—now often exceeds one hundred pages on weekdays and five hundred pages on Sundays; and its daily circulation, at the beginning fewer than five hundred copies, now tops one million and is the second largest (after the tabloid New York *Daily News*) of any general audience newspaper in the nation. From its shaky start in a tiny printing shop and bindery located only one block from its present headquarters in central Los Angeles, the *Times* has become a dynamic leader in the swiftly changing world of modern journalism.

Harrison Gray Otis, who pioneered it, created a holding company in 1884 in partnership with Colonel H. H. Boyce. Borrowing the name of the printing shop and bindery, the outfit was called The Times Mirror Company, and it was capitalized at $40,000. Hand in hand with the newspaper, Times Mirror has shared in a century of spectacular growth. The original $40,000 investment by 1984 has multiplied to a value of nearly $3 billion, as measured by the price of Times Mirror's shares (trading symbol: TMC) on the New York Stock Exchange, making the holding company one of the five largest publishing conglomerates in the world.

Sparked into life by Harrison Gray Otis, pushed forward by his son-in-law Harry Chandler and grandson Norman Chandler, Times Mirror has now embarked on its second century, led this time by the founder's great-grandson, Otis Chandler. The dynastic torch burns brightly, the flame taller than ever.

Acknowledgments

So many kind and generous persons contributed in so many ways to this book that it would require a special supplement to mention all by name. But special thanks must be expressed to a few: to the late associate editor James Bassett, for an early unpublished history of the *Times*; to archivists Lois Markwith and Carolyn Strickler, who provided valuable research assistance; to Stanley Gordon, a former Sunday editor of the *Times* who first advanced the idea of the book and thereafter continued to scout the past; to John Foley, who lent important help in gathering pictures, a task at which he was assisted by Joan Stern; to Joseph Guiteras, who introduced me to the magic of computers; to Merrie Campion, who deserves special recognition for her cheerful, efficient assistance with a great many secretarial chores; to Evelyn Peterson and her staff, who typed the manuscript; to Sherry Huber, Susan Leon, and Ted Johnson, who demonstrated uncommon skill at editing and copy editing; to Martin P. Levin, who provided fresh insights to the fascinating world of book publishing.

Bibliography

Certain books were especially valuable. Among them:

Adler, Ruth. *The Working Press.* New York: G. P. Putnam's Sons, 1966.

Allen, Frederick L. *Only Yesterday: An Informal History of the Nineteen Twenties.* New York: Harper & Row, 1957.

Bagdikian, Ben. *Information Machines: Their Impact on Men and the Media.* New York: Harper & Row, 1971.

Burns, William J. *The Masked War.* New York: Doran & Co., 1913.

Carr, Harry. *Los Angeles, City of Dreams.* New York: Appleton-Century, 1935.

Chapman, John L. *Incredible Los Angeles.* New York: Harper & Row, 1965.

Crouse, Timothy. *The Boys on the Bus.* New York: Random House, 1973.

Darrow, Clarence. *The Story of My Life.* New York: Charles Scribner's Sons, 1932.

Downie, Leonard, Jr. *The New Muckrakers.* Washington, D.C.: New Republic Books, 1976.

Elson, Robert T. *Time Inc.: The Intimate History of a Publishing Empire.* 2 vols. New York: Atheneum, 1968, 1973.

Emery, Edwin. *The Press and America: An Interpretative History of the Mass Media.* Englewood Cliffs, N.J.: Prentice-Hall, 1972.

Finney, Guy W. *Angel City in Turmoil.* Los Angeles: Amer Press, 1945.

Governor's Commission on the Los Angeles Riots. *Violence in the City: An End or a Beginning?* Sacramento, Calif.: California State Printing Office, 1965.

Halberstam, David. *The Powers That Be.* New York: Alfred A. Knopf, 1979.

Hart, Jack R. *The Information Empire.* Washington, D.C.: University Press of America, 1981.

Hill, Gladwin. *Dancing Bear.* New York: World, 1968.

Hoffman, Abraham. *Vision or Villainy: Origins of the Owens Valley–Los Angeles Water Controversy.* Texas A&M University Press, 1981.

Hoge, Alice. *Cissy Patterson.* New York: Random House, 1966.

Hopkins, Ernest Jerome. *Our Lawless Police: A Study of the Unlawful Enforcement of the Law.* New York: Viking Press, 1931.

Keogh, James. *President Nixon and the Press.* New York: Funk & Wagnalls, 1972.

Krock, Arthur. *Memoirs.* New York: Funk & Wagnalls, 1968.

Lindstrom, Carl. *The Fading American Newspaper.* Gloucester, Mass.: Peter Smith, 1964.

McLuhan, Marshall. *Understanding Media: The Extension of Man.* New York: New American Library, 1964.

McNulty, John Bard. *Older Than the Nation: The Life and Times of The Hartford Courant.* Stonington, Conn.: Pequot Press, 1964.

McWilliams, Carey. *The Great Exception.* New York: A. A. Wyn, 1950.

McWilliams, Carey. *Southern California: Island on the Land.* Layton, Utah: Peregrine Smith, 1946.

Mayo, Morrow. *Los Angeles.* New York: Alfred A. Knopf, 1933.

Mazo, Earl. *Richard Nixon.* New York: Harper & Row, 1959.

Merrill, John C. *The Elite Press.* New York: Pitman, 1968.

Mowry, George. *California Progressives.* New York: Quadrangle/New York Times Book Co., 1963.

Nadeau, Remi. *The Water Seekers.* New York: Doubleday, 1950.

Nixon, Richard. *Six Crises.* New York: Doubleday, 1962.

Olin, Spencer C. *California's Prodigal Sons: Hiram Johnson and the Progressives.* Los Angeles: University of California Press, 1968.

Rivers, William L. *The Opinion Makers.* Boston: Beacon Press, 1965.

Seitz, Don C. *Joseph Pulitzer, His Life & Letters.* New York: Simon & Schuster, 1924.

Seldes, George. *Lords of the Press.* New York: Blue Ribbon Books, 1941.

Spalding, William A. *Los Angeles Newspaperman*. Los Angeles: Huntington Library, 1961.

Steel, Ronald. *Walter Lippmann and the American Century*. Boston: Little, Brown, 1980.

Steffens, Lincoln. *Autobiography of Lincoln Steffens*. New York: Harcourt Brace Jovanovich, 1958.

Stone, Irving. *Clarence Darrow for the Defense*. New York: Bantam Books, 1958.

Talese, Gay. *The Kingdom and the Power*. New York: World, 1969.

White, Theodore H. *In Search of History*. New York: Harper & Row, 1978.

White, Theodore H. *The Making of the President*. 3 vols. New York: Atheneum, 1961, 1965, 1969.

Woodward, Bob, and Bernstein, Carl. *All the President's Men*. New York: Simon & Schuster, 1974.

Index

About the Author

Marshall Berges is a veteran journalist who has reported *Time* magazine cover stories on Ronald Reagan, John Kennedy, David Rockefeller, Norton Simon, Dag Hammarskjöld, Teamster boss Dave Beck and many other well-known figures. He has also written more than three hundred wide-ranging personality portraits for the *Los Angeles Times,* and his by-line has appeared in major magazines and newspapers around the world. He is the author of *Corporations and the Quality of Life.*